Better Homes and Gardens®

SUPER MARKET SHORTCUTS

SHOP SMART! 365 RECIPES TO SAVE TIME AND MONEY

WILEY

John Wiley & Sons, Inc.

Copyright © 2009 by Meredith Corporation, Des Moines, IA. All rights reserved

Published by John Wiley & Sons, Inc., Hoboken, New Jersey

Published simultaneously in Canada

For general information on our other products and services or for technical support, please contact our Customer Care Department within the United States at (800) 762-2974, outside the United States at (317) 572-3993 or fax (317) 572-4002.

Wiley also publishes its books in a variety of electronic formats. Some content that appears in print may not be available in electronic books. For more information about Wiley products, visit our web site at www.wiley.com.

Library of Congress Cataloging-in-Publication Data:

Better homes and gardens supermarket shortcuts : shop smart! : 365 recipes to save time and money / by Better homes and gardens.

p. cm.

Includes index.

ISBN 978-0-470-50068-2 (cloth)

1. Quick and easy cookery. 2. Grocery shopping. I. Better homes and gardens. II. Title: Supermarket shortcuts.

TX833.5.B48825 2009

641.5'55--dc22

Printed in China.

10 9 8 7 6 5 4 3 2 1

Our seal assures you that every recipe in *Supermarket Shortcuts* has been tested in the Better Homes and Gardens Test Kitchen®. This means that each recipe is practical and reliable and meets our high standards of taste appeal. We guarantee your satisfaction with this book for as long as you own it.

Meredith Corporation

Editors: Jan Miller, Tricia Laning, and Lois White
Contributing Editors: Mary Williams and Winifred Moranville
Recipe Development and Testing: Better Homes and Gardens Test Kitchen

John Wiley & Sons, Inc.

Publisher: Natalie Chapman
Executive Editor: Anne Ficklen
Editor: Adam Kowit
Production Director: Diana Cisek
Cover Design: Doug Samuelson, Waterbury Publications, Inc.; Suzanne Sunwoo
Design and Layout: Doug Samuelson, Waterbury Publications, Inc.
Manufacturing Manager: Tom Hyland

TABLE OF CONTENTS

HOW MANY TIMES HAVE YOU ORDERED TAKEOUT, hit the drive-through, or taken the family out for an ordinary, overpriced meal when what you really wanted was to share a satisfying home-cooked dinner?

And what was it that stood between you and your goal of getting a good meal on your family's table?

Often, it's not the actual time it takes to cook something—many dishes can be made in less time that it takes for a delivery car to arrive. Rather, it's those time-eating, energy-zapping last-minute trips to the supermarket that can make us throw up our hands, reach for the phone, and order a pizza. Again.

Your cookbook shelf may be filled with books that promise 20- and 30-minute meals, but in recent years, home cooks have told us they need more than quick recipes. They want strategies—surefire ways to get organized and inspired to bring family-pleasing dinners on the table night after night.

Supermarket Shortcuts is all about strategies. We've come up with four proven plans of action, each with its own winning way to break down any barriers between you and a wholesome home-cooked meal. Look for:

SHORTCUTS TO SUPPER: We've chosen almost 50 best-loved convenience products—such as meatballs, stir-fry peppers, polenta, and cooked pot roast—and offer five ways to transform each into a creative, one-of-a-kind recipe.

ONE GROCERY BAG: FIVE MEALS: Sometimes when you're at the supermarket, you don't really know what you're going to crave for dinner a day or two later. That's where this chapter comes in! Buy a handful of ingredients, and decide later how you want to serve them—perhaps as a stir-fry, a noodle dish, a salad, or a soup.

MAKE NOW, SERVE LATER: When you have a few extra minutes, get a jump-start on the next days' dinners—whether by making a whole casserole, a homemade pesto, or by marinating steaks. You'll be amazed at how quickly meals come together when you have most of it ready to go in advance.

WORKDAY DINNERS: Here's a stash of our all-time best 30-minute, 10-ingredient-or-less recipes. All are savvy combinations of fresh and prepared foods to satisfy a great range of tastes.

Thanks to this book, no matter how chock-full your days are, you can enjoy many nights of meaningful and nourishing family meals together. At last, going out to dinner will be for the sheer joy of it—rather than as a last-ditch attempt to get everyone fed.

Enjoy!
The Editors

TRICKS, TIPS AND KNOW-HOW TO A FAST DINNER

Pair the strategies on these pages with the recipes in the book, and a nourishing family meal will always be within reach.

KEEP MEATS THAT KEEP LONGER

Next time you shop, stock up on meats like pepperoni, kielbasa, and packaged corned beef. Check out the "sell by" and/or "use by" dates, and you'll see that these meats have a long shelf life in the fridge, making them great choices for ever-changing schedules. Kielbasa takes just minutes to heat. Pepperoni can be tossed with pasta or into salads, or used as a topper for pizza and sandwiches, or sliced and folded into an omelet. Put corned beef into a slow-cooker in the morning and it will be waiting for you at the end of your day (most packages give slow-cooker directions).

FISH IS YOUR FRIEND

Whether broiled, baked, or pan fried, fish fillets may be the speediest main dish around. Keep a stash of frozen fish fillets in the freezer, and place them in the refrigerator overnight to thaw all day while you're at work. Pair with quick-cooking couscous and cooked frozen vegetables, and you can truly have dinner on the table in five minutes—and a healthy one, at that!

SERVE EGGS—ENGLISH STYLE

Sometimes, all you need between soccer practice and dance lessons is a quick stop at home for a nourishing meal of fried or scrambled eggs. To make eggs into a filling meal for growing kids, serve with toast, brown-and serve sausages, and your family's favorite brand of baked beans. Eggs and baked beans may sound like an odd duo, but it's a classic combo in Great Britain. Try it once, and it may become a family favorite.

SERVE EGGS—EURO STYLE

When you want to have a stylish meal in minutes, an omelet or scrambled eggs with a few special stir-ins can be just the ticket. Keep some of these favorite flavor duos on hand:

- Feta cheese and dill weed
- Prosciutto and Parmigiano-Reggiano cheese
- Goat cheese and purchased black olive tapenade (top the cooked eggs with the tapenade rather than stirring the tapenade in).
- Sliced green onion and cheddar cheese
- Slivered ham and Brie

A tossed salad with a garlicky dressing works as a contrast to the rich eggs. Serve baguette-style bread alongside.

ANYTHING CAN BE BRUSCHETTA

Just about anything under the sun goes well atop bruschetta, and hefty slices can morph a soup or salad into a full meal. Simply toast French bread slices, rub with garlic and brush olive oil, then top with whatever you have handy. Some idea to start with:

- Purchased pesto, sundried tomatoes, and a sprinkling of grated cheese. Run under the broiler until cheese melts.

- A slather of purchased hummus and a sprinkling of herbs.

- Purchased tapenade with or without a sprinkling of cheese.

- Chopped cherry tomatoes tossed with some onions, herbs, and olive oil.

- A slather of cream cheese and some leftover roasted or stir-fried veggies; run under the broiler to heat.

- Canned tuna mixed with a little mayo and mustard, then topped with cheese and broiled for fast miniature tuna melts (these go especially well with tomato soup).

FREEZE THAT FRENCH BREAD

Sometimes the missing piece of the dinner puzzle is simply a good bread to jump-start or round out a meal. Crosswise-cut baguette-style bread slices make perfect bases for bruschetta. Sliced lengthwise, the long loaves are great for piling with deli meats and cheeses, then running under the broiler for terrifically oozy open-face sandwiches.

Trouble is, most baguettes only stay fresh a day or two. Fortunately, they freeze well. Use one half for one meal and wrap the other half well and store it in the freezer until needed. Thaw at room temperature, then toast or broil as needed.

TONIGHT'S LEFTOVERS = TOMORROW'S TACOS

Extra chicken, pork roast, steak, and seafood tuck tastily into or on top of tortillas for satisfying tacos and quesadillas. Just keep a few extras ingredients on hand, such as olives, roasted red peppers, and your favorite cheeses. Stash a few cans of refried beans, a couple jars of salsa, and a box or two of Spanish rice mix in your pantry, and you'll always have good go-withs for a family-friendly Tex-Mex feast—all more quick and more economical than a taco dinner out.

SAVE EVERY LAST LEFTOVER

A cup of chili and a dab of taco meat here, a half-bowl of stew and some leftover roasted chicken there—these may not look like a lot, but they may also be just the ticket on those nights when everyone's eating in shifts. Reheat them and serve atop cornbread, quick-cooking couscous, or baked potatoes to help stretch them into a meal. Keep little cans of veggies around for quick side dishes when you're cooking for one or two at a time.

Load up a cupboard with a variety of sizes of freezer containers along with adhesive labels to make it easier to label and stash the leftovers.

BE CREATIVE WITH BEANS

Canned black beans, garbanzo beans, and cannellini beans have a long shelf life and can all be transformed into quick, fiber-packed sides with just a few ingredients. Be sure to rinse and drain them well to remove as much salt as possible. Then, sauté some onions and garlic in some olive oil until tender. Add the rinsed and drained beans and some herbs and stir until heated through. From there, use your imagination—and what you have on hand—to flavor them your style. Basil, oregano, and Parmigiano-Reggiano cheese go great with garbanzos; sage and rosemary meld nicely with cannnellini beans. Black beans go well with Tex-Mex flavors, such as tomatoes, green onions, cilantro, and chile peppers. Add extra olive oil as needed, and serve these concoctions warm or at room temperature.

MUSTARD COUNTS AS A SAUCE

Check out all the varieties of mustard out there. Whether coarse or fine, flecked with herbs or flavored fruit, a spoonful or more can add just enough interest to grilled chops, steaks, or sausages to make the dish veer off the beaten path, so keep a few jars in the fridge. Creative mustards are also a way to transform an ordinary bottle of vinaigrette into your own specialty house dressing.

COUNT ON THE DELI COUNTER

When you know you have a few exceptionally busy days ahead, stock up on a few containers of hearty sides, such as pasta salad, potato salad, baked beans, and macaroni salad. These can be cook-free accompaniments to broiled or grilled steaks, fried chicken breasts or pork chops, or heated polish sausage.

REMEMBER THE RANCH

If you're having trouble getting kids to eat vegetables no matter how you cook them, save a step and don't cook them at all! Instead, try serving uncooked vegetables, such as sliced carrots, celery, lettuce, cauliflower and maybe (just maybe!) even broccoli with a bowl of ranch dressing. Kids really seem to go for its tangy, creamy appeal.

BONUS POINTS FOR A BIG BOWL OF FRUIT

To get more color and nutrients into your diet, place a bowl of in-season fruits at the center of your table. After you've finished your main course, peel and slice whatever fruits your family craves as you sit and linger a while at the table.

FRESH HERBS ADD FINESSE

A sprinkling of chopped fresh herbs will freshen up leftover soups and stews as well as readymade purchased entrees such as pork roasts, pot roasts, and chicken breasts in gravy. Keep fresh parsley on hand—it goes with so many foods. Also consider making a gremolata—a blend of parsley, fresh garlic, and lemon peel, all finely chopped together. Sprinkle this mixture over anything that could use a dose of bold, super-fresh flavor.

10 ITEMS = 7 SUPPERS

If you have these groceries in your fridge, freezer, and cupboard, you'll always have something good ready to go in minutes.

1. Frozen meatballs
2. Jars of pasta sauce
3. Boxes of dried pasta
4. A stash of frozen vegetables in bags
5. Bottles of salad dressing, including one vinaigrette-style dressing
6. Bags of mixed green salad
7. A sack of russet potatoes
8. Frozen fish fillets
9. Chicken breast halves
10. Pork chops

Stock up on the usual pantry ingredients (such as salt, pepper, butter, olive oil and cooking oil, milk, and your favorite cheese) and from the above list, you can easily bring one week's worth of meals to the table every night, including:

Spaghetti and meatballs served with a tossed green salad

Pasta tosssed with cooked chicken, cooked frozen vegetables, and olive oil

Pan-fried pork chops served with vegetables and fried potatoes

Pan-fried chicken breasts with vegetable and cheesy mashed potatoes

Mixed green salad topped with chicken breasts that have been marinated in vinaigrette-style dressing then broiled

Fish fillets brushed with vinaigrette-style dressing then broiled and served with vegetables and butter-tossed pasta

Broiled chicken breasts topped with cheese and broiled until cheese is melted, then placed on a bed of sauced pasta (serve with cooked frozen vegetables or a tossed salad)

SHORTCUTS TO SUPPER

With today's jam-packed schedules, moms rely more and more on convenience foods. Precut fresh vegetables, refrigerated cooked entrées, and heat-and-bake frozen meats are just some of the products available to make life easier for time-pressed cooks. This chapter showcases almost fifty of these tasty timesavers by providing five recipes for each that add home-cooked goodness to packaged fare.

BEEF AND BOK CHOY

Toasted sesame oil and sesame seeds lend a wonderful nutty flavor to this stir-fry. Toast the seeds in a heavy skillet over medium heat for 3 to 5 minutes or until a deep golden color, shaking the pan often.

Start to Finish: 20 minutes

12 ounces packaged beef stir-fry strips

4 teaspoons toasted sesame oil

1 teaspoon red chili paste

6 cups sliced bok choy

1 teaspoon bottled minced garlic (2 cloves)

1 tablespoon reduced-sodium soy sauce

2 teaspoons sesame seeds, toasted

1 Cut any thick pieces of beef to make thin strips. In a very large nonstick skillet heat 2 teaspoons of the oil over medium-high heat. Add beef strips and chili paste; cook and stir about 3 minutes or until beef is desired doneness. Remove skillet from heat. Reduce heat to medium. Remove beef from pan with a slotted spoon, reserving liquid in pan; cover beef to keep warm.

2 Add remaining 2 teaspoons oil to skillet. Add bok choy and garlic; cook and stir for 2 to 3 minutes or until bok choy is crisp-tender. Transfer to serving plates. Top with warm beef mixture. Drizzle with soy sauce and sprinkle with toasted sesame seeds.

Makes 4 servings

Nutrition Facts per serving: 179 cal., 9 g total fat (2 g sat. fat), 52 mg chol., 271 mg sodium, 4 g carbo., 1 g fiber, 20 g pro.

BLACKENED BEEF STIR-FRY

A melding of Cajun and Asian influences translates into intense flavor.
Who needs take-out when you can create superb fusion flavor at home
in minutes?

Start to Finish: 25 minutes

12	ounces packaged beef stir-fry strips
2¼	teaspoons blackened steak seasoning
⅔	cup water
2	tablespoons tomato paste
2	teaspoons cornstarch
½	teaspoon instant beef bouillon granules
1	tablespoon cooking oil
1	16-ounce package frozen stir-fry vegetables (any combination)
	Hot cooked rice (optional)

1 Cut any thick pieces of beef to make thin strips. Sprinkle beef strips with 2 teaspoons of the blackened seasoning; toss to coat well. Set beef strips aside.

2 For sauce, in a small bowl stir together the remaining ¼ teaspoon blackened seasoning, the water, tomato paste, cornstarch, and bouillon granules. Set aside.

3 In a wok or large skillet heat oil over medium-high heat. Add stir-fry vegetables. Cook and stir for 2 to 3 minutes or until crisp-tender. Remove vegetables from wok. Add beef strips to hot wok. (Add more oil as necessary during cooking.) Cook and stir about 3 minutes or until beef is desired doneness.

4 Push meat from center of wok. Stir sauce; add to center of wok. Cook and stir until thickened and bubbly. Return vegetables to wok. Stir to coat all ingredients with sauce. Heat through. If desired, serve with hot cooked rice.

Makes 4 servings

Nutrition Facts per serving: 190 cal., 6 g total fat (2 g sat. fat), 40 mg chol., 373 mg sodium, 10 g carbo., 3 g fiber, 21 g pro.

BARBECUE BEEF SANDWICHES

Slices of pepper cheese top saucy beef strips in these robust sandwiches.
Placate a tender palate by using plain Monterey Jack cheese rather than
cheese with jalapeños.

Start to Finish: 20 minutes

12	**ounces packaged beef stir-fry strips**
1	**tablespoon cooking oil**
1	**medium onion, sliced and separated into rings**
½	**cup red or green sweet pepper cut into thin bite-size strips**
½	**cup bottled barbecue sauce**
4	**hoagie buns, split and toasted**
3	**slices Monterey Jack cheese with jalapeño peppers or Monterey Jack cheese, quartered (about 3 ounces)**

1 Cut any thick pieces of beef to make thin strips; set aside.

2 In a large skillet heat oil over medium-high heat. Add onion and sweet pepper; cook about 3 minutes or until tender. Add beef strips. Cook and stir for 2 to 3 minutes or until beef is desired doneness.

3 Stir in barbecue sauce. Cook, uncovered, over medium heat until heated through, stirring occasionally. Spoon beef mixture onto hoagie bun bottoms. Top with cheese and then bun tops.

Makes 4 sandwiches

Nutrition Facts per sandwich: 716 cal., 25 g total fat (10 g sat. fat), 57 mg chol., 1223 mg sodium, 87 g carbo., 5 g fiber, 35 g pro.

FIVE-SPICE STEAK WRAPS

Forget the chopsticks! Wrap stir-fried beef, fresh veggies, and yogurt in a tortilla for easy and flavorful dining.

Start to Finish: 25 minutes

2	**cups packaged shredded cabbage with carrot (coleslaw mix)**
¼	**cup red and/or green sweet pepper cut into thin bite-size strips**
¼	**cup carrot cut into thin bite-size strips**
¼	**cup snipped fresh chives**
2	**tablespoons rice vinegar**
½	**teaspoon toasted sesame oil**
12	**ounces packaged beef stir-fry strips**
½	**teaspoon five-spice powder**
¼	**teaspoon salt**
	Nonstick cooking spray
¼	**cup plain low-fat yogurt or light dairy sour cream**
4	**8-inch flour tortillas**

1 In a medium bowl combine coleslaw mix, sweet pepper, carrot, and chives. In a small bowl combine vinegar and sesame oil. Pour vinegar mixture over coleslaw mixture; toss to coat. Set aside.

2 Cut any thick pieces of beef to make thin strips. Sprinkle beef strips with five-spice powder and salt. Coat an unheated large nonstick skillet with nonstick cooking spray. Preheat skillet over medium-high heat. Add beef strips; cook and stir about 3 minutes or until beef is desired doneness.

3 To assemble, spread 1 tablespoon of the yogurt down the center of each tortilla. Top with beef. Stir coleslaw mixture; spoon over beef. Fold in sides of tortillas. If desired, secure with wooden toothpicks.

Makes 4 servings

Nutrition Facts per serving: 237 cal., 7 g total fat (2 g sat. fat), 51 mg chol., 329 mg sodium, 20 g carbo., 2 g fiber, 22 g pro.

BEEF AND ASPARAGUS SAUTÉ

Herbes de Provence, Marsala, and lemon peel lend Mediterranean notes
to this beef and asparagus stir-fry.

Start to Finish: 20 minutes

12   **ounces fresh asparagus**

1   **pound packaged beef
stir-fry strips**

2   **teaspoons olive oil**

    **Salt and ground black
pepper**

1   **medium carrot, shredded
(½ cup)**

1   **teaspoon dried herbes
de Provence, crushed**

½   **cup dry Marsala**

¼   **teaspoon finely shredded
lemon peel**

1 Snap off and discard woody bases from asparagus. Bias-slice asparagus into 2-inch pieces; set aside. Cut any thick pieces of beef to make thin strips; set aside.

2 In a large nonstick skillet heat 1 teaspoon of the oil over medium-high heat. Add half of the beef strips to hot oil. Sprinkle with salt and pepper. Cook and stir about 3 minutes or until beef is desired doneness. Remove beef from skillet. Repeat with the remaining 1 teaspoon oil and the remaining beef strips.

3 Return all of the beef to the skillet. Add asparagus, carrot, and herbes de Provence; cook and stir for 2 minutes more. Add Marsala and lemon peel; reduce heat. Cook for 3 to 5 minutes more or until asparagus is crisp-tender.

Makes 4 servings

Nutrition Facts per serving: 327 cal., 7 g total fat (2 g sat. fat), 69 mg chol., 209 mg sodium, 29 g carbo., 2 g fiber, 28 g pro.

CALIENTE POT ROAST

Caliente means "hot to the touch" in Spanish. The fiery Tex-Mex influence is the ultimate complement to succulent beef pot roast. Avocado and sour cream offer a creamy, cooling counterpart to the picante sauce. Pictured on page 129.

Start to Finish: 25 minutes

1 **16- or 17-ounce package refrigerated cooked beef pot roast with juices**

1½ **cups packaged sliced fresh mushrooms**

1 **8-ounce bottle picante sauce**

1 **14-ounce can reduced-sodium chicken broth**

1 **cup quick-cooking couscous**

2 **tablespoons snipped fresh cilantro**

Dairy sour cream (optional)

Chopped fresh tomato (optional)

Sliced avocado (optional)

1 Transfer liquid from pot roast package to a large skillet; add mushrooms and picante sauce. Cut pot roast into 1- to 1½-inch pieces; add to mushrooms in skillet. Bring to boiling; reduce heat. Cover and simmer for 10 minutes.

2 Meanwhile, in a medium saucepan bring broth to boiling; stir in couscous. Remove from heat. Cover and let stand for 5 minutes. Fluff with a fork; stir in cilantro.

3 Spoon pot roast mixture over hot cooked couscous mixture. If desired, serve with sour cream, tomato, and/or avocado.

Makes 4 to 6 servings

Nutrition Facts per serving: 479 cal., 13 g total fat (4 g sat. fat), 120 mg chol., 1,000 mg sodium, 43 g carbo., 3 g fiber, 46 g pro.

BEEF ROAST with VEGETABLES

Hungry for slow-cooked roast, but you're just now thinking about it? Tap a package of cooked beef pot roast and simmer it with veggies and seasoning. You'll have what you're after in just 35 minutes.

Prep: 15 minutes   Cook: 20 minutes

1   **16- or 17-ounce package refrigerated cooked beef pot roast with juices**

1½   **cups packaged peeled baby carrots**

8   **ounces tiny new potatoes, quartered**

2   **stalks celery, cut into 1-inch pieces**

¼   **cup water**

½   **teaspoon dried thyme, crushed**

½   **teaspoon garlic pepper seasoning**

1 Transfer liquid from pot roast package to a large skillet. Halve any large carrots lengthwise. Add carrots, potatoes, celery, and water to skillet.

2 Place roast on top of vegetables. Sprinkle thyme and garlic pepper seasoning over all. Bring to boiling; reduce heat. Cover and simmer about 20 minutes or until vegetables are tender and meat is heated through. Serve meat with vegetables and juices.

Makes 4 servings

Nutrition Facts per serving: 239 cal., 9 g total fat (4 g sat. fat), 64 mg chol., 591 mg sodium, 18 g carbo., 3 g fiber, 25 g pro.

TARRAGON POT ROAST WITH FRUIT

Fresh fruit, shallot, and fresh tarragon add elegant notes to a packaged beef roast.

Start to Finish: 25 minutes

1 **tablespoon butter**

2 **tablespoons finely chopped shallot**

1 **16- to 17-ounce package refrigerated cooked beef pot roast with juices**

2 **tablespoons tarragon vinegar**

2 **cups fresh fruit wedges (such as apples, plums, pears, and/or peeled peaches)**

  Hot cooked wide noodles or spaetzle (optional)

1 **teaspoon snipped fresh tarragon**

1 In a large skillet melt butter over medium heat. Add shallot; cook for 1 minute. Add beef roast and juices from package; reduce heat. Cover and simmer about 10 minutes or until beef roast is heated through.

2 Add vinegar to skillet. Spoon fruit on top. Cover and heat about 4 minutes or until heated through. If desired, serve with hot cooked noodles. Sprinkle with tarragon.

Makes 4 servings

Nutrition Facts per serving: 225 cal., 11 g total fat (6 g sat. fat), 68 mg chol., 422 mg sodium, 12 g carbo., 1 g fiber, 22 g pro.

MEXICAN-STYLE HASH

Introduce a package of refrigerated precooked roast beef to a few simple ingredients to produce an especially satisfying hash. Toss together a simple salad to serve on the side and dinner's good to go.

Prep: 20 minutes   Cook: 15 minutes

1	**16- or 17-ounce package refrigerated cooked beef pot roast with juices**
2	**medium potatoes, finely chopped (1½ cups)**
1	**11-ounce can whole kernel corn, drained**
1	**10.75-ounce can condensed tomato soup**
1	**small onion, chopped (⅓ cup)**
1½	**teaspoons chili powder**
¼	**teaspoon ground black pepper**

1 Remove pot roast from package, reserving juices. Chop meat.

2 In a large skillet combine chopped meat, reserved meat juices, potatoes, corn, soup, onion, chili powder, and pepper. Bring to boiling; reduce heat. Cover and simmer for 15 to 20 minutes or until potato is tender, stirring occasionally to prevent sticking.

Makes 4 servings

Nutrition Facts per serving: 334 cal., 10 g total fat (4 g sat. fat), 64 mg chol., 1069 mg sodium, 40 g carbo., 4 g fiber, 27 g pro.

MEXICAN BEEF AND TORTILLAS

The beauty of packaged cooked pot roast is that it's ready to heat and serve right from the package, plus it takes to easy fix-ups like this Mexican-style one.

Start to Finish: 20 minutes

8   6-inch corn tortillas

1   16- or 17-ounce package refrigerated cooked beef pot roast with juices

1   14.5-ounce can diced tomatoes with green chiles, undrained

1   green sweet pepper, cut into strips

1   lime, cut into wedges

    Dairy sour cream (optional)

1 Wrap tortillas in microwave-safe paper towels. Microwave on 100% power (high) for 45 to 60 seconds or until warm. Cover; set aside.

2 Microwave beef according to package directions. Meanwhile, place undrained tomatoes in a small saucepan; heat through.

3 Remove meat, reserving juices; slice meat. Serve meat on the warm tortillas with tomatoes and sweet pepper strips. Drizzle with reserved juices. Pass lime wedges and, if desired, sour cream.

Makes 4 servings

Nutrition Facts per serving: 319 cal., 10 g total fat (5 g sat. fat), 64 mg chol., 857 mg sodium, 34 g carbo., 5 g fiber, 27 g pro.

BEEF TIPS WITH CORNICHONS

Look for small sour pickles called cornichons with other pickles at your supermarket or food specialty store.

Start to Finish: 35 minutes

| tablespoon cooking oil

| medium onion, chopped (½ cup)

| teaspoon bottled minced garlic (2 cloves)

¼ cup dry white wine

| 17-ounce package refrigerated cooked beef tips with gravy

⅓ cup cornichons, sliced lengthwise

½ teaspoon dried tarragon, crushed

½ cup dairy sour cream

Hot cooked noodles or rice

1 In a large skillet heat oil over medium heat. Add onion and garlic; cook and stir until onion is tender. Add wine. Bring to boiling; reduce heat. Simmer, uncovered, until reduced by half.

2 Add beef tips with gravy, cornichons, and tarragon to skillet; cook until heated through. Stir in sour cream. Serve immediately over hot cooked noodles.

Makes 4 servings

Nutrition Facts per serving: 347 cal., 16 g total fat (6 g sat. fat), 84 mg chol., 828 mg sodium, 28 g carbo., 2 g fiber, 22 g pro.

BEEF RAGOUT

Few things are more comforting on a cold day than a steaming hot, thick, and savory beef stew. A can of cheddar cheese soup and sour cream add a rich creaminess.

Start to Finish: 25 minutes

10   **ounces dried wide egg noodles (5 cups)**

1   **17-ounce package refrigerated cooked beef tips with gravy**

1   **10.75-ounce can condensed cheddar cheese soup**

1   **9-ounce package frozen Italian-style green beans**

1   **4.5-ounce jar (drained weight) whole mushrooms, drained**

½   **cup water**

3   **tablespoons tomato paste**

2   **tablespoons dried minced onion**

½   **cup dairy sour cream**

1 Cook noodles according to package directions; drain. Return noodles to pan; cover and keep warm.

2 Meanwhile, in a 4-quart Dutch oven combine beef tips with gravy, soup, green beans, drained mushrooms, water, tomato paste, and minced onion. Bring to boiling; reduce heat. Cover and simmer for 10 to 15 minutes or until green beans are crisp-tender, stirring occasionally. Stir in sour cream; cook for 2 to 3 minutes more or until heated through. Serve over hot cooked noodles.

Makes 6 servings

Nutrition Facts per serving: 378 cal., 13 g total fat (5 g sat. fat), 90 mg chol., 954 mg sodium, 49 g carbo., 4 g fiber, 22 g pro.

BEEF BURGUNDY

Packed with all the flavor of the classic slow-simmered stew, this shortcut beef Burgundy comes together in just 15 minutes, then cooks for another 20.

Prep: 15 minutes   Cook: 20 minutes

12   ounces dried wide egg
     noodles (6 cups)

1   17-ounce package
     refrigerated cooked beef
     tips with gravy

½   teaspoon dried basil,
     crushed

¼   teaspoon ground black
     pepper

1   10.75-ounce can condensed
     golden mushroom soup

½   cup Burgundy wine

1½   cups packaged sliced fresh
     mushrooms

1   cup packaged peeled baby
     carrots, halved lengthwise

1   cup frozen small whole
     onions

1 Cook noodles according to package directions; drain. Return noodles to pan; cover and keep warm.

2 In a large saucepan combine beef tips with gravy, basil, and pepper. Stir in soup and wine. Bring to boiling. Add mushrooms, carrots, and onions. Return to boiling; reduce heat to low. Cover and simmer for 20 to 25 minutes or until vegetables are tender, stirring frequently. Serve meat mixture over noodles.

Makes 5 or 6 servings

Nutrition Facts per serving: 458 cal., 10 g total fat (3 g sat. fat), 106 mg chol., 1017 mg sodium, 63 g carbo., 5 g fiber, 26 g pro.

ROAST BEEF AND MASHED POTATO STACKS

Here's a comfort food dish that recalls chrome-shiny diners and sassy waitstaff:
It's a layered concoction of white bread, prepared mashed potatoes, and purchased
cooked beef tips with gravy.

Start to Finish: 15 minutes

1	**17-ounce package refrigerated cooked beef tips with gravy**
½	**cup onion-seasoned beef broth**
1	**20-ounce package refrigerated mashed potatoes**
2	**tablespoons butter**
⅛	**teaspoon ground black pepper**
4	**slices thick-sliced white bread**

1 In a large skillet combine beef tips with gravy and broth. Cook and stir over medium heat until heated through.

2 Meanwhile, prepare mashed potatoes according to package directions, adding the butter and the pepper.

3 To serve, place bread slices on 4 plates. Divide mashed potatoes among bread slices. Ladle beef mixture over potatoes and bread. Serve immediately.

Makes 4 servings

Nutrition Facts per serving: 372 cal., 15 g total fat (6 g sat. fat), 64 mg chol., 1174 mg sodium, 36 g carbo., 2 g fiber, 23 g pro.

BEEF TIPS ON TOAST

Zucchini slices, red onion, and a feta cheese topper freshen hot roast beef sandwiches giving a Mediterranean spin to an American classic.

Start to Finish: 25 minutes

1 tablespoon olive oil or cooking oil

2 small zucchini and/or yellow summer squash, thinly sliced (about 2 cups)

½ of a medium red onion, cut into thin wedges (about ¾ cup)

1 17-ounce package refrigerated cooked beef tips with gravy

4 1-inch slices white or wheat bread, toasted

½ cup crumbled feta cheese (2 ounces)

1 In a large skillet heat oil over medium heat. Add zucchini and onion; cook just until tender. Add beef tips with gravy; heat through, breaking up meat with a spoon.

2 To serve, spoon beef mixture on top of bread slices. Sprinkle with feta cheese.

Makes 4 servings

Nutrition Facts per serving: 354 cal., 14 g total fat (5 g sat. fat), 60 mg chol., 1157 mg sodium, 34 g carbo., 3 g fiber, 24 g pro.

ITALIAN WEDDING SALAD

Reminiscent of the famous Italian wedding soup, this warm pasta salad combines hearty meatballs, spinach, and orzo pasta.

Start to Finish: 25 minutes

- **6 ounces dried orzo pasta**
- **I 16-ounce package frozen cooked meatballs (32 bite-size meatballs), thawed**
- **½ cup bottled Italian salad dressing**
- **I 6-ounce jar marinated artichoke hearts, drained and chopped**
- **I 6-ounce package prewashed baby spinach**
- **¼ cup chopped walnuts, toasted**
- **Salt and ground black pepper**
- **Finely shredded Parmesan or Romano cheese (optional)**

1 Cook pasta according to package directions; drain well.

2 Meanwhile, in a 4-quart Dutch oven combine meatballs and salad dressing. Cook over medium heat until meatballs are heated through, stirring occasionally. Stir in cooked pasta, artichoke hearts, spinach, and walnuts. Heat and stir just until spinach is wilted. Season to taste with salt and pepper. If desired, sprinkle with cheese.

Makes 4 servings

Nutrition Facts per serving: 730 cal., 52 g total fat (I5 g sat. fat), 40 mg chol., I383 mg sodium, 48 g carbo., 8 g fiber, 23 g pro.

QUICK MEATBALL MINESTRONE

Use the smaller ½-ounce meatballs for this soup as they are easier to eat with a spoon.

Start to Finish: 25 minutes

1   16-ounce package frozen cooked Italian-style meatballs (32 bite-size meatballs)

3   14-ounce cans reduced-sodium beef broth

1   15- to 16-ounce can Great Northern beans or cannellini (white kidney) beans, rinsed and drained

1   14.5-ounce can diced tomatoes with basil, garlic, and oregano, undrained

1   10-ounce package frozen mixed vegetables

1   cup dried small pasta (such as macaroni, small shell, mini penne, or rotini)

1   teaspoon sugar

Finely shredded Parmesan cheese (optional)

In a 4-quart Dutch oven stir together meatballs, beef broth, beans, undrained tomatoes, and frozen vegetables. Bring to boiling. Stir in pasta. Return to boiling; reduce heat. Simmer, uncovered, about 10 minutes, or until pasta is tender and meatballs are heated through. Stir in sugar. If desired, sprinkle individual servings with Parmesan cheese.

Makes 6 to 8 servings

Nutrition Facts per serving: 413 cal., 15 g total fat (7 g sat. fat), 40 mg chol., 1242 mg sodium, 47 g carbo., 8 g fiber, 24 g pro.

SWEET-AND-SOUR MEATBALLS

Pineapple juice and maple syrup make an easy sweet and sour sauce
to rival any sauce out of a bottle.

Start to Finish: 30 minutes

1   20-ounce can pineapple
    chunks

¾   cup maple syrup or maple-
    flavored syrup

½   cup cider vinegar

1   16-ounce package frozen
    cooked meatballs

2   medium red and/or green
    sweet peppers, cut into
    ¾-inch pieces

¼   cup cold water

2   tablespoons cornstarch

½   teaspoon salt

2   cups hot cooked Asian
    noodles or rice

    Sliced green onion
    (optional)

1 Drain pineapple, reserving liquid. Set pineapple chunks aside. In a large saucepan stir together pineapple liquid, syrup, and vinegar. Add meatballs. Bring to boiling; reduce heat. Cover and simmer for 15 minutes.

2 Add sweet pepper to meatballs. Cover and simmer for 5 minutes more.

3 In a small bowl stir together water, cornstarch, and salt until smooth. Stir into meatball mixture. Cook and stir until thickened and bubbly. Stir in pineapple chunks; cook about 2 minutes more or until pineapple is heated through. Serve over hot cooked noodles. If desired, sprinkle individual servings with green onion.

Makes 4 servings

Nutrition Facts per serving: 667 cal., 23 g total fat (9 g sat. fat), 30 mg chol., 972 mg sodium, 107 g carbo., 5 g fiber, 14 g pro.

GERMAN MEATBALLS WITH SPAETZLE

Look for dried spaetzle with the dried pasta and noodles in your supermarket. In a pinch, any small pasta will make a good substitute.

Prep: 20 minutes   Cook: 16 minutes

1	**10.5-ounce package dried spaetzle**
1	**16-ounce package frozen cooked meatballs (32 bite-size meatballs)**
1	**14-ounce can beef broth**
1	**4-ounce can (drained weight) mushroom stems and pieces, drained**
1	**medium onion, chopped (½ cup)**
1	**8-ounce carton dairy sour cream**
2	**tablespoons all-purpose flour**
½	**to 1 teaspoon caraway seeds**
	Snipped fresh parsley (optional)

1 Cook spaetzle according to package directions. Drain.

2 Meanwhile, in a large saucepan combine meatballs, beef broth, mushrooms, and onion. Bring to boiling; reduce heat. Cover and simmer for 15 to 20 minutes or until meatballs are heated through.

3 In a small bowl combine sour cream, flour, and caraway seeds; stir into meatball mixture. Cook and stir until mixture is thickened and bubbly. Cook and stir for 1 minute more.

4 To serve, spoon meatball mixture over spaetzle. If desired, sprinkle with parsley.

Makes 4 to 6 servings

Nutrition Facts per serving: 796 cal., 44 g total fat (20 g sat. fat), 122 mg chol., 2128 mg sodium, 70 g carbo., 7 g fiber, 30 g pro.

MEATBALL STEW

Fast, delicious, and sure to please, this stew has everything your family wants for a weeknight dinner. Make an extra batch and freeze in individual containers for busy nights.

Start to Finish: 30 minutes

2   14-ounce cans reduced-sodium beef broth

1   14.5-ounce can diced tomatoes, undrained

½   cup water

2   medium carrots, coarsely chopped (1 cup)

2   stalks celery, sliced (1 cup)

1   large onion, chopped (1 cup)

⅓   cup quick-cooking barley

1   teaspoon dried basil, crushed

1   bay leaf

1   16-ounce package frozen cooked meatballs (32 bite-size meatballs)

1 In a large saucepan combine beef broth, undrained tomatoes, water, carrots, celery, onion, barley, basil, and bay leaf. Bring to boiling, stirring occasionally; reduce heat. Cover and simmer for 5 minutes.

2 Add frozen meatballs. Return to boiling; reduce heat. Cover and simmer about 5 minutes more or until meatballs are heated through and barley is tender, stirring once or twice. Remove and discard bay leaf.

Makes 6 to 8 servings

Nutrition Facts per serving: 299 cal., 20 g total fat (8 g sat. fat), 27 mg chol., 1001 mg sodium, 19 g carbo., 5 g fiber, 13 g pro.

CRANBERRY–BLUE CHEESE BURGERS

Tangy cranberries and pungent blue cheese–flavored sour cream make
these easy-to-make hamburgers extra special.

Prep: 15 minutes   Grill: 10 minutes

6 **4-ounce purchased uncooked ground beef or ground turkey patties**

Salt and ground black pepper

1 **8-ounce dairy sour cream blue cheese–flavor dip**

½ **cup dried cranberries**

6 **kaiser rolls or hamburger buns, split and toasted**

Lettuce leaves, tomato slices, onion slices (optional)

1 Measure thickness of patties; sprinkle lightly with salt and pepper. For a charcoal grill, place patties on the greased rack of an uncovered grill. Grill directly over medium coals until done (160°F), turning once. Allow about 10 minutes for ½-inch-thick patties or 14 to 18 minutes for ¾-inch-thick patties. (For a gas grill, preheat grill. Reduce heat to medium. Place patties on a greased grill rack. Cover and grill as above.)

2 Meanwhile, stir together dip and dried cranberries.

3 Place each patty on the bottom of a bun. Top with cranberry mixture, and if desired, lettuce, tomato, and/or onion. Top each burger with a bun top.

Makes 6 burgers

Nutrition Facts per burger: 698 cal., 49 g total fat (20 g sat. fat), 95 mg chol., 702 mg sodium, 39 g carbo., 2 g fiber, 24 g pro.

CAESAR SALAD BEEF BURGERS ON GARLIC CROSTINI

Hail, Caesar! The garlic, Parmesan, and the Mediterranean greens that have made Caesar salad a champion give burgers the royal treatment.

Prep: 15 minutes   Grill: 10 minutes

4   **4-ounce purchased uncooked ground beef or ground turkey patties**

Salt and ground black pepper

8   **½-inch slices sourdough bread**

½   **cup bottled Caesar salad dressing**

4   **cups packaged Mediterranean-blend torn mixed salad greens**

½   **cup bottled roasted red sweet peppers, drained and cut into thin strips**

¼   **cup shredded Parmesan cheese (2 ounces)**

1 Measure thickness of patties; sprinkle lightly with salt and pepper. For a charcoal grill, place patties on the greased rack of an uncovered grill. Grill directly over medium coals until done (160°F)* turning once. Allow about 10 minutes for ½-inch-thick patties or 14 to 18 minutes for ¾-inch-thick patties. (For a gas grill. preheat grill. Reduce heat to medium. Place patties on the greased grill rack. Cover and grill as above.)

2 Meanwhile, brush both sides of each bread slice with 2 tablespoons of the dressing. Place bread slices on grill rack. Grill for 1 to 2 minutes per side until lightly toasted; remove from grill.

3 To serve, toss greens with remaining dressing. Divide greens among 4 of the bread slices. Top each with a burger and some of the roasted pepper strips. Sprinkle each with Parmesan cheese. Top with remaining bread slices.

Makes 4 burgers

Nutrition Facts per burger: 573 cal., 36 g total fat (11 g sat. fat), 79 mg chol., 809 mg sodium, 32 g carbo., 2 g fiber, 32 g pro.

*NOTE: The internal color of a burger is not a reliable doneness indicator. A beef or turkey patty cooked to 160°F is safe, regardless of color. To measure the doneness of a patty, insert an instant-read thermometer through the side of the patty to a depth of 2 to 3 inches.

BROILER METHOD: Preheat broiler. Place patties on unheated rack of a broiler pan. Broil in preheated broiler 3 to 4 inches from heat for 12 to 14 minutes or until done (160°F), turning once.

BURGERS ITALIANO

In this recipe, two American favorites—pizza and hamburgers—come together in complete harmony.

Prep: 15 minutes   Broil: 11 minutes

4   **4-ounce purchased uncooked ground beef or ground turkey patties**

    Salt and ground black pepper

4   **¾-inch slices sourdough bread**

1   **cup purchased mushroom pasta sauce**

1   **cup shredded provolone or mozzarella cheese (4 ounces)**

2   **tablespoons thinly sliced fresh basil**

1 Preheat broiler. Sprinkle patties lightly with salt and pepper. Place patties on the unheated rack of a broiler pan. Broil 3 to 4 inches from the heat for 10 to 12 minutes or until done (160°F),* turning once halfway through cooking time. Add bread slices to broiler pan for the last 2 to 3 minutes of broiling, turning once to toast.

2 Meanwhile, in a medium saucepan heat pasta sauce over medium heat until bubbly, stirring occasionally.

3 Place patties on bread slices. Spoon pasta sauce over patties; sprinkle with cheese. Place on the rack of the broiler pan. Return to broiler; broil for 1 to 2 minutes more or until cheese melts. Sprinkle with basil.

Makes 4 burgers

Nutrition Facts per burger: 504 cal., 30 g total fat (13 g sat. fat), 96 mg chol., 815 mg sodium, 27 g carbo., 2 g fiber, 30 g pro.

*NOTE: The internal color of a burger is not a reliable doneness indicator. A beef or turkey patty cooked to 160°F is safe, regardless of color. To measure the doneness of a patty, insert an instant-read thermometer through the side of the patty to a depth of 2 to 3 inches.

GREEK-STYLE BURGERS

The tang of feta cheese and a hint of fresh mint complement these deliciously different grilled patties. Pictured on page 130.

Prep: 10 minutes   Grill: 10 minutes

4   **4-ounce purchased uncooked ground beef or ground turkey patties**

   Salt and ground black pepper

⅓   **cup bottled cucumber ranch salad dressing**

½   **cup crumbled feta cheese (2 ounces)**

1   **tablespoon snipped fresh mint**

4   **lettuce leaves**

4   **kaiser rolls, split and toasted**

4   **tomato slices**

1 Measure thickness of patties; sprinkle patties lightly with salt and pepper. For a charcoal grill, place patties on the greased rack of an uncovered grill. Grill directly over medium coals until done (160°F), turning once. Allow about 10 minutes for ½-inch-thick patties or 14 to 18 minutes for ¾-inch-thick patties. (For a gas grill, preheat grill. Place patties on a greased grill rack over heat. Cover and grill as above.)

2 Meanwhile, for cucumber sauce, in a small bowl combine salad dressing, feta cheese, and mint.

3 Place lettuce on bottom halves of rolls. Top with patties, tomato, and cucumber sauce. Add roll tops.

Makes 4 burgers

Nutrition Facts per burger: 542 cal., 33 g total fat (11 g sat. fat), 88 mg chol., 837 mg sodium, 33 g carbo., 2 g fiber, 29 g pro.

CHILI BURGERS

Ever hear of Cincinnati chili? It's a spicy chili that's often served over spaghetti and topped with cheese—and sometimes onions and more beans. This fun version of burgers is patterned after that classic.

Start to Finish: 30 minutes

4	**4-ounce purchased uncooked ground beef or ground turkey patties**
½	**teaspoon salt**
	Dash ground black pepper
1	**tablespoon cooking oil**
¼	**cup chopped onion**
½	**teaspoon bottled minced garlic (1 clove)**
1	**15-ounce can chili with beans**
1	**14.5-ounce can diced tomatoes, undrained**
4	**slices Texas toast, toasted**
½	**cup shredded cheddar cheese (2 ounces)**

1 Sprinkle patties with salt and pepper. Heat a 12-inch skillet over medium-high heat. Add patties; reduce heat to medium. Cook, uncovered, for 6 to 8 minutes or until done (160°F), turning once. Remove patties from skillet and keep warm. Drain fat from skillet; carefully wipe out skillet.

2 Add oil to skillet. Return skillet to heat. Add onion and garlic; cook over medium heat until tender. Stir in chili and undrained tomatoes. Bring to boiling; reduce heat. Simmer, uncovered, for 5 to 10 minutes or until desired consistency, stirring occasionally.

3 To serve, place patties on top of toast. Spoon chili mixture over all. Sprinkle with cheese.

Makes 4 servings

Nutrition Facts per burger: 686 cal., 43 g total fat (16 g sat. fat), 168 mg chol., 1315 mg sodium, 39 g carbo., 5 g fiber, 37 g pro.

HAM AND POTATO SALAD IN PEPPERS

For more punch, add snipped fresh dill, celery seeds, and a grind or two of black pepper to the potato salad filling.

Start to Finish: 15 minutes

2   medium green sweet peppers

1   pint purchased deli potato salad

1   cup packaged cubed cooked ham (5 ounces)

½   cup frozen whole kernel corn, thawed

1   to 2 tablespoons dill pickle relish

1 Cut sweet peppers in half; remove and discard stems, seeds, and membranes. In a large saucepan cook pepper halves in a large amount of boiling water for 3 minutes. Drain. Chill pepper halves in a bowl of ice water.

2 Meanwhile, stir together potato salad, ham, corn, and pickle relish. Invert pepper halves onto paper towels to drain. Set pepper halves cut sides up; if necessary, pat dry with paper towels. Spoon potato mixture into pepper halves.

Makes 4 servings

Nutrition Facts per serving: 280 cal., 14 g total fat (3 g sat. fat), 106 mg chol., 1229 mg sodium, 23 g carbo., 3 g fiber, 12 g pro.

HAM AND BROCCOLI-TOPPED SPUDS

Wise moms have a ready stash of off-the-shelf ingredients for emergency meals. These saucy baked potatoes make a quick and filling supper with just four items that you can keep on hand.

Prep: 10 minutes   Bake: 40 minutes   Oven: 425°F

4   **medium baking potatoes (6 to 8 ounces each)**

2   **10-ounce packages frozen cut broccoli in cheese sauce**

2   **cups packaged cubed cooked ham (10 ounces)**

½   **teaspoon caraway seeds**

1 Preheat oven to 425°F. Scrub potatoes thoroughly; pat dry. Prick potatoes with a fork. (If desired, for soft skins, rub potatoes with shortening or wrap each potato in foil.) Bake potatoes for 40 to 60 minutes or until tender.*

2 Meanwhile, heat broccoli in pouches according to package directions. Place contents of pouches in a medium saucepan. Add ham and caraway seeds; heat through.

3 To serve, roll each potato gently under your hand. Using a knife, cut an X in top of each potato. Press in and up on the ends of each potato. Top with broccoli mixture.

Makes 4 servings

Nutrition Facts per serving: 338 cal., 10 g total fat (3 g sat. fat), 44 mg chol., 1713 mg sodium, 38 g carbo., 6 g fiber, 24 g pro.

*NOTE: To microwave potatoes, prick potatoes with a fork. Do not rub with shortening or wrap in foil. On a microwave-safe plate arrange potatoes spoke fashion. Microwave, uncovered, on 100% power (high) for 13 to 16 minutes or until tender, rearranging and turning potatoes over once. Let stand for 5 minutes. Continue as directed above.

Italian Vegetable and Sausage Topped Spuds: Substitute two 9-ounce packages Tuscan vegetables (zucchini, red and yellow peppers, carrots, and squash) in herbed tomato sauce for the broccoli in cheese sauce. Substitute 10 ounces chopped cooked Italian sausage for the ham. Omit the caraway seeds.

HEARTY HAM STEW

This sweet-and-saucy skillet meal works any time of year. When the weather's cold, it's ideal for chasing away the chills. During the summer, it's great fun to stir up over a campfire, camp stove, or grill.

Start to Finish: 15 minutes

2 **16-ounce cans pork and beans in tomato sauce**

1 **16-ounce package frozen mixed vegetables, thawed**

1½ **cups packaged cubed cooked ham (8 ounces)**

1 **tablespoon dried minced onion**

1 **cup broken corn chips (optional)**

In a large skillet stir together pork and beans, mixed vegetables, ham, and minced onion. Cook over medium heat until bubbly, stirring occasionally. If desired, top individual servings with broken corn chips.

Makes 6 to 8 servings

Nutrition Facts per serving: 255 cal., 5 g total fat (2 g sat. fat), 32 mg chol., 1189 mg sodium, 41 g carbo., 10 g fiber, 17 g pro.

CHEESE AND HAM CHOWDER

Russet or Idaho potatoes are perfect in this soup. Their starchy composition
adds just the right thickness.

Start to Finish: 30 minutes

1	**cup water**
2	**medium potatoes, peeled and chopped (1½ cups)**
1	**medium carrot, chopped (½ cup)**
1	**stalk celery, sliced (½ cup)**
¼	**cup chopped onion**
2	**tablespoons butter**
2	**tablespoons all-purpose flour**
1	**cup milk**
1	**cup packaged cubed cooked ham (5 ounces)**
8	**ounces process cheese spread, cubed**

1 In a large saucepan bring the water to boiling. Add potatoes, carrot, celery, and onion. Cover and cook for 12 to 15 minutes or until tender. Do not drain.

2 Meanwhile, in a small saucepan melt butter over medium heat; stir in flour until smooth. Add milk all at once. Cook and stir until mixture is thickened and bubbly. Stir milk mixture into potato mixture. Stir in ham and cheese. Cook and stir until cheese is melted and soup is heated through.

Makes 4 servings

Nutrition Facts per serving: 410 cal., 25 g total fat (15 g sat. fat), 88 mg chol., 1344 mg sodium, 24 g carbo., 2 g fiber, 23 g pro.

HAM AND CHEESE CALZONES

The melted cheese gets mighty hot, so let these turnovers cool for a few minutes before serving them.

Prep: 15 minutes   Bake: 15 minutes   Stand: 5 minutes   Oven: 400°F

1   **13.8-ounce package refrigerated pizza dough**

¼   **cup coarse-grain mustard**

6   **ounces sliced Swiss or provolone cheese**

1½   **cups packaged cubed cooked ham (8 ounces)**

½   **teaspoon caraway seeds**

1 Preheat oven to 400°F. Line a baking sheet with foil; lightly grease foil. Unroll pizza dough. On a lightly floured surface roll or pat dough to a 15×10-inch rectangle. Cut dough in half crosswise and lengthwise to make 4 rectangles. Spread mustard over rectangles.

2 Divide half of the cheese among the rectangles, placing cheese on half of each rectangle and cutting or tearing to fit as necessary. Top with ham and sprinkle with caraway seeds. Top with remaining cheese. Brush edges of rectangles with water. For each calzone, fold dough over filling to opposite edge, stretching slightly if necessary. Seal edges with the tines of a fork.

3 Place calzones on the prepared baking sheet. Prick tops to allow steam to escape. Bake about 15 minutes or until golden brown. Let stand for 5 minutes before serving.

Makes 4 calzones

Nutrition Facts per calzone: 421 cal., 21 g total fat (10 g sat. fat), 72 mg chol., 1390 mg sodium, 28 g carbo., 1 g fiber, 30 g pro.

Barbecue Chicken Calzones: Substitute ¼ cup bottled barbecue sauce for the mustard. Substitute 6 ounces shredded Monterey Jack cheese for the Swiss or provolone cheese. Substitute 1½ cups chopped cooked chicken for the ham and omit the caraway seeds.

CHICKEN, GOAT CHEESE, AND GREENS

Go ahead, invite guests over at the last minute. Dinner can be a cinch. Just stop at the supermarket to pick up a ready-to-eat deli-roasted chicken and a few other ingredients.

Prep: 15 minutes   Bake: 15 minutes   Oven: 350°F

1½ **pounds Swiss chard, beet greens, and/or mustard greens, trimmed and washed**

1   **2- to 2½-pound purchased deli-roasted chicken**

3   **tablespoons olive oil**

2   **tablespoons lemon juice**

2   **tablespoons snipped fresh dill, oregano, and/or sage**

¼   **teaspoon sea salt, kosher salt, or salt**

⅛   **teaspoon cracked black pepper**

1   **3- to 4-ounce log goat cheese (chèvre), sliced into rounds or coarsely crumbled**

⅛   **teaspoon cracked black pepper**

1 Preheat oven to 350°F. Reserve 1 or 2 small leaves of the greens. Tear remaining greens and place in a 3-quart rectangular baking dish. Remove string from chicken; use the string to tie the chicken legs together. Place chicken on greens in baking dish.

2 In a small bowl combine oil and lemon juice. Drizzle oil mixture over chicken and greens in baking dish. Sprinkle 1 tablespoon of the dill over the chicken and chard. Sprinkle the salt and ⅛ teaspoon pepper only over the torn greens.

3 Loosely cover dish with foil. Bake for 15 to 20 minutes or until torn greens are tender. Meanwhile, sprinkle cheese with remaining 1 tablespoon snipped dill and ⅛ teaspoon pepper.

4 Transfer chicken to a serving platter. Place some of the goat cheese on top of chicken. Add reserved greens. Toss cooked greens in dish to evenly coat with cooking liquid. Serve cooked greens and remaining cheese with chicken.

Makes 4 servings

Nutrition Facts per serving: 542 cal., 36 g total fat (10 g sat. fat), 143 mg chol., 620 mg sodium, 7 g carbo., 3 g fiber, 48 g pro.

NOTE: This recipe doubles easily to serve 8. Double the ingredients and prepare as directed, except place all the greens and both chickens in a large shallow roasting pan.

MEXICAN CHICKEN CASSEROLE

All it takes are four simple ingredients to dress up a store-bought roasted chicken for a Mexican fiesta. Serve some guacamole and Spanish rice on the side.

Prep: 15 minutes   Bake: 15 minutes   Oven: 350°F

- 1   **15-ounce can black beans, rinsed and drained**
- ½   **cup bottled chunky salsa**
- ½   **teaspoon ground cumin**
- 1   **2- to 2½-pound purchased deli-roasted chicken**
- ¼   **cup shredded Monterey Jack cheese with jalapeño peppers (1 ounce)**
-     **Dairy sour cream (optional)**

1 Preheat oven to 350°F. In a small bowl stir together beans, ¼ cup of the salsa, and the cumin. Divide bean mixture among 4 individual au gratin dishes or casseroles. Set aside.

2 Cut chicken into quarters. Place one piece on bean mixture in each dish. Spoon remaining ¼ cup salsa evenly over chicken pieces. Sprinkle evenly with cheese.

3 Bake for 15 to 20 minutes or until heated through. If desired, serve with sour cream.

Makes 4 servings

Nutrition Facts per serving: 468 cal., 23 g total fat (7 g sat. fat), 140 mg chol., 596 mg sodium, 16 g carbo., 5 g fiber, 50 g pro.

GINGER-LIME CHICKEN SALAD

Lime juice, fresh ginger, and pumpkin seeds update chicken salad with a breezy tropical flavor.

Start to Finish: 25 minutes

¼ **cup light mayonnaise or salad dressing**

¼ **teaspoon finely shredded lime peel**

2 **tablespoons lime juice**

1 **tablespoon finely chopped red onion**

2 **teaspoons grated fresh ginger**

½ **teaspoon bottled minced garlic (1 clove)**

1 **2- to 2½-pound purchased deli-roasted chicken**

2 **stalks celery, chopped (1 cup)**

Salt and ground black pepper

Lettuce leaves

1 **tablespoon salted pumpkin seeds (pepitas) or chopped peanuts**

1 In a medium bowl stir together mayonnaise, lime peel, lime juice, red onion, ginger, and garlic; set aside.

2 Cut enough of the chicken into bite-size strips (removing skin) to measure 1½ cups. (Reserve any remaining chicken for another use.) Add chicken strips and celery to mayonnaise mixture; toss to coat. Season to taste with salt and pepper. Serve immediately or cover and chill for up to 24 hours.

3 To serve, line 2 plates with lettuce leaves. Top with the chicken mixture; sprinkle with pumpkin seeds.

Makes 2 servings

Nutrition Facts per serving: 345 cal., 19 g total fat (4 g sat. fat), 103 mg chol., 636 mg sodium, 9 g carbo., 1 g fiber, 33 g pro.

ASIAN CHICKEN ROLL-UPS

Daikon is a large Asian radish with a pleasant, sweet, and zesty flavor and a mild bite. It is available year-round in many supermarkets and in Asian specialty stores.

Start to Finish: 30 minutes

1	**2- to 2½-pound purchased deli-roasted chicken**
8	**8- to 10-inch flour tortillas**
½	**cup bottled hoisin sauce**
¼	**cup finely chopped peanuts**
2	**green onions, finely chopped (¼ cup)**
½	**cup shredded daikon, well drained**
3	**tablespoons soy sauce**
3	**tablespoons Chinese black vinegar or rice vinegar**
1	**tablespoon water**
1	**teaspoon chili oil or toasted sesame oil**

1 Remove skin from chicken and discard. Remove chicken from bones and shred chicken (you should have about 4 cups); set aside.

2 Spread one side of each tortilla with some of the hoisin sauce; sprinkle with peanuts and green onion. Top with shredded chicken and daikon. Roll up; cut in half crosswise.

3 In a small bowl combine soy sauce, vinegar, water, and chili oil. Serve as a dipping sauce with chicken roll-ups.

Makes 8 roll-ups

Nutrition Facts per roll-up: 283 cal., 9 g total fat (2 g sat. fat), 50 mg chol., 869 mg sodium, 26 g carbo., 1 g fiber, 20 g pro.

DRIED TOMATO AND BASIL CHICKEN WRAPS

Make dinner fun with different colored tortillas. The kids will love filling up their white, green, and orange shells with the tomatoes, chicken, cheese, nuts, and basil leaves. Pictured on page 131.

Start to Finish: 25 minutes

½	**of a 3-ounce package (about ¾ cup) dried tomatoes (not oil-packed)**
1	**2- to 2½-pound purchased deli-roasted chicken**
1	**cup shredded mozzarella or Monterey Jack cheese (4 ounces)**
½	**cup chopped pecans, toasted**
⅔	**cup bottled creamy Italian or ranch salad dressing**
6	**10-inch dried tomato, spinach, and/or plain flour tortillas**
1	**cup large fresh basil leaves**
	Bottled creamy Italian or ranch salad dressing (optional)

1 Soak dried tomatoes in enough hot water to cover for 10 minutes. Meanwhile, using two forks, shred enough chicken to measure 3 cups. (Reserve any remaining chicken for another use.) Drain and chop the tomatoes.

2 In a large bowl combine the tomatoes, the shredded chicken, cheese, pecans, and the ⅔ cup salad dressing.

3 Line tortillas with basil leaves. Divide chicken mixture among the tortillas. Fold in sides and roll up. If desired, wrap in plastic wrap and chill for up to 4 hours. Cut each wrap diagonally in half to serve. If desired, serve with additional dressing for dipping.

Makes 6 wraps

Nutrition Facts per wrap: 501 cal., 34 g total fat (8 g sat. fat), 73 mg chol., 1318 mg sodium, 31 g carbo., 3 g fiber, 23 g pro.

TEQUILA-LIME CHICKEN

A bit of lime peel and a splash of tequila give purchased Alfredo sauce a Tex-Mex attitude.

Start to Finish: 15 minutes

- 1 **9-ounce package refrigerated fettuccine**
- 1 **10-ounce container refrigerated Alfredo pasta sauce or light Alfredo pasta sauce**
- ¼ **cup tequila or milk**
- 1 **teaspoon finely shredded lime peel**
- 2 **5.5-ounce packages refrigerated grilled chicken breast strips**
- 1 **lime, cut into 8 wedges**

1 Cook the fettuccine according to package directions; drain.

2 In a medium saucepan combine Alfredo sauce, tequila, and lime peel; cook and stir just until boiling. Stir in chicken strips; heat through. Toss chicken mixture with hot fettuccine. Serve with lime wedges.

Makes 4 servings

Nutrition Facts per serving: 547 cal., 24 g total fat (1 g sat. fat), 133 mg chol., 981 mg sodium, 39 g carbo., 2 g fiber, 11 g pro.

Cajun Chicken Fettuccine: Substitute bourbon for the tequila. Use 1 teaspoon Cajun seasoning instead of lime peel. Omit lime wedge garnish.

GARDEN TACOS

For a make-your-own taco supper, stir up the pesto sauce and set out the remaining ingredients. Everyone can fill their taco in their own style.

Start to Finish: 15 minutes

½ **cup mayonnaise or salad dressing**

3 **to 4 tablespoons purchased dried tomato pesto**

8 **to 12 6-inch corn or 7- to 8-inch flour tortillas**

2 **5.5-ounce packages refrigerated grilled chicken breast strips**

2 **small yellow summer squash or zucchini (8 ounces), cut into sticks**

1 **medium sweet pepper, cut into strips**

   Cilantro sprigs (optional)

1 In a small bowl stir together mayonnaise and pesto; set aside.

2 Place tortillas on a microwave-safe plate; cover with paper towels. Microwave on 100% power (high) for 30 to 45 seconds or until tortillas are warm.

3 Place warm tortillas on serving plates. Arrange chicken, squash, and sweet pepper on half of each tortilla. If desired, top with cilantro; add mayonnaise mixture. Fold tortillas over to cover filling.

Makes 4 servings

Nutrition Facts per serving: 481 cal., 30 g total fat (6 g sat. fat), 66 mg chol., 1021 mg sodium, 30 g carbo., 5 g fiber, 24 g pro.

BUFFALO CHICKEN PIZZAS

If the Southwest-flavor chicken breast strips aren't hot enough for you, add a few drops of bottled hot pepper sauce or buffalo wing sauce.

Start to Finish: 20 minutes   Oven: 450°F

4   **pita bread rounds**

¼   **cup bottled blue cheese salad dressing**

1   **9-ounce package refrigerated Southwest-flavor cooked chicken breast strips or two 5.5-ounce packages refrigerated grilled chicken breast strips**

¾   **cup thinly sliced celery**

Blue cheese crumbles (optional)

Bottled hot pepper sauce or buffalo wing sauce

1 Preheat oven to 450°F. Place pita rounds on baking sheet. Brush with salad dressing. Top with chicken strips and celery.

2 Bake, uncovered, about 10 minutes or until heated through and pitas are crisp. Transfer pizzas to plates. If desired, sprinkle with blue cheese crumbles. Pass hot pepper sauce.

Makes 4 servings

Nutrition Facts per serving: 353 cal., 14 g total fat (3 g sat. fat), 45 mg chol., 1084 mg sodium, 36 g carbo., 2 g fiber, 21 g pro.

SOUTHWESTERN CHICKEN WRAPS

These Tex-Mex-influenced sandwich rolls are perfect for a meal on a sweltering summer day. The precooked chicken strips allow you to put them together with no cooking.

Start to Finish: 15 minutes

½   cup dairy sour cream

2   tablespoons purchased guacamole

4   10-inch dried tomato, spinach, and/or plain flour tortillas

2   5.5-ounce packages refrigerated Southwest-flavor cooked chicken breast strips

2   roma tomatoes, sliced

2   cups shredded lettuce

In a small bowl stir together sour cream and guacamole. Divide sour cream mixture among tortillas, spreading over 1 side of each tortilla. Divide chicken, tomatoes, and lettuce among tortillas. Roll up. Serve immediately.

Makes 4 wraps

Nutrition Facts per wrap: 395 cal., 13 g total fat (4 g sat. fat), 49 mg chol., 1015 mg sodium, 45 g carbo., 2 g fiber, 25 g pro.

Light Southwestern Chicken Wraps: Substitute light dairy sour cream or plain lowfat yogurt for the sour cream.

COUSCOUS CHICKEN SALAD

Swift-cooking couscous is a tiny grain-shaped pasta made from semolina flour. Once cooked and fluffed up, it's a good substitute for rice or polenta. You'll find couscous near the rice and dried beans at your grocery store.

Start to Finish: 20 minutes

1 **14-ounce can reduced-sodium chicken broth**

1¼ **cups quick-cooking couscous**

½ **cup mango chutney (cut up large fruit pieces)**

¼ **cup bottled olive oil and vinegar salad dressing, white wine vinaigrette salad dressing, or roasted garlic vinaigrette salad dressing**

1 **6-ounce package refrigerated lemon-pepper or Italian-style cooked chicken breast strips, cut into bite-size pieces (about 1½ cups)**

1 **cup coarsely chopped seeded cucumber or radish**

½ **cup golden raisins**

Salt and ground black pepper

1 **small cucumber, cut into spears**

1 In a medium saucepan bring broth to boiling. Stir in couscous. Cover and remove from heat. Let stand for 5 minutes. Fluff couscous lightly with a fork.

2 In a medium bowl combine chutney and salad dressing. Add chicken, chopped cucumber, raisins, and couscous; toss to coat. Season to taste with salt and pepper. Serve with cucumber spears.

Makes 4 servings

Nutrition Facts per serving: 418 cal., 10 g total fat (1 g sat. fat), 28 mg chol., 873 mg sodium, 62 g carbo., 4 g fiber, 19 g pro.

EASY CHICKEN-PESTO MOCK POT PIE

These mini pot pies topped with breadstick pinwheels win in eye appeal as well as flavor.

Prep: 15 minutes   Bake: according to package directions   Oven: 375°F

- 1 **11-ounce package (12) refrigerated breadsticks**
- 1 **12-ounce jar chicken gravy**
- ½ **cup dairy sour cream**
- ⅓ **cup purchased basil or dried tomato pesto**
- 2 **9-ounce packages frozen chopped cooked chicken breast, thawed**
- 1 **16-ounce package frozen peas and carrots**

1 Preheat oven to 375°F. Unroll and separate breadsticks. Curl each breadstick into a spiral and place on an ungreased baking sheet. Bake the breadsticks according to package directions.

2 Meanwhile, in a large saucepan combine chicken gravy, sour cream, and pesto. Stir in chicken and peas and carrots. Bring to boiling, stirring frequently.

3 Spoon chicken mixture into 6 serving bowls. Top with baked breadsticks.

Makes 6 servings

Nutrition Facts per serving: 416 cal., 16 g total fat (6 g sat. fat), 58 mg chol., 1140 mg sodium, 39 g carbo., 4 g fiber, 30 g pro.

CILANTRO CHICKEN PASTA WITH TOMATOES

This bow-tie-and-chicken salad can be served either hot or chilled.

Start to Finish: 20 minutes

8   ounces dried bow tie or penne pasta

1   9-ounce package frozen chopped, cooked chicken breast, thawed

2   medium tomatoes, chopped (1 cup)

2   green onions, sliced (¼ cup)

⅓   cup snipped fresh cilantro

¾   cup bottled French salad dressing

1   tablespoon balsamic vinegar

2   slices packaged ready-to-serve cooked bacon, crumbled

¼   teaspoon salt

¼   teaspoon cracked black pepper

1 Cook pasta according to package directions; drain. In a large bowl combine cooked pasta, chicken, tomatoes, green onions, and cilantro.

2 In a small bowl stir together salad dressing, balsamic vinegar, bacon, salt, and pepper. Pour over pasta mixture; toss to coat. Return to pan and heat through. Serve immediately. (Or, cover and chill for up to 24 hours before serving.)

Makes 4 servings

Nutrition Facts per serving: 558 cal., 24 g total fat (6 g sat. fat), 57 mg chol., 894 mg sodium, 56 g carbo., 3 g fiber, 29 g pro.

SWEET CHICKEN TOSTADAS

Fruit salsa makes a nice change from the regular tomato version.
It complements the chicken and gives these tostadas a pleasant
sweetness. Look for pineapple or peach salsa.

Start to Finish: 20 minutes

- **8 tostada shells**
- **½ cup dairy sour cream**
- **1 cup bottled fruit salsa**
- **1 9-ounce package frozen chopped cooked chicken breast, thawed**
- **1 cup shredded Monterey Jack cheese with jalapeño chile peppers (4 ounces)**

1 Preheat broiler. Spread one side of each tostada shell with 1 tablespoon of the sour cream, spreading to edges. Spread 2 tablespoons of the salsa evenly over the sour cream on each tostada. Top each with 3 tablespoons of the chopped chicken and 2 tablespoons of the shredded cheese.

2 Place 4 of the tostadas on a large baking sheet. Broil 4 to 5 inches from the heat for 1 to 1½ minutes or until cheese is melted. Repeat with remaining tostadas. Serve warm.

Makes 4 servings

Nutrition Facts per serving: 5ll cal., 26 g total fat (l2 g sat. fat), 89 mg chol., 488 mg sodium, 42 g carbo., 4 g fiber, 27 g pro.

CHICKEN AND BROCCOLI SOUP WITH DUMPLINGS

If you think dumplings are something only your grandmother had the time and talent to make, think again! These dumplings stir together quickly and puff up magically on top of this family-pleasing soup.

Start to Finish: 30 minutes

2	**10.75-ounce cans condensed cream of chicken soup**
3	**cups milk**
1½	**cups frozen cut broccoli**
1	**9-ounce package frozen chopped cooked chicken breast**
1	**medium carrot, coarsely shredded (½ cup)**
1	**teaspoon Dijon-style mustard**
¼	**teaspoon dried thyme, crushed**
1	**recipe Easy Dumplings**
½	**cup shredded cheddar cheese (2 ounces)**

1 In a 4-quart Dutch oven combine soup, milk, broccoli, chicken, carrot, mustard, and thyme. Bring to boiling; reduce heat.

2 Meanwhile, prepare Easy Dumplings. Spoon dumpling batter in 4 or 5 mounds onto bubbling soup. Reduce heat. Cover and simmer for 10 to 12 minutes or until a wooden toothpick inserted into a dumpling comes out clean. Sprinkle with cheddar cheese.

Makes 4 or 5 servings

Nutrition Facts per serving: 535 cal., 26 g total fat (9 g sat. fat), 75 mg chol., 1701 mg sodium, 42 g carbo., 3 g fiber, 23 g pro.

Easy Dumplings: In a small bowl combine ⅔ cup all-purpose flour and 1 teaspoon baking powder. Add ¼ cup milk and 2 tablespoons cooking oil. Stir just until moistened.

CURRIED CHICKEN AND CORN CHOWDER

Curry powder leads this chicken soup in an exciting direction. Cooked chicken, chopped peanuts, and red pepper round out this lively soup.

Start to Finish: 15 minutes

- 1 **17-ounce can cream-style corn, undrained**
- 2 **cups milk**
- 1 **10.75-ounce can condensed cream of chicken soup**
- 1 **medium green or red sweet pepper, chopped (¾ cup)**
- 1 **tablespoon dried minced onion**
- 2 **to 3 teaspoons curry powder**
- 1 **9-ounce package frozen chopped cooked chicken breast**

 Coarsely chopped peanuts (optional)

1 In a large saucepan stir together undrained corn, milk, soup, sweet pepper, minced onion, and curry powder. Bring to boiling, stirring frequently.

2 Stir in frozen chicken; cook until heated through. If desired, sprinkle individual servings with peanuts.

Makes 4 servings

Nutrition Facts per serving: 324 cal., 11 g total fat (4 g sat. fat), 49 mg chol., 1201 mg sodium, 39 g carbo., 3 g fiber, 24 g pro.

CHICKEN with BUTTERMILK GRAVY

The aroma of broiled chicken and savory, herbed gravy will stir your senses while the flavor will satisfy your palate with each forkful.

Start to Finish: 15 minutes

6   **frozen cooked, breaded chicken breast patties**

1   **24-ounce package refrigerated mashed potatoes**

1   **1-ounce envelope chicken gravy mix**

1   **cup buttermilk**

¼   **to ½ teaspoon finely shredded lemon peel**

¼   **teaspoon dried sage leaves, crushed**

1 Bake chicken patties according to package directions. Heat potatoes according to package directions.

2 Meanwhile, for gravy, in a small saucepan prepare chicken gravy mix according to package directions, except use the 1 cup buttermilk in place of the water called for and add lemon peel and sage. Place chicken patties on serving plates. Mound potatoes on top of patties. Spoon some of the gravy over top. Pass remaining gravy.

Makes 6 servings

Nutrition Facts per serving: 301 cal., 13 g total fat (3 g sat. fat), 26 mg chol., 776 mg sodium, 33 g carbo., 2 g fiber, 14 g pro.

CHICKEN AND BISCUIT KABOBS

For the first step, heat the frozen chicken in the microwave oven to thaw slightly so you can easily thread the chicken chunks onto the skewers.

Start to Finish: 20 minutes   Oven: 400°F

- ½ **of a 13.5-ounce package (12) frozen cooked, breaded chicken breast chunks**
- 1 **4.5-ounce package (6) refrigerated buttermilk or country biscuits**
- 1 **medium zucchini or yellow summer squash, cut into 3×¾-inch strips**
- ⅓ **cup butter, melted**
- 3 **tablespoons honey**

1 Preheat oven to 400°F. Arrange chicken chunks in a single layer on a microwave-safe plate. Microwave, uncovered, on 100% power (high) for 1 minute (chicken will not be heated through).

2 Using kitchen scissors, snip each biscuit in half. On each of four wooden or metal skewers, alternately thread chicken pieces, biscuit halves, and squash strips, leaving a ¼-inch space between pieces. Place on ungreased baking sheet. Bake about 10 minutes or until biscuits are golden brown and chicken is heated through.

3 Meanwhile, whisk together melted butter and honey. Drizzle some of the butter mixture over kabobs. Pass remainder for dipping.

Makes 4 servings

Nutrition Facts per serving: 376 cal., 22 g total fat (9 g sat. fat), 57 mg chol., 649 mg sodium, 37 g carbo., 1 g fiber, 10 g pro.

SWEET-AND-SOUR CHICKEN

Bottled sweet-and-sour sauce and frozen breaded chicken make this perennial favorite doable any night of the week. Bake a package of frozen egg rolls to serve alongside.

Prep: 15 minutes   Cook: 5 minutes

1	**11-ounce package frozen cooked, breaded chicken breast strips or nuggets**
1	**tablespoon cooking oil**
1	**medium red sweet pepper, cut into bite-size strips**
1	**medium carrot, thinly sliced (½ cup)**
1	**cup fresh pea pods, tips and strings removed**
1	**8-ounce can pineapple chunks (juice pack), undrained**
½	**cup bottled sweet-and-sour sauce**
2	**to 3 cups hot cooked rice**

1 Bake chicken strips according to package directions.

2 Meanwhile, in a large nonstick skillet heat oil over medium-high heat. Add sweet pepper and carrot; cook and stir for 3 minutes. Add pea pods; cook and stir about 1 minute more or until vegetables are crisp-tender.

3 Add undrained pineapple chunks and sweet-and-sour sauce to skillet; heat through. Spoon vegetable mixture over hot cooked rice and top with chicken.

Makes 4 to 6 servings

Nutrition Facts per serving: 322 cal., 6 g total fat (1 g sat. fat), 45 mg chol., 791 mg sodium, 48 g carbo., 2 g fiber, 19 g pro.

CHICKEN AND SWEET PEPPER WRAPS

Red sweet pepper, breaded chicken strips, and shredded cheese rolled up in a tortilla make a colorful wrap with a pleasing crunch.

Start to Finish: 20 minutes

- ½ **of a 28-ounce package frozen cooked, breaded chicken strips (about 24 strips)**
- ½ **of an 8-ounce tub light cream cheese**
- 1 **green onion, thinly sliced (2 tablespoons)**
- 1 **tablespoon snipped fresh cilantro**
- 6 **7- to 8-inch flour tortillas**
- 1 **red sweet pepper, cut into bite-size strips**
- ½ **cup shredded reduced-fat or regular Monterey Jack cheese (2 ounces)**

    Bottled salsa (optional)

1 Bake chicken strips according to package directions.

2 Meanwhile, in a small bowl stir together cream cheese, green onion, and cilantro. Spread over tortillas. Top with sweet pepper strips and cheese. Top with hot chicken strips. Fold in sides and roll up. Cut in half to serve. Secure tortillas with toothpicks. If desired, serve with salsa.

Makes 6 servings

Nutrition Facts per serving: 356 cal., 20 g total fat (6 g sat. fat), 54 mg chol., 610 mg sodium, 27 g carbo., 1 g fiber, 18 g pro.

CHICKEN SALAD WITH STRAWBERRIES

Another time, try this salad with fresh raspberries instead of strawberries
and bottled raspberry vinaigrette salad dressing instead of the balsamic
vinaigrette.

Start to Finish: 20 minutes

1   **11-ounce package frozen
    cooked, breaded chicken
    nuggets**

1   **10-ounce package mixed
    salad greens**

2   **cups sliced fresh
    strawberries**

¼   **cup fresh basil leaves, cut
    into strips**

½   **cup bottled balsamic
    vinaigrette salad dressing**

1 Bake chicken nuggets according to package directions.

2 Meanwhile, in a very large bowl toss together greens,
strawberries, and basil. Divide among serving plates. Top
with chicken. Drizzle salad dressing over top of each serving.

Makes 6 servings

Nutrition Facts per serving: 244 cal., 15 g total fat (3 g sat. fat), 29 mg chol., 487 mg sodium, 19 g carbo.,
2 g fiber, 8 g pro.

GERMAN SWEET-AND-SOUR STIR-FRY

This is a dish that will have you coming back for more. The smokiness of the sausage is a wonderful counterpart to the tangy, vinegary dressing, and the red cabbage and carrot add intense color and crunch.

Start to Finish: 20 minutes

- 2 **tablespoons cooking oil**
- 1 **pound cooked smoked turkey sausage, cut into 1-inch slices**
- 4 **green onions, bias-sliced into 1-inch pieces**
- 1 **tablespoon all-purpose flour**
- 1 **tablespoon sugar**
- ½ **teaspoon salt**
- ½ **teaspoon celery seeds**
- ½ **teaspoon dry mustard**
- ¼ **teaspoon ground black pepper**
- ⅔ **cup water**
- ¼ **cup cider vinegar**
- 1 **10-ounce package shredded red cabbage (5 cups)**
- 2 **cups packaged coarsely shredded carrot**

1 In a very large skillet heat oil over medium heat. Add sausage and green onion; cook and stir for 5 minutes. Using a slotted spoon, remove sausage and onion from skillet.

2 For dressing, stir flour, sugar, salt, celery seeds, dry mustard, and pepper into drippings in skillet. Stir in the water and vinegar. Cook and stir until thickened and bubbly. Stir in the cabbage and carrot. Cover and simmer about 3 minutes or until cabbage is crisp-tender, stirring once. Top with sausage mixture. Cover and cook for 1 to 2 minutes more or until heated through.

Makes 4 to 6 servings

Nutrition Facts per serving: 313 cal., 17 g total fat (5 g sat. fat), 60 mg chol., 1405 mg sodium, 22 g carbo., 5 g fiber, 19 g pro.

VERMICELLI WITH SAUSAGE AND SPINACH

Quickly wilting fresh spinach in the pasta mixture is a great way
to introduce kids to this nutrient-rich green since it's not overcooked.
Pictured on page 132.

Start to Finish: 25 minutes

2   teaspoons olive oil

1   pound cooked smoked
    turkey sausage, halved
    lengthwise and cut into
    ½-inch slices

1   large onion, chopped (1 cup)

1½ teaspoons bottled minced
    garlic (3 cloves)

2   14-ounce cans reduced-
    sodium chicken broth

¼   cup water

8   ounces dried vermicelli or
    angel hair pasta, broken

1   9-ounce package
    prewashed fresh baby
    spinach

¼   teaspoon freshly ground
    black pepper

⅓   cup whipping cream

1 In a 4-quart Dutch oven heat oil over medium-high heat. Add
sausage, onion, and garlic; cook until onion is tender and
sausage is light brown.

2 Add broth and water; bring to boiling. Add pasta; cook for
3 minutes, stirring frequently. Add spinach and pepper;
cook about 1 minute more or until spinach is wilted. Stir in cream.
Serve immediately.

Makes 4 to 6 servings

Nutrition Facts per serving: 524 cal., 21 g total fat (9 g sat. fat), 87 mg chol., 1586 mg sodium, 56 g carbo.,
5 g fiber, 30 g pro.

WHITE BEAN AND SAUSAGE RIGATONI

Reminiscent of a wonderful baked Italian casserole that comes bubbling from the oven, this dish cooks on the stovetop instead, so it's ready to put on the table in less than half the time.

Start to Finish: 20 minutes

- 8 **ounces dried rigatoni pasta or medium shell pasta**

- 1 **15- to 19-ounce can white kidney (cannellini), Great Northern, or navy beans, rinsed and drained**

- 1 **14.5-ounce can Italian-style stewed tomatoes, undrained**

- 6 **ounces cooked smoked turkey sausage, halved lengthwise and cut into ½-inch slices**

- ⅓ **cup snipped fresh basil**

- 1 **ounce Asiago or Parmesan cheese, shaved or finely shredded (optional)**

1 Cook pasta according to package directions; drain. Return pasta to hot saucepan; cover to keep warm.

2 Meanwhile, in a large saucepan combine beans, undrained tomatoes, and sausage; heat through. Add cooked pasta and basil; toss gently to combine. If desired, sprinkle individual servings with cheese.

Makes 4 servings

Nutrition Facts per serving: 378 cal., 6 g total fat (1 g sat. fat), 29 mg chol., 760 mg sodium, 65 g carbo., 7 g fiber, 21 g pro.

TURKEY SAUSAGE AND ASPARAGUS SOUP

Cheddar cheese soup is normally a side dish, but here it gets transformed
into a hearty one-pot meal thanks to smoked turkey sausage and asparagus.

Start to Finish: 25 minutes

- **1 tablespoon butter**
- **¼ cup chopped celery**
- **¼ cup chopped onion**
- **3 cups milk**
- **1 10.75-ounce can condensed cheddar cheese soup**
- **1 teaspoon dry mustard**
- **½ teaspoon Worcestershire sauce**
- **14 to 16 ounces cooked smoked turkey sausage or kielbasa, halved lengthwise and sliced**
- **1 10-ounce package frozen cut asparagus**

1 In a large saucepan melt butter over medium heat. Add celery and onion; cook until tender. Stir in milk, soup, dry mustard, and Worcestershire sauce. Bring just to boiling.

2 Stir in sausage and asparagus. Return to boiling; reduce heat. Cook, uncovered, about 6 minutes more or until asparagus is tender, stirring occasionally.

Makes 5 or 6 servings

Nutrition Facts per serving: 281 cal., 16 g total fat (7 g sat. fat), 79 mg chol., 1294 mg sodium, 17 g carbo., 2 g fiber, 22 g pro.

TURKEY-BEAN SOUP

Keep the fixings on hand for this creamy and delicious soup.
It's perfect on cold days for lunch or supper.

Start to Finish: 30 minutes

2   15-ounce cans Great Northern or white kidney (cannellini) beans, rinsed and drained

1   10.75-ounce can condensed cream of celery soup

8   ounces cooked smoked turkey sausage, halved lengthwise and sliced

1½ cups milk

1   teaspoon dried minced onion

½   teaspoon dried thyme, crushed

⅛   to ¼ teaspoon ground black pepper

1   teaspoon bottled minced garlic (2 cloves) or ¼ teaspoon garlic powder

1 In a large saucepan combine beans, soup, and sausage. Stir in milk, minced onion, thyme, pepper, and garlic.

2 Bring to boiling over medium-high heat, stirring occasionally; reduce heat. Cover and simmer for 10 minutes, stirring occasionally.

Makes 4 servings

Nutrition Facts per serving: 434 cal., 11 g total fat (3 g sat. fat), 54 mg chol., 1129 mg sodium, 57 g carbo., 11 g fiber, 29 g pro.

ALFREDO DELI SANDWICHES

When you need a quick but delicious dinner, fix this kid-friendly,
easy-to-make hot sandwich.

Prep: 10 minutes   Bake: 5 minutes   Oven: 350°F

1   **16-ounce jar Alfredo pasta
     sauce**

6   **hoagie buns, split**

12   **ounces thinly sliced deli
     roast beef, ham, or turkey**

6   **slices provolone cheese
     (about 6 ounces)**

1 Preheat oven to 350°F. Spread 1 tablespoon Alfredo sauce
over the bottom half of each bun. Top with deli meat and cheese.
Replace bun tops. Place sandwiches on a large baking sheet.

2 Bake for 5 to 7 minutes or until buns are toasted and
cheese melts.

3 Meanwhile, heat remaining Alfredo sauce. Serve hot sandwiches
with sauce on the side for dipping.

Makes 6 sandwiches

Nutrition Facts per sandwich: 774 cal., 36 g total fat (16 g sat. fat), 108 mg chol., 1493 mg sodium,
76 g carbo., 4 g fiber, 36 g pro.

Marinara Spicy Deli Sandwich: Substitute a 14- to 17-ounce jar
marinara sauce for the Alfredo sauce. Substitute 12 ounces thinly
sliced salami, capicola, or sandwich pepperoni for the roast beef,
ham, or turkey.

FOCACCIA SANDWICH

Make some extra sandwiches and pack for the next day's lunch. Serve with a deli pasta salad or slices of cantaloupe and honeydew melon.

Start to Finish: 10 minutes

4   ciabatta rolls or individual
     Italian flatbreads (focaccia)

¼   cup bottled creamy garlic
     salad dressing

4   ounces thinly sliced deli
     roast beef, ham, or turkey

8   cherry tomatoes, thinly
     sliced

4   slices provolone cheese

¼   cup chopped bottled
     roasted red sweet peppers

4   romaine lettuce leaves

1 Slice the rolls in half horizontally. Spread salad dressing on the bottom halves of the rolls. Layer meat, tomato slices, cheese, roasted peppers, and romaine on bottom halves of rolls. Cover with top halves of rolls.

2 Serve right away or wrap sandwiches individually in plastic wrap and chill for up to 24 hours.

Makes 4 sandwiches

Nutrition Facts per sandwich: 461 cal., 19 g total fat (7 g sat. fat), 45 mg chol., 1235 mg sodium, 54 g carbo., 4 g fiber, 22 g pro.

DELI GREEK-STYLE PITAS

Pita bread rounds are great for meals on the go because they make tidy, fun-to-eat sandwiches.

Prep: 10 minutes   Chill: 1 hour

¼   **cup plain low-fat yogurt**

2   **teaspoons vinegar**

1   **teaspoon snipped fresh dill**

½   **teaspoon sugar**

1   **small cucumber, thinly sliced (1 cup)**

1   **roma tomato, chopped (½ cup)**

½   **of a small red onion, thinly sliced**

4   **whole wheat or white pita bread rounds**

12   **ounces thinly sliced deli roast beef, turkey, or chicken**

1 In a medium bowl combine yogurt, vinegar, dill, and sugar. Add cucumber, tomato, and onion; toss gently to combine. Cover and chill for 1 hour.

2 Cut pita rounds in half crosswise. Line pita halves with meat. Spoon the cucumber mixture into each half.

Makes 4 sandwiches

Nutrition Facts per sandwich: 400 cal., 15 g total fat (5 g sat. fat), 67 mg chol., 703 mg sodium, 39 g carbo., 6 g fiber, 30 g pro.

Easy Muffaletta Pitas: Omit yogurt, vinegar, dill, sugar, cucumber, tomato, and red onion. Omit step 1. Drain and chop a 16-ounce jar of pickled mixed vegetables (giardiniera). Stir in ¼ cup chopped green olives. Spoon mixture into pita halves in place of cucumber mixture.

DELI-STYLE SUBMARINES

To make these ahead of time, assemble the sandwich as directed, except do not cut into pieces. Wrap sandwich in plastic wrap and chill for up to 4 hours. Cut and serve as directed.

Start to Finish: 20 minutes

1	**16-ounce loaf French bread**
½	**of an 8-ounce carton dairy sour cream ranch dip**
1	**cup shredded lettuce**
¾	**cup shredded carrot**
8	**ounces thinly sliced deli roast beef, ham, or turkey**
½	**of a medium cucumber, seeded and shredded**
4	**ounces thinly sliced mozzarella or provolone cheese**

Cut the French bread in half horizontally. Spread dip on cut sides of bread. On the bottom half of the bread, layer lettuce, carrot, meat, cucumber, and cheese. Add top half of bread. Cut sandwich into 8 portions. Secure portions with decorative toothpicks.

Makes 8 sandwiches

Nutrition Facts per sandwich: 286 cal., 10 g total fat (5 g sat. fat), 41 mg chol., 551 mg sodium, 33 g carbo., 2 g fiber, 17 g pro.

ALL-WRAPPED-UP CHEF'S SALAD

These wraps allow you to enjoy a chef's salad on the run.
Pictured on page 133.

Prep: 20 minutes

4	**8-inch flour or whole wheat tortillas**
1½	**cups torn romaine**
8	**ounces thinly sliced deli roast beef, ham, or turkey**
1	**avocado, halved, seeded, peeled, and sliced**
½	**of a cucumber, seeded and thinly sliced**
½	**cup shredded Monterey Jack cheese with jalapeño peppers (2 ounces)**
	Bottled Thousand Island or ranch salad dressing (optional)

1 On each tortilla layer lettuce, meat, avocado, cucumber, and cheese. Roll up tightly. If desired, halve tortillas diagonally. Serve immediately or wrap individually in plastic wrap and chill for up to 6 hours.

2 If desired, serve wraps with salad dressing.

Makes 4 wraps

Nutrition Facts per wrap: 351 cal., 15 g total fat (5 g sat. fat), 39 mg chol., 1081 mg sodium, 33 g carbo., 6 g fiber, 20 g pro.

SWEET-AND-SOUR FISH STICKS

A package of precooked rice is a real timesaver in this complete-meal recipe. Fresh snow peas and sweet pepper keep the flavor fresh.

Start to Finish: 25 minutes

¾   **cup bottled sweet and sour sauce**

1   **11- to 12-ounce package (18) frozen baked, breaded fish sticks**

1   **tablespoon cooking oil**

1   **red sweet pepper, cut into strips**

1   **cup snow pea pods, trimmed**

1   **8.8-ounce pouch cooked brown or white rice**

1 Place ¼ cup of the sweet and sour sauce in a small microwave-safe bowl or measuring cup; set aside. Bake fish sticks according to package directions.

2 Meanwhile, in a large skillet heat oil over medium-high heat. Add sweet pepper strips and cook for 3 minutes. Add pea pods and cook for 1 to 2 minutes more or until vegetables are crisp-tender. Stir in the remaining ½ cup sweet and sour sauce to coat; heat through.

3 Prepare rice according to package directions.

4 To serve, heat reserved sweet and sour sauce in microwave oven on 100% power (high) for 30 to 40 seconds or until heated through. Spoon vegetable mixture over rice. Top with fish sticks. Drizzle all with warm sweet and sour sauce.

Makes 4 servings

Nutrition Facts per serving: 406 cal., 17 g total fat (3 g sat. fat), 16 mg chol., 643 mg sodium, 52 g carbo., 2 g fiber, 11 g pro.

PIZZA-STYLE FISH STICKS

You'll be surprised at how four ingredients come together and result in a flavorful, Italian-inspired fish dish.

Prep: 15 minutes   Bake: 20 minutes   Oven: 425°F

1   **11- to 12-ounce package (18) frozen baked, breaded fish sticks**

1   **8-ounce can pizza sauce**

1   **cup shredded provolone or mozzarella cheese (4 ounces)**

2   **tablespoons shredded fresh basil (optional)**

1 Preheat oven to 425°F. Arrange fish sticks in a 2-quart square or rectangular baking dish. Spoon sauce over fish sticks. Sprinkle with cheese.

2 Bake, uncovered, about 20 minutes or until heated through. If desired, sprinkle with basil.

Makes 4 servings

Nutrition Facts per serving: 336 cal., 20 g total fat (7 g sat. fat), 36 mg chol., 839 mg sodium, 22 g carbo., 1 g fiber, 17 g pro.

FISH TACOS

For an even faster preparation, substitute creamy deli coleslaw for the mayonnaise, lime juice, and coleslaw mix.

Start to Finish: 20 minutes

1	**11- to 12-ounce package (18) frozen baked, breaded fish sticks**
3	**tablespoons low-fat mayonnaise or salad dressing**
1	**teaspoon lime juice**
1½	**cups packaged shredded cabbage with carrot (coleslaw mix) or shredded cabbage**
8	**taco shells**
1	**recipe Mango Salsa**

1 Bake fish according to package directions. Cut each fish stick in half crosswise.

2 Meanwhile, in a medium bowl stir together mayonnaise and lime juice. Add cabbage; toss to coat. Spoon some of the coleslaw mixture into each taco shell. Add fish and top with Mango Salsa.

Makes 4 servings

Nutrition Facts per serving: 334 cal., 12 g total fat (2 g sat. fat), 22 mg chol., 655 mg sodium, 47 g carbo., 4 g fiber, 10 g pro.

Mango Salsa: In a medium bowl stir together 1 cup seeded, peeled, and chopped mango; 1 medium red sweet pepper, finely chopped (¾ cup); 2 green onions, sliced (¼ cup); ½ teaspoon finely shredded lime peel; 1 tablespoon lime juice; ¼ teaspoon salt; and ¼ teaspoon ground black pepper. Makes about 1½ cups.

SOMETHING'S FISHY SANDWICHES

Cool, creamy salad dressing complements the hot, crispy fish in these tantalizing sandwiches.

Start to Finish: 20 minutes

1	**11- to 12-ounce package (18) frozen baked, breaded fish sticks**
4	**thin slices tomato**
½	**teaspoon dried basil, crushed**
⅛	**teaspoon ground black pepper**
1	**cup shredded mozzarella, cheddar, Swiss, or American cheese (4 ounces)**
2	**tablespoons bottled buttermilk ranch, creamy cucumber, or creamy Parmesan salad dressing**
4	**kaiser rolls, split and toasted**

1 Arrange fish sticks close together on a baking sheet. Bake fish according to package directions.

2 Top fish with tomato slices. Sprinkle with basil and pepper; top with cheese. Bake for 2 to 3 minutes more or until cheese is melted.

3 Spread the salad dressing over the bottom halves of rolls. Top with fish and the top halves of rolls.

Makes 4 sandwiches

Nutrition Facts per sandwich: 414 cal., 14 g total fat (5 g sat. fat), 35 mg chol., 875 mg sodium, 50 g carbo., 1 g fiber, 20 g pro.

WILTED SPINACH AND FISH SALAD

The balsamic vinegar may darken the fish sticks a bit where it hits them, but it adds a real flavor punch.

Start to Finish: 25 minutes

- 1 **11- to 12-ounce package (18) frozen baked, breaded fish sticks**
- 4 **cups packaged prewashed fresh baby spinach**
- 1 **tablespoon olive oil or cooking oil**
- 1 **medium onion, cut into thin wedges**
- 1 **medium red or yellow sweet pepper, cut into thin strips**
- 3 **tablespoons balsamic vinegar**
- 1 **tablespoon honey**

1 Bake fish according to package directions. Place spinach in a large bowl. Top with baked fish; cover to keep warm.

2 Meanwhile, in a large skillet heat oil over medium heat. Add onion and cook for 5 to 6 minutes or until tender and slightly golden. Add sweet pepper; cook and stir for 1 minute more. Remove from heat. Add onion mixture to spinach and fish; toss to combine. Transfer to a serving platter.

3 In a small bowl stir together balsamic vinegar and honey. Add to skillet. Cook and stir about 1 minute or until heated through. Spoon vinegar mixture over fish and spinach; serve immediately.

Makes 4 servings

Nutrition Facts per serving: 279 cal., 14 g total fat (2 g sat. fat), 25 mg chol., 356 mg sodium, 29 g carbo., 3 g fiber, 10 g pro.

SHRIMP AND ARTICHOKE SKILLET

Skillet dinners aren't usually known for their elegance, but here, the already upscale title ingredients get tweaked with sherry and cream for a dish that travels well beyond the ordinary.

Start to Finish: 25 minutes

- 1   **14-ounce can artichoke hearts, drained**
- 1   **tablespoon butter**
- ⅓   **cup chopped onion (1 small)**
- 1   **10.75-ounce can condensed golden mushroom soup**
- ¾   **cup half-and-half or light cream**
- ¼   **cup dry sherry**
- ½   **cup finely shredded Parmesan cheese (2 ounces)**
- 1   **10- to 12-ounce package frozen peeled, cooked shrimp, thawed**
- 2   **cups hot cooked rice**

1 Quarter artichoke hearts; set aside. In a large skillet melt butter over medium heat. Add onion; cook until tender. Add soup, half-and-half, and sherry, stirring until smooth. Add Parmesan cheese; heat and stir until melted.

2 Add artichoke hearts and shrimp; heat through. Serve shrimp mixture over hot cooked rice.

Makes 4 servings

Nutrition Facts per serving: 422 cal., 14 g total fat (8 g sat. fat), 202 mg chol., 1349 mg sodium, 38 g carbo., 4 g fiber, 28 g pro.

SHORTCUT SHRIMP RISOTTO

Traditional risotto requires a cook's full attention, an ideal not always possible for a busy cook. This simplified main-dish version cooks on its own. Pictured on page 134.

Start to Finish: 30 minutes

2 14-ounce cans reduced-sodium chicken broth

1⅓ cups arborio rice or short grain white rice

1 medium onion, finely chopped (½ cup)

1 tablespoon snipped fresh basil or ¾ teaspoon dried basil, crushed

1 10- to 12-ounce package frozen peeled, cooked shrimp, thawed

1½ cups frozen peas

¼ cup grated Parmesan cheese

1 In a large saucepan combine broth, rice, onion, and dried basil (if using). Bring mixture to boiling; reduce heat. Cover and simmer for 18 minutes.

2 Stir in shrimp and peas. Cover and cook for 3 minutes more (do not lift lid). Stir in fresh basil (if using). Sprinkle individual servings with cheese.

Makes 4 servings

Nutrition Facts per serving: 305 cal., 3 g total fat (1 g sat. fat), 143 mg chol., 767 mg sodium, 45 g carbo., 3 g fiber, 25 g pro.

SHRIMP ALFREDO

Sliced fresh zucchini and shrimp give a package of Alfredo noodle mix a sophisticated flavor edge. Try this recipe with shrimp on one occasion, crabmeat on another.

Start to Finish: 25 minutes

3 **cups water**

1 **cup milk**

¼ **cup butter**

2 **4.4-ounce packages noodles with Alfredo-style sauce**

2 **medium zucchini, thinly sliced (3 cups)**

1 **10- to 12-ounce package frozen peeled, cooked shrimp, thawed, or 12 ounces chunk-style imitation crabmeat**

1 In a large saucepan combine water, milk, and butter. Bring to boiling. Stir in noodle mix. Return to boiling; reduce heat. Simmer, uncovered, for 5 minutes.

2 Stir in zucchini. Return to a gentle boil; cook, uncovered, about 3 minutes more or until noodles are tender.

3 Gently stir in shrimp. Heat through. Remove from heat; let stand for 3 to 5 minutes or until slightly thickened.

Makes 4 servings

Nutrition Facts per serving: 486 cal., 21 g total fat (12 g sat. fat), 264 mg chol., 1279 mg sodium, 44 g carbo., 2 g fiber, 30 g pro.

SHRIMP AND AVOCADO HOAGIES

Dinner al fresco calls for a fresh-tasting meal in a roll, such as this one. And the coolest part is the 15-minute prep time.

Start to Finish: 15 minutes

1 **10- to 12-ounce package frozen peeled, cooked shrimp, thawed**

2 **large avocados, pitted, peeled, and chopped**

1 **medium carrot, shredded (½ cup)**

⅓ **cup bottled coleslaw salad dressing**

4 **hoagie buns**

Lemon wedges (optional)

1 Coarsely chop shrimp. In a large bowl combine shrimp, avocados, carrot, and salad dressing; set aside.

2 Halve hoagie buns. Using a spoon, slightly hollow out bottoms and tops of hoagie buns, leaving ½-inch shells. Discard excess bread. Toast buns.

3 Spoon shrimp mixture into hoagie buns. If desired, serve with lemon wedges.

Makes 4 sandwiches

Nutrition Facts per sandwich: 560 cal., 24 g total fat (4 g sat. fat), 144 mg chol., 825 mg sodium, 63 g carbo., 8 g fiber, 25 g pro.

SPINACH AND PASTA SALAD WITH SHRIMP

If you prefer, make the pasta-and-shrimp mixture up to 24 hours ahead and chill it. At serving time, simply line the plates with spinach and dish up the pasta salad.

Start to Finish: 25 minutes

1   **cup dried shell pasta or elbow macaroni**

1   **10- to 12-ounce package frozen peeled, cooked shrimp, thawed**

1   **large red sweet pepper, chopped (1 cup)**

⅓   **cup bottled creamy onion or Caesar salad dressing**

2   **tablespoons snipped fresh dill (optional)**

   Salt and ground black pepper

1   **6-ounce package prewashed fresh baby spinach**

4   **ounces goat cheese (chèvre), sliced, or feta cheese, crumbled**

1 Cook pasta according to package directions; drain. Rinse with cold water; drain again.

2 In an extra-large bowl combine cooked pasta, shrimp, and sweet pepper. Drizzle with salad dressing. If desired, sprinkle with dill. Toss to coat. Season to taste with salt and black pepper.

3 Divide spinach among 6 salad plates or bowls. Top with shrimp mixture and cheese.

Makes 6 servings

Nutrition Facts per serving: 247 cal., 10 g total fat (4 g sat. fat), 156 mg chol., 435 mg sodium, 17 g carbo., 2 g fiber, 23 g pro.

SPEEDY SPICY TUNA NOODLE CASSEROLE

Canned tuna has long been a staple in busy cooks' pantries. Today's time-pressed moms can turn to shelf-stable pouches of tuna in either plain or flavored styles. This updated tuna-mac supper showcases the product.

Start to Finish: 25 minutes

8 **ounces dried wagon wheel and/or elbow macaroni (2⅔ cups)**

1 **10.75-ounce can condensed fiesta nacho cheese soup**

½ **cup milk**

2 **7- to 7.1-ounce pouches chunk light tuna**

1 **4- to 4.5-ounce can diced green chile peppers**

Rich round crackers, tortilla chips, or corn chips, coarsely crushed (optional)

1 In a large saucepan cook pasta according to package directions; drain. Return pasta to saucepan.

2 Stir soup and milk into cooked pasta. Gently fold in tuna and chile peppers. Heat through. If desired, top individual servings with crushed crackers.

Makes 4 servings

Nutrition Facts per serving: 410 cal., 7 g total fat (3 g sat. fat), 61 mg chol., 1026 mg sodium, 51 g carbo., 3 g fiber, 33 g pro.

MEXICAN TUNA WRAPS

The beauty of the tuna filling is that in addition to using it for these yummy wraps, you can spoon it over lettuce for a refreshing salad or spread it on bread slices for filling sandwiches.

Start to Finish: 15 minutes

⅓ **cup mayonnaise or salad dressing**

¼ **cup chopped red sweet pepper**

2 **green onions, chopped (¼ cup)**

1 **teaspoon lime juice (optional)**

   Dash bottled hot pepper sauce

1 **7- to 7.1-ounce pouch chunk light tuna**

4 **8-inch flour tortillas**

1¼ **cups shredded lettuce**

¾ **cup finely shredded Mexican cheese blend (3 ounces)**

1 In a medium bowl stir together mayonnaise, sweet pepper, green onions, lime juice (if desired), and bottled hot pepper sauce. Add the tuna and mix gently to combine.

2 Divide tuna mixture among the tortillas. Top with lettuce and cheese. Roll up tightly. Serve immediately.

Makes 4 wraps

Nutrition Facts per wrap: 363 cal., 24 g total fat (7 g sat. fat), 52 mg chol., 599 mg sodium, 17 g carbo., 1 g fiber, 18 g pro.

TUNA AND WHITE BEAN PANINI

Keep the ingredients on hand for this uptown alternative to a tuna melt.
The recipe easily doubles for unexpected dinner guests.

Start to Finish: 25 minutes

2   7- to 7.1-ounce pouches
    chunk light tuna

1   15-ounce can cannellini
    (white kidney) beans,
    rinsed, drained, and
    slightly mashed

¼   cup mayonnaise or salad
    dressing

1   teaspoon bottled minced
    garlic (2 cloves)

8   ½-inch slices country Italian
    or hearty multigrain bread

¼   cup thinly sliced red onion

1   tomato, thinly sliced

4   ounces thinly sliced Havarti
    or mozzarella cheese

2   tablespoons olive oil

1 Preheat an electric sandwich press, a covered indoor grill, a grill pan, or a skillet.

2 Meanwhile, in a medium bowl stir together tuna, beans, mayonnaise, and garlic. To assemble sandwiches, spread tuna mixture on 4 of the bread slices. Top with red onion, tomato, and cheese. Top each with another bread slice. Brush both sides of each sandwich with oil.

3 Place sandwiches (half at a time, if necessary) in the sandwich press or indoor grill; cover and cook about 6 minutes or until bread is toasted. (If using a grill pan or skillet, place sandwiches on grill pan. Weight sandwiches down* and grill about 2 minutes or until bread is lightly toasted. Turn sandwiches over, weight down, and grill until remaining side is lightly toasted.)

Makes 4 sandwiches

Nutrition Facts per sandwich: 347 cal., 18 g total fat (3 g sat. fat), 53 mg chol., 315 mg sodium, 30 g carbo., 9 g fiber, 22 g pro.

*NOTE: Use a heavy skillet on top of sandwiches to weight down.

HOT TUNA HOAGIES

This may be a sandwich, but provide knives and forks for eating it!

Start to Finish: 15 minutes

2 **tablespoons mayonnaise
or salad dressing**

2 **tablespoons buttermilk
ranch, creamy cucumber,
or creamy Parmesan
salad dressing**

2 **cups packaged shredded
cabbage with carrot
(coleslaw mix)**

1 **7- to 7.1-ounce pouch
chunk light tuna**

2 **hoagie buns, split**

4 **slices cheddar cheese
or Swiss cheese (about
3 ounces)**

1 Preheat broiler. In a medium mixing bowl stir together mayonnaise and ranch dressing. Add cabbage and tuna; stir gently to coat. Set aside.

2 Place bun halves, split side up, on unheated rack of broiler pan. Broil 4 to 5 inches from the heat about 1 minute or until toasted. Spread tuna mixture evenly on the four halves. Broil 2 to 3 minutes more or until heated through. Top with cheese. Broil 30 to 60 seconds more or until cheese melts.

Makes 4 sandwiches

Nutrition Facts per sandwich: 434 cal., 21 g total fat (7 g sat. fat), 53 mg chol., 802 mg sodium, 39 g carbo., 3 g fiber, 23 g pro.

CURRIED TUNA CUPS

Tuna, tomato, and curry powder give store-bought coleslaw a winning
edge. The mixture also makes a great sandwich or wrap filling.

Start to Finish: 15 minutes

1½ **cups purchased creamy
     coleslaw**

 1   **small tomato, seeded and
     chopped (⅓ cup)**

 1   **teaspoon curry powder**

 1   **7- to 7.1-ounce pouch
     chunk light tuna, drained**

 4   **large butterhead (Bibb or
     Boston) lettuce leaves**

¼   **cup chopped peanuts**

     **Dairy sour cream dip
     with chives (optional)**

1 In a small bowl stir together coleslaw, tomato, and curry powder.
Gently fold in tuna.

2 Spoon tuna mixture onto lettuce leaves. Sprinkle with peanuts.
If desired, top with dip.

Makes 4 servings

Nutrition Facts per serving: 148 cal., 7 g total fat (1 g sat. fat), 21 mg chol., 213 mg sodium, 9 g carbo., 2 g fiber,
14 g pro.

CHILI WITH POLENTA

If you like the combination of corn bread and chili, you'll love the idea of a polenta topper! And it's so easy, thanks to refrigerated cooked polenta, usually found in tubes in the produce aisle.

Start to Finish: 25 minutes

12 ounces lean ground beef

 1 medium onion, chopped
    (½ cup)

 1 15-ounce can hot-style
    chili beans with chili gravy,
    undrained

 1 15-ounce can black beans,
    rinsed and drained

 1 8-ounce can tomato sauce

½ teaspoon ground cumin

 1 16-ounce tube refrigerated
    cooked polenta, crumbled

½ cup shredded taco cheese
    (2 ounces)

    Sliced green onion
    (optional)

    Dairy sour cream (optional)

1 In a large skillet cook ground beef and onion over medium heat until beef is brown. Drain off fat.

2 Stir undrained chili beans, drained black beans, tomato sauce, and cumin into beef mixture in skillet. Bring to boiling. Sprinkle the crumbled polenta over the beef mixture. Cover and simmer about 5 minutes or until heated through. Sprinkle with cheese. If desired, sprinkle with green onion and serve with sour cream.

Makes 4 servings

Nutrition Facts per serving: 497 cal., 15 g total fat (7 g sat. fat), 65 mg chol., 1464 mg sodium, 58 g carbo., 14 g fiber, 34 g pro.

SAUSAGE AND POLENTA WITH BALSAMIC VINAIGRETTE

Layers of flavors compose this unforgettable dish. A slice of baked polenta on a bed of mixed greens is crowned by sweet Italian sausages cooked in balsamic vinegar.

Start to Finish: 30 minutes   Oven: 400°F

½ **of a 16-ounce tube refrigerated cooked polenta (plain or flavored)**

1 **tablespoon olive oil**

4 **uncooked sweet Italian sausage links (about 1 pound), each cut into 4 pieces**

½ **cup apple juice or apple cider**

¼ **cup balsamic vinegar**

2 **tablespoons snipped dried tomatoes**

1 **8-ounce package mixed salad greens**

¼ **cup pine nuts or slivered almonds, toasted (optional)**

1 Preheat oven to 400°F. Cut polenta crosswise into ¼-inch slices; cut each slice in half. Brush polenta with oil. Arrange in a single layer in a shallow baking pan. Bake about 15 minutes or until light brown, turning once halfway through baking.

2 Meanwhile, in a large skillet cook sausage over medium heat for 5 minutes, turning to brown evenly. Remove sausage from skillet. Drain off fat; wipe skillet with paper towels.

3 Return sausage to skillet; add apple juice, vinegar, and dried tomato. Bring to boiling; reduce heat. Cover and simmer for 8 to 10 minutes or until sausage is no longer pink (160°F).

4 To serve, divide greens among 4 serving plates. Arrange polenta slices and sausage next to greens. Spoon tomato mixture over greens, polenta, and sausage. If desired, sprinkle with nuts.

Makes 4 servings

Nutrition Facts per serving: 380 cal., 22 g total fat (8 g sat. fat), 57 mg chol., 741 mg sodium, 23 g carbo., 4 g fiber, 15 g pro.

POLENTA WITH
TURKEY SAUSAGE FLORENTINE

For 4 servings, double all ingredients and cook the polenta in 2 batches.

Start to Finish: 25 minutes

1	9- or 10-ounce package frozen creamed spinach
8	ounces bulk turkey sausage
1	tablespoon olive oil
½	of a 16-ounce tube refrigerated cooked plain polenta or polenta with wild mushrooms, cut crosswise into ¾-inch slices
2	tablespoons sliced almonds or pine nuts, toasted

1 Cook the creamed spinach according to package directions.

2 Meanwhile, in a medium skillet cook sausage until brown. Drain sausage in a colander.

3 In the same skillet heat oil over medium heat. Add polenta slices; cook about 6 minutes or until golden, turning once. Transfer polenta to a serving platter or plates.

4 Stir cooked sausage into hot creamed spinach; heat through. Serve sausage mixture over polenta. Sprinkle with toasted nuts.

Makes 2 servings

Nutrition Facts per serving: 607 cal., 41 g total fat (8 g sat. fat), 119 mg chol., 1586 mg sodium, 33 g carbo., 6 g fiber, 28 g pro.

SAUCY SHRIMP over POLENTA

A tube of prepared polenta is your leg up on getting a simple but brilliant spicy shrimp sauté to the table to enjoy dinner with friends. Put this one in your "quick great meals to share" file.

Start to Finish: 25 minutes

18   **fresh or frozen peeled and deveined, cooked shrimp, tails removed (about 8 ounces)**

1   **tablespoon cooking oil**

1   **16-ounce tube refrigerated cooked polenta, cut crosswise into 12 slices**

2   **cups frozen whole kernel corn**

4   **roma tomatoes, chopped (about 1½ cups)**

3   **tablespoons balsamic vinegar**

1   **teaspoon dried thyme, crushed**

½   **teaspoon ground cumin**

¼   **teaspoon salt**

1 Thaw shrimp, if frozen. Rinse shrimp; pat dry with paper towels. Set shrimp aside.

2 In a large skillet heat oil over medium heat. Add polenta slices and cook for 5 to 8 minutes or until golden brown, turning once. Transfer polenta to a serving platter or plates; keep warm.

3 In the same large skillet combine corn, tomato, balsamic vinegar, thyme, cumin, and salt. Cook and stir about 5 minutes or until heated through. Stir in shrimp. Cook and stir until heated through. Using a slotted spoon, spoon shrimp mixture over polenta slices.

Makes 6 servings

Nutrition Facts per serving: 196 cal., 3 g total fat (1 g sat. fat), 74 mg chol., 483 mg sodium, 30 g carbo., 4 g fiber, 12 g pro.

TOMATO, MOZZARELLA, AND POLENTA PLATTER

Let your imagination run wild when it comes to tonight's salad supper. Instead of bread, try toasty polenta croutons. Use lettuce as the bowl and indulge in slices of fresh mozzarella, garden tomatoes, and tangy kalamata olives.

Start to Finish: 20 minutes

1 large head butterhead (Boston or Bibb) lettuce

8 ounces fresh mozzarella cheese, sliced

2 medium red tomatoes, cut into wedges

2 medium yellow tomatoes, sliced

¼ cup fresh basil leaves

2 teaspoons olive oil

1 16-ounce tube refrigerated cooked polenta, cut crosswise into ¾-inch slices

⅓ cup kalamata olives

¼ cup bottled red wine vinegar and oil salad dressing

1 Line a platter with lettuce leaves. (Or make a basket out of the head of butterhead lettuce by removing center leaves.) Arrange cheese, tomato wedges, tomato slices, and basil leaves on the lettuce, leaving room for polenta slices; set aside.

2 In a large skillet heat oil over medium heat. Cook polenta slices in hot oil for 4 to 6 minutes or until warm and light brown, turning once. Arrange polenta and olives on lettuce. Serve with salad dressing.

Makes 4 servings

Nutrition Facts per serving: 395 cal., 25 g total fat (9 g sat. fat), 44 mg chol., 928 mg sodium, 30 g carbo., 5 g fiber, 16 g pro.

BEEF AND VEGETABLES WITH FETTUCCINE

If refrigerated fettuccine isn't available at your supermarket, substitute 6 to 8 ounces dried fettuccine for a 9-ounce package of refrigerated pasta. Pictured on page 135.

Start to Finish: 25 minutes

- 1 **9-ounce package refrigerated fettuccine or linguine**
- 12 **ounces packaged beef stir-fry strips**
- 1 **teaspoon dried Italian seasoning, crushed**
- 1 **tablespoon olive oil**
- 1 **medium onion, cut into thin wedges**
- 2 **teaspoons bottled minced garlic (4 cloves)**
- ¼ **teaspoon crushed red pepper**
- 1 **14.5-ounce can diced tomatoes with basil, garlic, and oregano, undrained**
- 1 **cup bottled roasted red sweet peppers, drained and coarsely chopped**
- 1 **tablespoon balsamic vinegar**
- 2 **cups packaged prewashed fresh baby spinach**
- ¼ **cup finely shredded Parmesan cheese (1 ounce)**

1 Cook pasta according to package directions. Drain well. Return pasta to hot pan. Using kitchen shears, snip pasta in a few places to break up the long pieces. Cover and keep warm. Meanwhile, sprinkle meat with Italian seasoning; toss to coat.

2 In a large skillet heat oil over medium-high heat. Add meat; cook and stir for 3 to 4 minutes or until desired doneness. Remove meat from skillet. Add onion, garlic, and crushed red pepper to skillet. Cook about 5 minutes or until onion is tender, stirring occasionally.

3 Stir meat, undrained tomatoes, roasted peppers, and balsamic vinegar into onion mixture in skillet. Heat through. Add meat mixture and spinach to hot pasta; toss to mix. Serve with Parmesan cheese.

Makes 4 servings

Nutrition Facts per serving: 413 cal., 10 g total fat (3 g sat. fat), 123 mg chol., 687 mg sodium, 50 g carbo., 3 g fiber, 30 g pro.

FETTUCCINE WITH CHERRY TOMATOES

This quick-to-fix pasta toss is perfect for the dog days of summer. Fresh-from-the-vine cherry tomatoes are guaranteed to energize your taste buds.

Start to Finish: 20 minutes

I	**9-ounce package refrigerated fettuccine**
I	**6- to 9-ounce package refrigerated or frozen Italian-flavor cooked or grilled chicken breast strips, thawed if frozen**
½	**cup finely shredded Parmesan cheese (2 ounces)**
2	**tablespoons olive oil**
I	**pint cherry tomatoes, halved**
½	**cup pitted ripe olives, halved**
	Salt and ground black pepper

1 Cut strands of fettuccine into thirds. In a Dutch oven cook pasta according to package directions. Drain and return pasta to pan.

2 Add chicken, cheese, and oil to pasta in pan; toss to mix. Cook over low heat until heated through. Remove from heat. Add the tomato halves and olives; toss to mix. Season to taste with salt and pepper; toss again. Serve immediately.

Makes 4 servings

Nutrition Facts per serving: 371 cal., 15 g total fat (4 g sat. fat), 76 mg chol., 866 mg sodium, 39 g carbo., 3 g fiber, 22 g pro.

SALMON with TARRAGON CREAM SAUCE

A simple sauce of cream cheese, milk, and a snip of fresh tarragon coats chunks of salmon, garden veggies, and pasta for this ultra-rich entrée. Pictured on page 136.

Start to Finish: 25 minutes

12	ounces fresh or frozen salmon fillets or steaks
1	9-ounce package refrigerated fettuccine
1	cup sliced zucchini and/or yellow summer squash
1	cup red sweet pepper cut into bite-size strips
1	teaspoon cooking oil
¾	cup milk
½	of a 3-ounce package cream cheese, cut up
1	tablespoon snipped fresh tarragon or 1 teaspoon dried tarragon, crushed
¼	teaspoon salt
¼	teaspoon ground black pepper

1 Thaw fish, if frozen. Skin fish, if necessary. Rinse fish; pat dry with paper towels. Cut fish into 1-inch pieces. Set aside.

2 Cook pasta according to package directions, adding squash and sweet pepper to pasta for the last minute of cooking. Drain and keep warm.

3 Meanwhile, in a large nonstick skillet heat oil over medium-high heat. Add fish; cook, stirring gently, for 3 to 5 minutes or until fish begins to flake when tested with fork. Remove fish from skillet. Add milk, cream cheese, tarragon, salt, and pepper to skillet. Cook and whisk until cream cheese is melted and sauce is smooth. Stir in pasta mixture and fish. Heat through, gently tossing mixture.

Makes 3 servings

Nutrition Facts per serving: 554 cal., 23 g total fat (8 g sat. fat), 142 mg chol., 356 mg sodium, 51 g carbo., 3 g fiber, 37 g pro.

SHRIMP WITH BASIL ON FETTUCCINE

For convenience, keep a supply of dried herbs on hand but remember they can quickly lose their pungency. Store dried herbs away from moisture and replace them regularly.

Start to Finish: 25 minutes

1 **pound frozen peeled and deveined medium shrimp (1½ pounds medium shrimp in shells)**

1 **9-ounce package refrigerated plain or spinach fettucine or linguine**

2 **tablespoons butter**

2 **teaspoons snipped fresh basil or tarragon or 1 teaspoon dried basil or tarragon, crushed**

1 Thaw shrimp. Cook pasta according to package directions.

2 In a large skillet melt butter over medium-high heat. Add shrimp and basil; cook for 2 to 3 minutes or until shrimp turn opaque, stirring frequently. Serve warm shrimp over pasta.

Makes 4 servings

Nutrition Facts per serving: 366 cal., 10 g total fat (5 g sat. fat), 244 mg chol., 291 mg sodium, 35 g carbo., 2 g fiber, 32 g pro.

FETTUCCINE VEGETABLE TOSS

Feta cheese packs plenty of tanginess on its own, but versions made with herbs or peppercorns intensify the taste of this colorful fettuccine one-dish meal.

Start to Finish: 20 minutes

1   **9-ounce package refrigerated plain or spinach fettuccine**

1   **tablespoon olive oil**

1   **green onion, chopped (2 tablespoons)**

4   **red and/or yellow medium tomatoes, chopped (2 cups)**

1   **medium carrot, finely chopped (½ cup)**

¼   **cup oil-packed dried tomatoes, drained and snipped**

½   **cup crumbled garlic-and-herb feta cheese, peppercorn feta cheese, or plain feta cheese (2 ounces)**

1 Cook the pasta according to package directions; drain. Return the pasta to hot pan.

2 Meanwhile, in a large skillet heat olive oil over medium heat. Add green onion; cook 30 seconds. Stir in fresh tomatoes, carrot, and dried tomatoes. Cover and cook for 5 minutes, stirring once. Spoon tomato mixture and cheese over cooked pasta; toss gently to mix.

Makes 4 servings

Nutrition Facts per serving: 299 cal., 10 g total fat (3 g sat. fat), 54 mg chol., 241 mg sodium, 43 g carbo., 4 g fiber, 16 g pro.

TIP: If refrigerated spinach fettuccine isn't available at your supermarket, substitute 6 to 8 ounces dried spinach or plain fettuccine for a 9-ounce package of refrigerated pasta.

SAUCY ONE-PAN RAVIOLI

Convenient refigerated ravioli makes this an easy meal to prepare but don't let that stop you from serving it to guests on a special occasion. The flavors are fresh and lively; the presentation is impressive.

Start to Finish: 20 minutes

2   **cups cherry tomatoes**

½   **teaspoon bottled minced garlic (1 clove)**

¾   **cup chicken broth**

¼   **teaspoon salt**

¼   **teaspoon ground black pepper**

1   **9-ounce package refrigerated cheese- or meat-filled ravioli**

2   **tablespoons snipped fresh basil**

1   **tablespoon snipped fresh flat-leaf parsley**

¼   **cup finely shredded Romano or Parmesan cheese (1 ounce)**

1 In a food processor or blender combine cherry tomatoes and garlic. Cover and process or blend until smooth. Transfer to a large saucepan. Add chicken broth, salt, and pepper. Bring to boiling.

2 Add ravioli to tomato mixture in pan. Return to boiling; reduce heat. Cover and simmer for 7 to 9 minutes or just until pasta is tender, stirring gently once or twice. Stir in basil and parsley. Spoon into shallow serving bowls; sprinkle with cheese.

Makes 2 servings

Nutrition Facts per serving: 491 cal., 20 g total fat (10 g sat. fat), 121 mg chol., 1356 mg sodium, 53 g carbo., 2 g fiber, 26 g pro.

RAVIOLI SKILLET LASAGNA

Cheese-filled ravioli is the quick and cinchy route to a lasagna-like casserole that's a family pleaser. The ravioli replaces the layers of cheese and lasagna noodles.

Start to Finish: 30 minutes

2 **cups bottled tomato-based pasta sauce**

⅓ **cup water**

1 **9-ounce package refrigerated cheese- or meat-filled ravioli**

1 **egg, lightly beaten**

1 **15-ounce carton ricotta cheese**

¼ **cup grated Romano or Parmesan cheese**

1 **10-ounce package frozen chopped spinach, thawed and well drained**

Grated Romano or Parmesan cheese

1 Preheat broiler. In a 10-inch broilerproof skillet combine pasta sauce and the water. Bring to boiling. Stir in ravioli. Cover and cook over medium heat about 5 minutes or until ravioli are nearly tender, stirring once to prevent sticking.

2 Meanwhile, in a medium bowl combine egg, ricotta cheese, and the ¼ cup Romano cheese. Dot ravioli with spinach. Spoon ricotta mixture on top of spinach.

3 Cover and cook over low heat about 10 minutes more or until ricotta layer is set and ravioli are tender.

4 Broil 4 to 5 inches from the heat for 4 to 5 minutes or until top is light brown. Sprinkle individual servings with additional Romano cheese.

Makes 4 servings

Nutrition Facts per serving: 556 cal., 29 g total fat (18 g sat. fat), 163 mg chol., 1222 mg sodium, 46 g carbo., 6 g fiber, 29 g pro.

TURKEY RAVIOLI SOUP

Need a quick meal? This soup is a slick way to use leftover turkey
(or substitute frozen diced cooked chicken). The ravioli adds some fun
and will satisfy kids of all ages.

Start to Finish: 25 minutes

6   cups reduced-sodium
     chicken broth

1   medium red sweet pepper,
     chopped (¾ cup)

1   medium onion, chopped
     (½ cup)

1½   teaspoons dried Italian
     seasoning, crushed

1½   cups chopped cooked
     turkey (8 ounces)

1   9-ounce package
     refrigerated
     cheese-filled ravioli

2   cups packaged prewashed
     shredded fresh spinach

     Finely shredded Parmesan
     cheese (optional)

1 In a Dutch oven combine chicken broth, sweet pepper, onion,
and Italian seasoning. Bring to boiling; reduce heat. Cover and
simmer for 5 minutes.

2 Add turkey and ravioli to broth mixture. Return to boiling;
reduce heat. Simmer, uncovered, about 6 minutes or just until
ravioli are tender. Stir in spinach. If desired, sprinkle individual
servings with Parmesan cheese.

Makes 6 servings

Nutrition Facts per serving: 251 cal., 9 g total fat (5 g sat. fat), 58 mg chol., 912 mg sodium, 24 g carbo.,
2 g fiber, 20 g pro.

RAVIOLI SAUCED WITH PUMPKIN AND SAGE

Here's proof that fine dining and off-the-shelf cooking can go hand-in-hand. White wine, shallots, hazelnuts, and a creamy pumpkin sauce elevate refrigerated ravioli to a trendy, restaurant-style offering.

Start to Finish: 25 minutes

½   **cup dry white wine or chicken broth**

¼   **cup finely chopped shallot**

1⅓   **cups refrigerated Alfredo pasta sauce**

½   **cup canned pumpkin**

1½   **teaspoons dried sage, crushed**

2   **9-ounce packages refrigerated cheese-filled ravioli**

2   **tablespoons snipped fresh flat-leaf parsley**

2   **tablespoons chopped hazelnuts, toasted**

1 For sauce, in a large skillet combine wine and shallot. Cook over medium heat for 5 to 8 minutes or until most of the liquid is evaporated, stirring frequently. Stir in Alfredo sauce, pumpkin, and sage. Cook until mixture is heated through, stirring occasionally.

2 Meanwhile, cook ravioli according to package directions. Before draining ravioli, remove ½ cup of the cooking water and set aside. Drain ravioli; return to pan.

3 Stir the reserved cooking water into sauce. Stir in parsley. Pour the sauce over cooked ravioli; toss gently to coat. Sprinkle individual servings with hazelnuts.

Makes 4 servings

Nutrition Facts per serving: 687 cal., 38 g total fat (20 g sat. fat), 162 mg chol., 1436 mg sodium, 69 g carbo., 6 g fiber, 22 g pro.

PASTA AND PEAS AU GRATIN

Another time, try bite-size pieces of asparagus instead of the peas. Add the asparagus to the pasta 3 or 4 minutes before it's done cooking.

Start to Finish: 15 minutes

1	**9-ounce package refrigerated cheese-filled ravioli or cheese-filled tortellini**
1	**cup frozen peas**
2	**tablespoons all-purpose flour**
⅛	**teaspoon ground black pepper**
1	**cup half-and-half, light cream, or milk**
1	**14.5-ounce can diced tomatoes with basil, garlic, and oregano, undrained**
2	**tablespoons shredded Parmesan cheese**

1 In a large saucepan cook pasta according to package directions, except add peas for the last 1 minute of cooking. Drain. Return pasta and peas to the saucepan.

2 Meanwhile, in a medium saucepan stir together flour and pepper. Gradually stir in half-and-half. Cook and stir over medium heat until thickened and bubbly. Cook and stir for 1 minute more. Gradually stir in the undrained tomatoes. Pour over pasta mixture. Toss to coat. Sprinkle individual servings with Parmesan cheese.

Makes 4 servings

Nutrition Facts per serving: 413 cal., 18 g total fat (11 g sat. fat), 72 mg chol., 1099 mg sodium, 49 g carbo., 4 g fiber, 15 g pro.

MAC AND CHEESE WITH SMOKED SAUSAGE

A box of macaroni and cheese dinner mix is an economical start to this easy family pleaser.

Start to Finish: 25 minutes

1   **7.25-ounce package macaroni and cheese dinner mix**

6   **ounces cooked smoked sausage, halved lengthwise and sliced**

¾   **cup bottled roasted red sweet peppers, drained and coarsely chopped**

    Snipped fresh flat-leaf parsley

1 Prepare dinner mix according to package directions.

2 Stir in sausage and roasted peppers. Heat through. Sprinkle individual servings with parsley.

Makes 4 servings

Nutrition Facts per serving: 466 cal., 24 g total fat (11 g sat. fat), 58 mg chol., 965 mg sodium, 46 g carbo., 2 g fiber, 16 g pro.

CREAMY TUNA MAC

Peas, tuna, and flavored sour cream dip rev up the appeal of already beloved mac 'n cheese. A simple salad or apple slices is all you need to round out this meal.

Start to Finish: 25 minutes

I **7.25-ounce package macaroni and cheese dinner mix**

I **cup frozen peas**

¼ **cup butter**

¼ **cup milk**

½ **cup ranch-, onion-, or chive-flavor sour cream dip**

I **6-ounce can solid white tuna, drained and broken into chunks**

Crushed potato chips (optional)

1 Cook macaroni from dinner mix according to package directions, except add peas for the last 2 minutes of cooking. Drain. Continue according to package directions, adding the butter and milk.

2 Stir sour cream dip into macaroni mixture; stir in tuna. Heat through. If desired, sprinkle individual servings with crushed potato chips.

Makes 4 to 6 servings

Nutrition Facts per serving: 368 cal., 9 g total fat (4 g sat. fat), 47 mg chol., 888 mg sodium, 50 g carbo., 2 g fiber, 23 g pro.

PIZZA-STYLE MAC AND CHEESE

Brimming with pizza toppings, this saucepan dinner makes a good option for the kid who wants pizza every day.

Start to Finish: 25 minutes

1 **7.25-ounce package macaroni and cheese dinner mix**

¼ **cup butter**

¼ **cup milk**

½ **cup canned or bottled pizza sauce or Italian cooking sauce**

1 **6-ounce can or jar (drained weight) sliced or chopped mushrooms, drained**

¼ **cup chopped, pitted ripe olives**

¼ **cup chopped pepperoni**

   Grated Parmesan cheese

1 Prepare dinner mix with the butter and milk according to package directions.

2 Stir pizza sauce into macaroni mixture in saucepan. Stir in mushrooms, olives, and pepperoni. Heat through. Sprinkle individual servings with Parmesan cheese.

Makes 4 servings

Nutrition Facts per serving: 404 cal., 47 g total fat (8 g sat. fat), 45 mg chol., 1174 mg sodium, 49 g carbo., 2 g fiber, 14 g pro.

MACARONI AND CHEESE CHOWDER

Macaroni replaces potatoes in this cheesy, kid-pleasing chowder.

Start to Finish: 25 minutes

1   14-ounce can reduced-
     sodium chicken broth

2   cups water

1   7.25-ounce package
     macaroni and cheese
     dinner mix

1   14.75-ounce can cream-
     style corn

1   cup chopped cooked ham
     (5 ounces)

1   cup milk

½   cup frozen peas (optional)

1 In a large saucepan bring chicken broth and water to boiling. Gradually add macaroni from dinner mix. Reduce heat to medium-low. Cover and simmer for 7 to 8 minutes or until macaroni is tender. Do not drain.

2 Stir the contents of the cheese packet, the corn, ham, milk, and, if desired, peas into the macaroni mixture. Cook and stir over medium heat until heated through.

Makes 4 servings

Nutrition Facts per serving: 349 cal., 5 g total fat (2 g sat. fat), 28 mg chol., 1571 mg sodium, 59 g carbo., 3 g fiber, 21 g pro.

ITALIAN-STYLE MACARONI SALAD

Transform mac 'n cheese into a summertime favorite that would make a simple entree or side for grilled burgers or hot dogs.

Prep: 20 minutes   Freeze: 30 minutes

1   **7.25-ounce package macaroni and cheese dinner mix**

2   **cups frozen stir-fry vegetables (yellow, green, and red sweet peppers and onion)**

¼   **cup butter**

¼   **cup milk**

4   **ounces sliced salami, cut into bite-size pieces**

1   **large tomato, seeded and chopped (¾ cup)**

⅓   **cup bottled Italian salad dressing**

1 Cook the macaroni from the dinner mix according to package directions and adding the frozen vegetables during the last 2 minutes of cooking (return water to boiling after adding the frozen vegetables). Drain. Continue according to package directions, adding the butter and milk.

2 Transfer pasta mixture to a large bowl. Stir in salami, tomato, and salad dressing. Cover and chill in freezer for 30 minutes, stirring once or twice.

Makes 4 servings

Nutrition Facts per serving: 501 cal., 30 g total fat (14 g sat. fat), 67 mg chol., 1680 mg sodium, 51 g carbo., 2 g fiber, 16 g pro.

QUICK SAUSAGE AND NOODLE SOUP

Seasoned tomatoes and ramen noodles make this dish extra easy while adding lots of snappy flavor.

Start to Finish: 20 minutes

4   cups water

1   14.5-ounce can diced
    tomatoes with green
    pepper and onion,
    undrained

8   ounces cooked smoked
    sausage, halved lengthwise
    and thinly sliced

1   medium sweet pepper,
    cut into bite-size strips

2   3-ounce packages chicken-
    flavor ramen noodles

In a large saucepan combine water, undrained tomatoes, sausage, sweet pepper, and seasoning packets from the noodles (set noodles aside). Bring to boiling. Break up noodles; add to saucepan. Return to boiling; cook for 2 to 3 minutes or until noodles are tender.

Makes 4 servings

Nutrition Facts per serving: 462 cal., 27 g total fat (6 g sat. fat), 39 mg chol., 2001 mg sodium, 36 g carbo., 2 g fiber, 19 g pro.

SIMPLY RAMEN CHICKEN SOUP

Simple definitely describes this soup. In just 15 minutes you can have hot, nourishing soup on the table. It doesn't get much simpler, or more satisfying, than this!

Start to Finish: 15 minutes

- 2 **14-ounce cans reduced-sodium chicken broth**
- 2 **3-ounce packages chicken-flavor ramen noodles**
- ½ **teaspoon dried oregano or basil, crushed**
- 1 **10-ounce package frozen cut broccoli**
- 2 **cups shredded cooked chicken or turkey (10 ounces)**
- ¼ **cup sliced almonds, toasted**

In a large saucepan combine chicken broth, seasoning packets from ramen noodles, and oregano. Bring to boiling. Break up noodles. Add noodles and broccoli to mixture in saucepan. Return to boiling; reduce heat. Simmer, uncovered, for 3 minutes. Stir in chicken; heat through. Sprinkle individual servings with almonds.

Makes 4 servings

Nutrition Facts per serving: 416 cal., 18 g total fat (2 g sat. fat), 62 mg chol., 1300 mg sodium, 32 g carbo., 3 g fiber, 30 g pro.

CURRIED CHICKEN AND NOODLES

Coconut milk and curry powder make a delightful sauce for a package
of ramen noodles and chicken.

Start to Finish: 15 minutes

5   **cups water**

2   **3-ounce packages chicken-
     flavor ramen noodles**

½   **of a 16-ounce package
     frozen broccoli,
     cauliflower, and carrots
     (2 cups)**

½   **cup purchased coconut milk**

1   **to 2 teaspoons curry
     powder**

     Dash cayenne pepper

1   **cup cubed cooked chicken
     (5 ounces)**

1 In a large saucepan bring water to boiling. Add ramen noodles
with seasoning packets and frozen vegetables to saucepan.
Cook, uncovered, about 3 minutes or until noodles and vegetables
are tender. Drain. Return noodle mixture to saucepan.

2 Stir together coconut milk, curry powder, and cayenne pepper.
Stir coconut milk mixture and chicken into saucepan. Heat
through.

Makes 4 servings

Nutrition Facts per serving: 340 cal., 16 g total fat (10 g sat. fat), 31 mg chol., 945 mg sodium, 32 g carbo.,
3 g fiber, 17 g pro.

EASY ORIENTAL CHICKEN SOUP

Chicken thighs are often overlooked in favor of breast halves, but they are just as convenient and even more flavorful.

Start to Finish: 15 minutes

1 tablespoon cooking oil

8 ounces skinless, boneless chicken thighs or breast halves, cut into thin bite-size strips

3 cups water

½ of a 16-ounce package frozen broccoli, carrots, and water chestnuts (2 cups)

1 3-ounce package chicken-flavor ramen noodles

2 tablespoons reduced-sodium soy sauce

1 In a large saucepan heat oil over medium-high heat. Add chicken; cook and stir for 2 to 3 minutes or until no longer pink. Remove from heat. Drain off fat.

2 Carefully add water, frozen vegetables, and seasoning packet from ramen noodles to chicken in saucepan. Bring to boiling. Break up noodles; add to saucepan. Reduce heat. Cover and simmer about 3 minutes or until noodles are tender. Stir in soy sauce. Skim off fat, if necessary.

Makes 3 servings

Nutrition Facts per serving: 288 cal., 13 g total fat (1 g sat. fat), 65 mg chol., 1046 mg sodium, 21 g carbo., 2 g fiber, 19 g pro.

QUICK AND CRUNCHY TURKEY SALAD

This has to be one of the fastest salads you'll ever prepare! Toss fresh crunchy cabbage slaw, tender cooked turkey, sweet mandarin oranges, and crispy ramen noodles with a vibrant orange vinaigrette dressing and you're ready to eat. Pictured on page 137.

Start to Finish: 10 minutes

1   16-ounce package shredded cabbage with carrot (coleslaw mix)

6   ounces sliced cooked turkey breast, cut into bite-size pieces

1   3-ounce package ramen noodles (any flavor)

⅔   cup bottled Asian vinaigrette salad dressing

1   11-ounce can mandarin orange sections, drained

In a large salad bowl combine cabbage and turkey. Remove seasoning packet from noodles; discard or reserve for another use. Crumble noodles and add to cabbage mixture. Pour the dressing over the salad; toss to coat. Gently fold in orange sections.

Makes 4 servings

Nutrition Facts per serving: 527 cal., 23 g total fat (1 g sat. fat), 15 mg chol., 1552 mg sodium, 67 g carbo., 3 g fiber, 17 g pro.

OVEN-FRIED PORK CHOPS

Coating the chops with either herbed or corn bread stuffing mix gives them
a delightful crispy crust, keeping the meat juicy and moist.

Prep: 10 minutes   Bake: 20 minutes   Oven: 425°F

3 **tablespoons butter**

1 **egg**

2 **tablespoons milk**

1 **cup packaged herb-
seasoned or corn bread
stuffing mix, crushed**

4 **pork loin chops,
cut ½ inch thick**

Applesauce (optional)

1 Preheat oven to 425°F. Place butter in a 13×9×2-inch baking pan
in the preheated oven about 3 minutes or until butter is melted.

2 Meanwhile, in a shallow dish lightly beat egg with a fork; stir
in milk. Place dry stuffing mix in another shallow dish. Trim fat
from chops. Dip pork chops into egg mixture. Coat both sides with
stuffing mix. Place chops in the baking pan with the butter.

3 Bake for 20 to 25 minutes or until pork chops are tender and
juices run clear (160°F), turning once halfway through baking.
If desired, serve pork chops with applesauce.

Makes 4 servings

Nutrition Facts per serving: 306 cal., 15 g total fat (8 g sat. fat), 123 mg chol., 357 mg sodium, 17 g carbo.,
0 g fiber, 23 g pro.

STUFFED PORK CHOPS

The stuffing mix provides the foundation for the pork chop stuffing
plus a tasty side dish.

Prep: 25 minutes   Cook: 20 minutes

1	tablespoon olive oil
1	small Granny Smith apple, chopped (½ cup)
¼	cup chopped red onion
¾	cup water
½	teaspoon salt
2	cups packaged herb-seasoned stuffing mix
4	bone-in pork top loin chops, cut 1½ inches thick
⅛	teaspoon ground black pepper
1	teaspoon olive oil
½	cup water
1	10-ounce package frozen honey-glazed carrots

1 For stuffing, in a large nonstick skillet heat the 1 tablespoon oil over medium-high heat. Add apple and onion; cook and stir about 4 minutes or until tender. Add the ¾ cup water and ¼ teaspoon of the salt; bring to boiling. Place stuffing mix in a large microwave-safe bowl. Pour water mixture over stuffing mix. Toss to combine. Remove 1 cup of the stuffing mixture. Cover remaining stuffing and set aside.

2 Cut 2½-inch long slits (about 1½-inch deep) along the fat-side of chops. Fill each chop with ¼ cup of the reserved stuffing. Sprinkle chops with the remaining ¼ teaspoon salt and the pepper.

3 In the same skillet heat the 1 teaspoon oil over medium-high heat. Add chops; cook for 10 minutes, turning once. Add ½ cup water. Bring to boiling; reduce heat. Cover and simmer for 20 minutes or until done (160°F).

4 Meanwhile, microwave carrots according to package directions. Stir carrots and glaze into remaining stuffing in bowl. If necessary, microwave, uncovered, on 100% power (high) for 1 minute to heat through, stirring once. Serve chops with stuffing.

Makes 4 servings

Nutrition Facts per serving: 391 cal., 16 g total fat (3 g sat. fat), 51 mg chol., 800 mg sodium, 35 g carbo., 5 g fiber, 26 g pro.

NUTTY TURKEY TENDERLOINS

Brushed with mustard and topped with stuffing mix and pecans,
turkey tenderloins bake to perfection in less than 20 minutes.

Prep: 15 minutes Bake: 18 minutes   Oven: 375°F

- **2 turkey breast tenderloins
  (about 1 pound)**

- **2 tablespoons creamy
  Dijon-style mustard blend**

- **¾ cup packaged herb-
  seasoned or corn bread
  stuffing mix, crushed**

- **½ cup finely chopped pecans**

- **2 tablespoons butter, melted**

1 Preheat oven to 375°F. Split each turkey breast tenderloin in
half horizontally to make 4 turkey steaks. Spread one side
of each turkey steak with the mustard blend. In a shallow dish
combine dry stuffing mix and pecans; dip coated side of turkey in
stuffing mixture. Place turkey steaks, coated sides up, in a shallow
baking pan. Sprinkle with any remaining stuffing mixture. Drizzle
with melted butter.

2 Bake, uncovered, for 18 to 20 minutes or until turkey is no
longer pink (170°F).

Makes 4 servings

Nutrition Facts per serving: 332 cal., 18 g total fat (5 g sat. fat), 86 mg chol., 352 mg sodium, 12 g carbo.,
2 g fiber, 30 g pro.

TURKEY-SPINACH CASSEROLE

The individual au gratin dishes give an elegant touch to this home-style casserole, but the turkey and stuffing combo is just as delicious when baked in a 2-quart baking dish.

Prep: 30 minutes   Bake: 25 minutes   Oven: 350°F

1	**10-ounce package frozen chopped spinach or chopped broccoli**
1	**10.75-ounce can reduced-fat and reduced-sodium condensed cream of celery soup**
1	**cup water**
2	**tablespoons butter**
3	**cups packaged herb-seasoned stuffing mix**
2	**cups chopped cooked turkey or chicken (about 10 ounces)**
⅓	**cup milk**
1	**tablespoon grated Parmesan cheese**

1 Preheat oven to 350°F. In a large saucepan combine spinach or broccoli, half of the soup, the water, and butter. Bring to boiling. (If using spinach, separate it with a fork.) Cover and simmer for 5 minutes.

2 Add stuffing mix to spinach mixture; stir to moisten. Spread mixture into an ungreased 2-quart square baking dish or divide mixture among four 10-ounce au gratin dishes; top with turkey.

3 In a small bowl stir together milk and remaining soup; pour over turkey. Sprinkle with Parmesan cheese.

4 Bake, uncovered, about 25 minutes or until heated through.

Makes 4 servings

Nutrition Facts per serving: 375 cal., 12 g total fat (5 g sat. fat), 65 mg chol., 1065 mg sodium, 44 g carbo., 5 g fiber, 23 g pro.

EASY BAKED FISH

Easy says it all! Frozen fish portions plus stuffing mix are brightened with
a splash of lemon juice.

Prep: 10 minutes   Bake: 18 minutes   Oven: 425°F

½   **cup packaged herb-
     seasoned stuffing mix,
     finely crushed**

2   **tablespoons butter, melted**

2   **7.6-ounce packages
     frozen Caesar Parmesan or
     grill-flavored fish portions
     (4 portions)**

2   **teaspoons lemon juice**

1 Preheat oven to 425°F. In a small bowl combine dry stuffing mix
and melted butter, tossing until well mixed.

2 Lightly grease a 2-quart rectangular baking dish; place frozen
fish portions in prepared baking dish. Sprinkle with lemon
juice. Sprinkle stuffing mixture over fish.

3 Bake, uncovered, for 18 to 20 minutes or until fish begins to
flake when tested with a fork.

Makes 4 servings

Nutrition Facts per serving: 183 cal., 9 g total fat (4 g sat. fat), 76 mg chol., 401 mg sodium, 6 g carbo.,
1 g fiber, 18 g pro.

CANADIAN BACON PIZZA

Tomatoes are nowhere to be found on this pizza—but it is delicious just the same. While it bakes, toss together a mixed green salad. Dessert can be fresh fruit served with chocolate chip cookies. Pictured on page 138.

Prep: 15 minutes   Bake: 15 minutes   Oven: 350°F

- 1 **12-inch Italian bread shell (Boboli)**
- 1 **6-ounce jar marinated artichoke hearts**
- 1 **5.2-ounce container semisoft cheese with garlic and herb**
- 1 **3.5-ounce package pizza-style Canadian-style bacon (1½-inch-diameter slices)**
- 1 **medium red sweet pepper, cut into bite-size strips**

1 Preheat oven to 350°F. Place the bread shell on a large baking sheet. Drain artichoke hearts, reserving 1 tablespoon of the marinade. Coarsely chop artichokes; set aside.

2 In a small bowl combine cheese and reserved marinade. Spread half of the cheese mixture over bread shell; top with Canadian bacon, sweet pepper, and artichoke hearts. Spoon remaining cheese mixture over all.

3 Bake about 15 minutes or until pizza is heated through.

Makes 4 to 6 servings

Nutrition Facts per serving: 529 cal., 24 g total fat (9 g sat. fat), 54 mg chol., 1136 mg sodium, 58 g carbo., 2 g fiber, 23 g pro.

MUSHROOM-TOMATO PESTO PIZZA

Premade pizza shells are indispensable for the busy home cook—especially if you've got hungry kids to feed. The topping possibilities are endless! We've chosen a combination of pesto, cheese, mushrooms, and chicken strips. Pictured on page 138.

Prep: 15 minutes   Bake: 10 minutes   Oven: 400°F

1   **12-inch Italian bread shell (Boboli)**

½   **cup purchased dried tomato pesto**

1   **cup shredded pizza cheese (4 ounces)**

1   **6-ounce package refrigerated Italian flavor cooked chicken breast strips**

1½   **cups sliced fresh shiitake, crimini, and/or button mushrooms**

1 Preheat oven to 400°F. Place the bread shell on a 12-inch pizza pan. Spread pesto over bread shell. Sprinkle with half of the cheese. Top with the chicken strips and mushrooms. Sprinkle with remaining cheese.

2 Bake for 10 to 15 minutes or until pizza is heated through and cheese is melted.

Makes 4 servings

Nutrition Facts per serving: 585 cal., 24 g total fat (8 g sat. fat), 55 mg chol., 1382 mg sodium, 64 g carbo., 4 g fiber, 33 g pro.

PIZZA ALFREDO

Creamy garlicky Alfredo sauce instead of pizza sauce is a great change of pace for pizza. Buy two or three Italian bread shells and freeze them for quick-to-fix, satisfying pizzas.

Prep: 15 minutes **Bake: 10 minutes** **Oven: 425°F**

1   **12-inch Italian bread shell or four 6-inch Italian bread shells (Boboli)**

½   **of a 10-ounce container refrigerated Alfredo pasta sauce (about ⅔ cup)**

½   **teaspoon dried Italian seasoning, crushed**

1   **8-ounce package shredded pizza cheese (2 cups)**

1½   **cups shredded or chopped cooked chicken breast (8 ounces)**

1 Preheat oven to 425°F. Place bread shell(s) on an ungreased baking sheet. In a small bowl stir together Alfredo sauce and Italian seasoning. Spread sauce mixture over bread shell(s).

2 Sprinkle bread shell(s) with half of the cheese. Top with chicken. Sprinkle with remaining cheese.

3 Bake about 10 minutes or until heated through and cheese is melted.

Makes 4 servings

Nutrition Facts per serving: 695 cal., 34 g total fat (9 g sat. fat), 107 mg chol., 1169 mg sodium, 54 g carbo., 0 g fiber, 43 g pro.

HAWAIIAN-STYLE BARBECUE PIZZA

A can of tropical fruit salad brings island flavor to a pizza assembled on top of an Italian bread shell. Add chicken, or not, as you like.

Prep: 20 minutes   **Bake:** 10 minutes   **Oven:** 425°F

- **1   12-inch Italian bread shell (Boboli)**
- **½   cup bottled barbecue sauce**
- **1½   cups shredded pizza cheese (6 ounces)**
- **1   15.25-ounce can tropical fruit salad, drained**
- **½   of a 2- to 2½-pound purchased deli-roasted chicken, cut into strips or chunks (1 to 1½ cups)**
- **¼   of a small red or yellow onion, thinly sliced and separated into rings**
- **2   green onions, thinly sliced (¼ cup)**

1 Preheat oven to 425°F. Place bread shell on a baking sheet. Spread barbecue sauce over bread shell. Sprinkle with half of the cheese. Arrange drained fruit salad, chicken, and red or yellow onion on top. Sprinkle with the remaining cheese and the green onion.

2 Bake about 10 minutes or until pizza is heated through and cheese is melted.

Makes 4 servings

Nutrition Facts per serving: 573 cal., 16 g total fat (5 g sat. fat), 56 mg chol., 1104 mg sodium, 77 g carbo., 5 g fiber, 32 g pro.

PEASANT PIZZA WITH GOAT CHEESE

Using goat or feta cheese and cream cheese in place of the traditional mozzarella gives pizza a lighter, more fresh-tasting spin.

Prep: 15 minutes **Bake: 12 minutes** **Oven: 400°F**

1   12-inch Italian bread shell (Boboli)

2   ounces cream cheese

¼   cup crumbled semisoft goat cheese or feta cheese (about 2 ounces)

2   tablespoons snipped fresh basil or 2 teaspoons dried basil, crushed

½   teaspoon bottled minced garlic (1 clove)

⅛   teaspoon ground black pepper

3   roma tomatoes, thinly sliced

1   small yellow, orange, or green sweet pepper, cut into thin bite-size strips

1 Preheat oven to 400°F. Place the bread shell on a baking sheet.

2 In a small bowl stir together cream cheese, goat cheese, dried basil (if using), garlic, and black pepper. Spread mixture over the bread shell. Arrange tomato slices and sweet pepper strips on top of the cheese mixture.

3 Bake about 12 minutes or until heated through. Sprinkle with fresh basil (if using).

Makes 6 servings

Nutrition Facts per serving: 284 cal., 11 g total fat (4 g sat. fat), 21 mg chol., 493 mg sodium, 37 g carbo., 2 g fiber, 12 g pro.

ITALIAN-SAUSAGE PIZZA

Refrigerated dough makes this favorite pizza a cinch to prepare. If you have extra time, use sliced fresh mushrooms instead of canned.

Prep: 15 minutes   Bake: 15 minutes   Stand: 5 minutes   Oven: 425°F

- 1   **13.8-ounce package refrigerated pizza dough**
- 8   **ounces bulk Italian sausage**
- ½   **of a medium green sweet pepper, cut into thin strips**
- 1   **8-ounce can pizza sauce**
- 1   **4-ounce can (drained weight) sliced mushrooms, drained**
- 1   **8-ounce package shredded pizza cheese (2 cups)**

1 Preheat oven to 425°F. Grease a 12-inch pizza pan; press pizza dough into prepared pan, building up the side. Bake for 5 minutes.

2 Meanwhile, in a medium skillet cook sausage and sweet pepper until sausage is brown. Drain off fat. Stir in pizza sauce and mushrooms.

3 Sprinkle half of the cheese on the crust. Spoon sausage mixture over cheese. Top with remaining cheese. Bake for 10 to 15 minutes or until cheese is melted. Let stand for 5 minutes before serving.

Makes 6 servings

Nutrition Facts per serving: 403 cal., 21 g total fat (11 g sat. fat), 53 mg chol., 1049 mg sodium, 28 g carbo., 1 g fiber, 23 g pro.

BARBECUED CHICKEN PIZZA

A container of barbecue sauce with shredded chicken makes a tasty pizza topping. If you like a spicy barbecue, stir in a dash of bottled hot pepper sauce.

Prep: 20 minutes   **Bake:** 19 minutes   **Oven:** 425°F

- 1 **13.8-ounce package refrigerated pizza dough**
- 1 **18-ounce tub refrigerated barbecue sauce with shredded chicken**
- 1 **8-ounce package shredded pizza cheese (2 cups)**
- ¼ **cup snipped fresh cilantro**

1 Preheat oven to 425°F. In a greased 15×10×1-inch baking pan unroll the pizza dough. Press the dough into a 12×10-inch rectangle. Build up the edges slightly. Bake for 7 minutes. Remove from oven.

2 Spread the chicken in sauce evenly over the hot crust. Sprinkle cheese and cilantro over chicken. Bake for 12 to 15 minutes or until light brown.

Makes 6 servings

Nutrition Facts per serving: 324 cal., 13 g total fat (6 g sat. fat), 39 mg chol., 683 mg sodium, 33 g carbo., 1 g fiber, 20 g pro.

BEEFY CALZONES

Purchased refrigerated pizza dough makes these half-moon shaped delights
a quick and easy solution for dinner on a busy night.

Prep: 20 minutes   **Bake:** 8 minutes   **Oven:** 425°F

8   **ounces lean ground beef**

½   **cup packaged sliced fresh mushrooms**

¼   **cup chopped green sweet pepper**

½   **cup shredded mozzarella cheese (2 ounces)**

⅓   **cup purchased pizza sauce**

1   **13.8-ounce package refrigerated pizza dough**

1   **tablespoon milk**

Grated Parmesan cheese (optional)

Warmed pizza sauce (optional)

1 Preheat oven to 425°F. In a medium skillet cook ground beef, mushrooms, and sweet pepper over medium-high heat until meat is brown; drain off fat. Stir in the mozzarella cheese and the ⅓ cup pizza sauce.

2 Unroll pizza dough. Roll or stretch dough into a 10×15-inch rectangle. Cut dough into six 5-inch squares. Spoon some of the meat mixture onto half of each square. Brush dough edges with water. Lift a corner and stretch dough over meat mixture to opposite corner. Seal the edges by pressing with the tines of a fork.

3 Place calzones on a greased baking sheet. Prick tops with a fork to allow steam to escape. Brush with the milk. If desired, sprinkle with Parmesan cheese.

4 Bake for 8 to 10 minutes or until golden brown. Let stand for 5 minutes before serving. If desired, serve with warmed pizza sauce.

Makes 6 calzones

Nutrition Facts per calzone: 235 cal., 8 g total fat (3 g sat. fat), 31 mg chol., 358 mg sodium, 26 g carbo., 1 g fiber, 13 g pro.

PIZZA TURNOVERS

Let these turnovers stuffed with favorite pizza toppings star at your child's next slumber party.

Prep: 10 minutes   **Bake:** 15 minutes   **Stand:** 5 minutes   **Oven:** 400°F

- 1 **13.8-ounce package refrigerated pizza dough**
- ¼ **cup purchased pizza sauce or spaghetti sauce**
- 2 **slices mozzarella, American, or provolone cheese, halved diagonally**
- 20 **slices pepperoni**
- 1 **tablespoon milk**
- 2 **tablespoons grated Parmesan cheese**

1 Preheat oven to 400°F. Unroll pizza dough onto a greased large baking sheet. Use a pizza cutter to cut the dough into 4 squares. Spread 1 tablespoon of the pizza sauce over each square, leaving a ¼-inch border around the edges. Place half a cheese slice on half of each square. Top with pepperoni.

2 For each turnover, fold one corner of the square down over the opposite corner to make a triangle. Carefully slide triangles apart on the baking sheet, leaving about 2 inches between each. Seal edges by pressing with the tines of a fork. Brush tops of turnovers with the milk. Sprinkle with Parmesan cheese.

3 Bake for 15 to 17 minutes or until golden brown. Let stand for 5 minutes before serving.

Makes 4 turnovers

Nutrition Facts per turnover: 377 cal., 17 g total fat (7 g sat. fat), 32 mg chol., 1110 mg sodium, 35 g carbo., 0 g fiber, 17 g pro.

Ham and Pineapple Turnovers: Prepare as above, except substitute 2 ounces chopped thinly sliced cooked ham or 20 slices pizza-style Canadian-style bacon for pepperoni. Drain an 8-ounce can pineapple tidbits. Place pineapple on top of ham. Continue as directed in Step 2.

Nutrition Facts per turnover: 301 cal., 7 g total fat (3 g sat. fat), 18 mg chol., 736 mg sodium, 44 g carbo., 1 g fiber, 14 g pro.

THREE-CORNER CHICKEN SALAD BOWLS

All you need to do for these easy bread bowls is roll out the pizza dough, cut it into triangles, drape it over custard cups, and bake.

Prep: 10 minutes   Bake: 15 minutes   Oven: 400°F

- 1 **13.8-ounce package refrigerated pizza dough**
- 1 **9-ounce package frozen cooked chicken breast strips**
- 6 **cups packaged torn mixed salad greens**
- 1 **cup red seedless grapes, halved**
- ⅓ **cup bottled blue cheese salad dressing**
- 3 **tablespoons chopped walnuts, toasted**

1 For bread bowls, preheat oven to 400°F. Invert four 10-ounce custard cups in a shallow baking pan; generously grease the outside of each custard cup. Set aside. On a cutting board unroll refrigerated pizza dough. Shape into a 10-inch square. Cut the square diagonally into 4 triangles. Drape each triangle over a prepared custard cup. Bake about 15 minutes or until deep golden brown. Remove bread bowls from custard cups; cool on a wire rack.

2 Meanwhile, prepare frozen cooked chicken breast strips according to package directions.

3 To serve, divide the mixed salad greens, chicken, and grapes among bread bowls. Drizzle with salad dressing and sprinkle with walnuts.

Makes 4 servings

Nutrition Facts per serving: 419 cal., 21 g total fat (4 g sat. fat), 43 mg chol., 1333 mg sodium, 37 g carbo., 2 g fiber, 21 g pro.

Chinese Chicken Salad: Substitute 1 cup mandarin orange segments for the grapes. Substitute ⅓ cup bottled Asian salad dressing for the blue cheese salad dressing, and substitute 3 tablespoons toasted sliced almonds for the walnuts.

EASY GOULASH

Frozen hash brown potatoes come in a variety of forms. For this recipe use either the diced potatoes or for more flavor, those diced with onion and green pepper.

Prep: 10 minutes   Cook: 10 minutes   Stand: 5 minutes

1   **pound lean ground beef**

½   **of a 24-ounce package frozen diced hash brown potatoes or diced hash brown potatoes with onions and peppers (about 3½ cups)**

1   **15-ounce can tomato sauce**

1   **14.5-ounce can diced tomatoes with basil, garlic, and oregano, undrained**

½   **cup shredded cheddar cheese (2 ounces)**

2   **cups hot cooked noodles**

1 In a large skillet cook ground beef over medium heat until brown. Drain off fat.

2 Stir in hash brown potatoes, tomato sauce, and undrained tomatoes. Bring to boiling; reduce heat. Cover and simmer about 10 minutes or until potatoes are tender. Sprinkle with cheese. Let stand, covered, about 5 minutes or until cheese melts. Serve meat mixture with noodles.

Makes 4 servings

Nutrition Facts per serving: 503 cal., 18 g total fat (8 g sat. fat), 112 mg chol., 1272 mg sodium, 50 g carbo., 4 g fiber, 35 g pro.

PORK AND POTATO SKILLET

This one-dish dinner is a winner every time with the combination of pork chops, potatoes, and vegetables.

Prep: 10 minutes   Cook: 20 minutes

4	**4-ounce boneless pork loin chops**
¾	**teaspoon seasoned salt**
2	**tablespoons cooking oil**
1	**medium red sweet pepper, cut into ¾-inch pieces**
1	**small onion, chopped (⅓ cup)**
3	**cups frozen diced hash brown potatoes**
2	**cups frozen peas and carrots**
1	**teaspoon dried thyme, crushed**

1 Sprinkle chops with ½ teaspoon of the seasoned salt. In a 12-inch skillet heat 1 tablespoon of the oil over medium-high heat. Add chops; cook for 3 minutes. Turn chops. Cook about 3 minutes more or until brown. Remove chops from skillet.

2 Carefully add the remaining 1 tablespoon oil to skillet. Add sweet pepper and onion; cook and stir for 1 minute. Add hash brown potatoes, peas and carrots, thyme, and the remaining ¼ teaspoon seasoned salt; mix well. Cook for 6 minutes, stirring frequently.

3 Place chops on top of potato mixture in skillet; cover. Reduce heat to medium. Cook for 7 to 9 minutes more or until pork chops are no longer pink (160°F) and potatoes are brown.

Makes 4 servings

Nutrition Facts per serving: 406 cal., 15 g total fat (3 g sat. fat), 72 mg chol., 422 mg sodium, 39 g carbo., 5 g fiber, 29 g pro.

SHREDDED POTATOES
with SAUSAGE and APPLES

Choose a lean or lowfat sausage for a more healthful version of this delicious main dish.

Start to Finish: 30 minutes

- 2 tablespoons olive oil
- 2 tablespoons butter
- ½ of a 26-ounce package frozen shredded hash brown potatoes (about 5 cups)
- 1 tablespoon snipped fresh thyme or 1 teaspoon dried thyme, crushed
- ¼ teaspoon ground black pepper
- 6 ounces cooked smoked sausage, coarsely chopped
- 1 medium apple, cut into thin wedges

  Salt and ground black pepper

1 In a 10-inch nonstick skillet heat the oil and 1 tablespoon of the butter over medium heat. Add potatoes in an even layer. Cook about 8 minutes, stirring occasionally, until light brown. Stir in half the thyme and the ¼ teaspoon pepper. With a wide metal spatula press down firmly. Cook about 8 minutes more or until potatoes are tender.

2 Meanwhile, in a medium skillet melt remaining 1 tablespoon butter over medium heat. Add sausage and apple. Cook, stirring occasionally, about 10 minutes or until apple is tender. Stir in remaining thyme.

3 Slide potatoes onto a cool plate, cover with another plate and flip. Top with apple mixture. Season to taste with salt and additional pepper.

Makes 4 servings

Nutrition Facts per serving: 376 cal., 27 g total fat (10 g sat. fat), 45 mg chol., 866 mg sodium, 23 g carbo., 2 g fiber, 12 g pro.

SALMON POTATO SCRAMBLE

To save even more time, use canned salmon instead of poaching the fillets.
You also can substitute canned tuna.

Start to Finish: 25 minutes

1　**pound fresh or frozen skinless salmon fillets**

2　**tablespoons butter**

2　**cups frozen diced hash brown potatoes, thawed**

1　**medium green sweet pepper, seeded and chopped**

2　**to 3 teaspoons Old Bay® seasoning**

6　**eggs, lightly beaten**

⅓　**cup water**

1 Thaw salmon, if frozen. Rinse salmon; pat dry with paper towels. In a 12-inch skillet cook salmon, covered, in a small amount of boiling water for 6 to 9 minutes or just until fish begins to flake when tested with a fork. Remove salmon from skillet; discard liquid. Using a fork, break salmon into large chunks.

2 Wipe skillet with paper towels. Melt butter in the skillet over medium-high heat. Add hash brown potatoes, pepper, and Old Bay seasoning. Cook for 5 to 10 minutes or until potatoes start to brown, stirring occasionally.

3 In a medium bowl whisk together eggs and water; add to skillet. Cook over medium heat without stirring until mixture begins to set on the bottom and around edges. With a spatula or a large spoon, lift and fold partially cooked egg mixture so that the uncooked portion flows underneath. Continue cooking and folding over medium heat for 2 to 3 minutes or until egg mixture is cooked through but is still glossy and moist. Add salmon and toss gently to combine. Heat through.

Makes 6 servings

Nutrition Facts per serving: 294 cal., 17 g total fat (6 g sat. fat), 266 mg chol., 396 mg sodium, 12 g carbo., 1 g fiber, 23 g pro.

CALIENTE POT ROAST
page 15

VERMICELLI WITH SAUSAGE
AND SPINACH
page 61

**ALL-WRAPPED-UP
CHEF'S SALAD**
page 69

SHORTCUT SHRIMP RISOTTO
page 76

BEEF AND VEGETABLES WITH FETTUCCINE
page 90

SHREDDED PORK PIZZA
page 304

MUSHROOM-TOMATO PESTO PIZZA
page 116

CANADIAN BACON PIZZA
page 115

MAKE-AHEAD PIZZA
page 347

QUICK ITALIAN PEPPER STEAK
page 146

GARLIC PORK
page 152

SKILLET ROTINI WITH ZUCCHINI AND SAUSAGE
page 157

POACHED CHICKEN AND PASTA
WITH PESTO DRESSING
page 173

INDIVIDUAL SICILIAN MEAT LOAVES
page 177

GINGER NOODLE BOWL
page 192

144

SEAFOOD CHOWDER

You choose the fish fillets—salmon, cod, or other mild-tasting fish—then toss them in a saucepan with hash-brown potatoes and a handful of flavor-spiking ingredients. The soup's ready to ladle in less than a half an hour.

Start to Finish: 25 minutes

12 ounces fresh or frozen salmon, cod, or other fish fillets

3 cups frozen diced hash brown potatoes or hash brown potatoes with onions and peppers

1 cup water

1 12-ounce can evaporated milk

1 10.75-ounce can condensed cream of shrimp or cream of potato soup

⅓ of a 3-ounce can cooked bacon pieces (⅓ cup)

2 teaspoons snipped fresh dill or ¾ teaspoon dried dill

¼ teaspoon ground black pepper

1 2-ounce jar diced pimiento, drained

1 Thaw fish, if frozen. Rinse fish; pat dry with paper towels. Cut fish into 1-inch pieces. Set aside.

2 Meanwhile, in a large saucepan combine frozen potatoes and water. Bring to boiling; reduce heat. Cover and simmer about 5 minutes or until tender.

3 Stir in evaporated milk, soup, bacon, dill, and pepper. Return to boiling. Add fish and pimiento; reduce heat. Cover and simmer for 3 to 5 minutes or just until fish flakes begins to flake when tested with a fork.

Makes 4 servings

Nutrition Facts per serving: 366 cal., 15 g total fat (7 g sat. fat), 86 mg chol., 1045 mg sodium, 27 g carbo., 2 g fiber, 30 g pro.

QUICK ITALIAN PEPPER STEAK

Frozen vegetable medleys are a boon to today's busy cook. Keep a variety on hand for quick stir-fries and meals-in-minutes like this zesty and colorful dish. Pictured on page 139.

Start to Finish: 25 minutes

| 9-ounce package refrigerated fettuccine

12 ounces packaged beef stir-fry strips

¼ teaspoon crushed red pepper

2 tablespoons olive oil

| 16-ounce package frozen pepper stir-fry vegetables (yellow, green, and red sweet peppers and onion), thawed and well drained

2 tablespoons balsamic vinegar

| 15-ounce can chunky Italian-style tomato sauce

2 tablespoons pine nuts, toasted (optional)

Crushed red pepper (optional)

1 Cook pasta according to package directions; drain well. Return pasta to pan; cover and keep warm.

2 Meanwhile, cut any thick pieces of beef to make thin strips. Combine beef strips and ¼ teaspoon crushed red pepper; set aside.

3 In a large skillet heat 1 tablespoon of the oil over medium heat; add thawed vegetables. Stir-fry for 2 to 3 minutes or until crisp-tender. Carefully add balsamic vinegar; toss to coat. Remove from skillet. Cover and keep warm.

4 Heat remaining 1 tablespoon oil in the same skillet; add beef. Stir-fry for 2 to 3 minutes or until desired doneness. Stir in tomato sauce; heat through.

5 Toss beef mixture with pasta and vegetables. If desired, sprinkle with pine nuts and pass additional crushed red pepper.

Makes 4 or 5 servings

Nutrition Facts per serving: 415 cal., 11 g total fat (2 g sat. fat), 87 mg chol., 648 mg sodium, 50 g carbo., 6 g fiber, 28 g pro.

THAI BEEF STIR-FRY

No time to slice and cut for your stir-fry? It's no problem with frozen stir-fry vegetables and precut beef stir-fry strips.

Start to Finish: 15 minutes

4   ounces dried rice noodles

2   tablespoons cooking oil

1   16-ounce package frozen pepper stir-fry vegetables (yellow, green, and red sweet peppers and onion), thawed and well drained

12 ounces packaged beef stir-fry strips

½   cup bottled peanut sauce

1 Prepare the noodles according to package directions. Drain and set aside.

2 In a large skillet heat 1 tablespoon of the oil over medium-high heat. Add the stir-fry vegetables; cook and stir for 2 to 3 minutes or until tender. Drain; place stir-fry vegetables in a bowl.

3 Heat the remaining 1 tablespoon oil in the same skillet; add beef. Stir-fry for for 2 to 3 minutes or until desired doneness. Return stir-fry vegetables to skillet; add peanut sauce. Stir to combine; heat through. Serve over rice noodles.

Makes 4 servings

Nutrition Facts per serving: 404 cal., 16 g total fat (4 g sat. fat), 50 mg chol., 597 mg sodium, 39 g carbo., 3 g fiber, 23 g pro.

MU SHU STYLE PORK ROLL-UPS

Stir-fries come together in a flash once the prep work is complete. Here, starting with pre-cut vegetables means you're ready to cook almost immediately.

Start to Finish: 20 minutes

I	**teaspoon toasted sesame oil**
12	**ounces packaged pork stir-fry strips***
2	**cups frozen pepper stir-fry vegetables (yellow, green, and red sweet peppers and onion), thawed and well drained**
4	**10-inch flour tortillas, warmed**
¼	**cup bottled plum or hoisin sauce**

1 In a large skillet heat oil over medium-high heat. Add pork strips; stir-fry for 2 to 3 minutes or just until meat is slightly pink in center. Add the vegetables. Cook and stir for 2 to 3 minutes or until vegetables are crisp-tender.

2 To warm tortillas, wrap them in white microwave-safe paper towels; microwave on 100% power (high) for 15 to 30 seconds or until tortillas are softened. (Or preheat oven to 350°F. Wrap tortillas in foil. Heat in preheated oven for 10 to 15 minutes or until warmed.)

3 Spread each tortilla with 1 tablespoon of the plum sauce. Spoon one-fourth of the meat mixture onto each tortilla just below the center. Fold the bottom edge of each tortilla up and over the filling. Fold in the sides until they meet; roll up over the filling.

Makes 4 servings

Nutrition Facts per serving: 302 cal., 8 g total fat (2 g sat. fat), 53 mg chol., 311 mg sodium, 34 g carbo., 2 g fiber, 22 g pro.

*NOTE: If your supermarket doesn't sell pork strips, cut your own from pork loin.

JAMAICAN PORK STIR-FRY

Make your meal lively by adding some Caribbean heat. Jerk seasoning is a heady and fragrant combination of chiles, garlic, onion, and other seasonings, such as thyme, cinnamon, ginger, allspice, and cloves.

Start to Finish: 20 minutes

1 tablespoon cooking oil

1 16-ounce package frozen pepper stir-fry vegetables (yellow, green, and red sweet peppers and onion)

12 ounces packaged pork stir-fry strips*

2 to 3 teaspoons Jamaican jerk seasoning

½ cup bottled plum sauce

Soy sauce (optional)

2 cups hot cooked rice or pasta

Peanuts (optional)

1 In a large skillet heat oil over medium-high heat. Add frozen vegetables; stir-fry for 5 to 7 minutes or until vegetables are crisp-tender. Remove from skillet.

2 Toss pork with jerk seasoning; add to skillet. Add more oil if necessary. Stir-fry for 2 to 5 minutes or until pork is no longer pink.

3 Add plum sauce to skillet; return vegetables to skillet. Gently toss to coat; heat through. If desired, season to taste with soy sauce. Serve over rice. If desired, sprinkle individual servings with peanuts.

Makes 4 servings

Nutrition Facts per serving: 357 cal., 9 g total fat (2 g sat. fat), 54 mg chol., 405 mg sodium, 45 g carbo., 2 g fiber, 22 g pro.

***NOTE:** If your supermarket doesn't sell pork strips, cut your own from pork loin.

FIVE-SPICE TURKEY STIR-FRY

Use a wok if you have one, or a skillet, to get this sizzling stir-fry to the table in a flash. Five-spice powder—a seasoning blend of ground cinnamon, cloves, star anise, fennel seed, and Szechuan peppercorns—will lend a familiar Chinese flavor.

Start to Finish: 25 minutes

1	4.4-ounce package beef lo-mein noodle mix
12	ounces turkey breast tenderloin, cut into thin bite-size strips
¼	teaspoon five-spice powder
¼	teaspoon salt
¼	teaspoon ground black pepper
2	tablespoons cooking oil
½	of a 16-ounce package frozen pepper stir-fry vegetables (yellow, green, and red sweet peppers and onion)
2	tablespoons chopped honey-roasted peanuts or plain peanuts

1 Prepare noodle mix according to package directions. Set aside. In a small bowl toss together turkey strips, five-spice powder, salt, and black pepper; set aside.

2 In a large skillet heat 1 tablespoon of the oil over medium-high heat. Add frozen vegetables; stir-fry for 3 minutes. Remove vegetables from skillet. Add remaining 1 tablespoon oil to hot skillet. Add turkey mixture to skillet; stir-fry for 2 to 3 minutes or until turkey is no longer pink. Return cooked vegetables to skillet. Cook and stir about 1 minute more or until heated through.

3 To serve, divide noodle mixture among 4 dinner plates. Top with turkey mixture; sprinkle with peanuts.

Makes 4 servings

Nutrition Facts per serving: 314 cal., 11 g total fat (2 g sat. fat), 76 mg chol., 670 mg sodium, 26 g carbo., 3 g fiber, 27 g pro.

ROAST BEEF SANDWICHES
WITH HORSERADISH SLAW

Horseradish and beef, common sandwich partners, pair up once again.
Here the horseradish seasons crunchy broccoli slaw.

Start to Finish: 15 minutes

⅓ **cup dairy sour cream**

2 **tablespoons snipped fresh chives**

2 **tablespoons spicy brown mustard**

1 **teaspoon prepared horseradish**

½ **teaspoon sugar**

¼ **teaspoon salt**

1 **cup packaged shredded broccoli (broccoli slaw mix)**

8 **ounces thinly sliced cooked roast beef**

8 **½-inch slices sourdough bread, toasted**

1 In a medium bowl combine sour cream, chives, mustard, horseradish, sugar, and salt. Add shredded broccoli; toss to coat.

2 To assemble, divide roast beef among 4 of the bread slices. Top with broccoli mixture and remaining bread slices. If desired, secure sandwiches with wooden toothpicks.

Makes 4 servings

Nutrition Facts per serving: 312 cal., 12 g total fat (5 g sat. fat), 52 mg chol., 612 mg sodium, 29 g carbo., 2 g fiber, 21 g pro.

GARLIC PORK

The exotic flavors of the Orient—fresh ginger, sesame oil, and hoisin sauce—make this hearty stir-fry as delicious as it is easy. Using broccoli slaw saves precious prep time. Pictured on page 140.

Start to Finish: 25 minutes

1	**7.7-ounce package fresh stir-fry noodles or 8 ounces dried fine egg noodles**
12	**ounces ground pork or beef**
2	**teaspoons bottled minced garlic (4 cloves)**
2	**teaspoons peanut oil or cooking oil**
1	**teaspoon toasted sesame oil**
2	**cups packaged shredded broccoli (broccoli slaw mix)**
1	**medium carrot, cut into thin 2-inch strips**
1	**tablespoon grated fresh ginger**
¼	**teaspoon crushed red pepper**
¼	**cup chicken broth**
¼	**cup bottled hoisin sauce**
	Sliced green onion

1 Prepare fresh noodles to loosen according to package directions, saving seasoning packet for another use. Or, cook dried noodles according to package directions; drain.

2 Meanwhile, heat a wok large skillet or a wok over medium-high heat. Add ground meat and garlic; cook until meat is brown. Drain off fat. Remove meat from wok.

3 Add peanut oil and sesame oil to wok. Add shredded broccoli, carrot, ginger, and crushed red pepper; stir-fry for 2 minutes. Stir in broth and hoisin sauce. Cook and stir until bubbly.

4 Stir noodles into vegetable mixture. Stir in cooked meat; heat through. If desired, sprinkle individual servings with green onion.

Makes 4 servings

Nutrition Facts per serving: 500 cal., 23 g total fat (7 g sat. fat), 61 mg chol., 457 mg sodium, 51 g carbo., 2 g fiber, 23 g pro.

CHICKEN WITH BROCCOLI AND GARLIC

Broccoli slaw and pecans boost the flavor of these tender sweet-and-sour
chicken thighs.

Start to Finish: 35 minutes

¼ **cup all-purpose flour**

¼ **teaspoon salt**

¼ **teaspoon ground black pepper**

4 **skinless, boneless chicken thighs (about 12 ounces)**

1 **tablespoon olive oil**

1 **bulb garlic, separated into cloves, peeled, and sliced (about ¼ cup)**

1 **cup reduced-sodium chicken broth**

3 **tablespoons white wine vinegar**

2 **tablespoons honey**

1 **16-ounce package shredded broccoli (broccoli slaw mix)**

2 **tablespoons coarsely chopped pecans**

1 In a large resealable plastic bag combine flour, salt, and pepper. Add chicken; seal bag. Shake to coat.

2 In a large skillet heat oil over medium heat. Add chicken and cook for 10 to 12 minutes or until chicken is tender and no longer pink (180°F), turning once. Transfer chicken to a plate; cover and keep warm.

3 Add garlic to skillet. Cook and stir for 1 minute. Add broth, vinegar, and honey. Bring to boiling; reduce heat. Simmer, uncovered, for 5 minutes. Stir in shredded broccoli. Return to boiling; reduce heat. Cover and simmer for 8 to 10 minutes more or until broccoli is crisp-tender. Stir in pecans. Serve the broccoli mixture with the chicken.

Makes 4 servings

Nutrition Facts per serving: 270 cal., 10 g total fat (2 g sat. fat), 68 mg chol., 392 mg sodium, 24 g carbo., 3 g fiber, 23 g pro.

CHICKEN AND BROCCOLI SALAD

Bacon adds the crowning touch to a popular salad turned main dish.
To keep the kitchen cool, crisp bacon in the microwave or opt for bacon
pieces from a jar.

Prep: 15 minutes   Chill: 1 to 24 hours

½   **cup mayonnaise or salad dressing**

2   **tablespoons cider vinegar**

4   **cups packaged shredded broccoli (broccoli slaw mix)**

2   **cups chopped cooked chicken (10 ounces)**

2   **medium red apples, cored and chopped (2 cups)**

3   **slices bacon, crisp-cooked, drained, and crumbled**

   Bacon, crisp-cooked, drained, and crumbled (optional)

1 For dressing, in a small bowl stir together mayonnaise and vinegar; set aside.

2 In a large bowl toss together shredded broccoli, chicken, apple, and 3 slices crumbled bacon. Pour dressing over chicken mixture; toss lightly to coat. Cover and chill for 1 to 24 hours.

3 If desired, sprinkle with additional crumbled bacon before serving.

Makes 4 servings

Nutrition Facts per serving: 426 cal., 30 g total fat (6 g sat. fat), 79 mg chol., 382 mg sodium, 16 g carbo., 4 g fiber, 25 g pro.

BEAN AND CHEESE QUESADILLAS

On nights the family must eat in shifts, assemble all the quesadillas but
bake them one or two at a time as needed.

Prep: 15 minutes   Bake: 12 minutes   Oven: 400°F

½ **of a 16-ounce can refried
beans (¾ cup)**

1 **8-ounce can whole kernel
corn, drained**

¼ **cup bottled salsa**

1 **canned chipotle chile
pepper in adobo sauce,
drained and chopped*
(optional)**

8 **8-inch flour tortillas**

2 **tablespoons cooking oil**

1 **cup packaged shredded
broccoli (broccoli slaw mix)**

1 **4- to 4.25-ounce can or
container diced peaches,
drained**

1 **cup finely shredded
Mexican cheese blend
(4 ounces)**

**Purchased guacamole dip,
dairy sour cream, and/or
bottled salsa**

1 Preheat oven to 400°F. In a small bowl combine refried beans,
corn, the ¼ cup salsa, and, if desired, chipotle chile pepper.
Brush 1 side of each tortilla with some of the oil. Spread bean
mixture over the plain side of 4 of the tortillas; set aside.

2 In another bowl combine shredded broccoli and peaches. Top
bean mixture with broccoli mixture. Top with cheese. Top with
remaining tortillas, oiled sides up; press down lightly. Place on a
large baking sheet.

3 Bake for 12 to 15 minutes or until golden brown and cheese is
melted. Cut into quarters to serve. Serve with guacamole dip,
sour cream, and/or additional salsa.

Makes 4 servings

Nutrition Facts per serving: 444 cal., 21 g total fat (7 g sat. fat), 25 mg chol., 825 mg sodium, 50 g carbo.,
5 g fiber, 14 g pro.

*NOTE: Because chile peppers contain volatile oils that can burn your
skin and eyes, avoid direct contact with them as much as possible. When
working with chile peppers, wear plastic or rubber gloves. If your bare
hands do touch the peppers, wash your hands and nails well with soap
and warm water.

TEX-MEX SKILLET

Chorizo sausage, made with garlic, chili powder, and other spices, is the star here surrounded by the vibrant colors of tomatoes, green chile peppers, corn, and cheddar cheese.

Start to Finish: 30 minutes

8   **ounces ground uncooked pork**

4   **ounces uncooked chorizo sausage**

1   **10-ounce can diced tomatoes and green chile peppers, undrained**

1   **cup frozen whole kernel corn**

¾   **cup water**

1   **small red sweet pepper, chopped (½ cup)**

1   **cup uncooked instant rice**

½   **cup shredded cheddar or Monterey Jack cheese (2 ounces)**

Flour tortillas, warmed (optional)

Dairy sour cream (optional)

1 In a large skillet cook pork and sausage until brown. Drain off fat. Stir in undrained tomatoes, corn, the water, and sweet pepper. Bring to boiling.

2 Stir uncooked rice into the meat mixture in skillet. Remove skillet from heat. Sprinkle with cheese. Cover and let stand about 5 minutes or until rice is tender.

3 Meanwhile, if desired, wrap tortillas in white microwave-safe paper towels; microwave on 100% power (high) for 15 to 30 seconds or until tortillas are softened. (Or preheat oven to 350°F. Wrap tortillas in foil. Heat in preheated oven for 10 to 15 minutes or until warm.) Serve in flour tortillas and top with sour cream.

Makes 4 servings

Nutrition Facts per serving: 395 cal., 20 g total fat (9 g sat. fat), 66 mg chol., 748 mg sodium, 33 g carbo., I g fiber, 2I g pro.

SKILLET ROTINI
WITH ZUCCHINI AND SAUSAGE

Sausage makes it savory, green pepper and zucchini make it fresh, chopped
tomatoes with green chile peppers make it just a little spicy,
and you make it all in just one skillet. Pictured on page 141.

Start to Finish: 35 minutes

1   pound bulk pork sausage
    or ground turkey sausage

2   medium onions, chopped
    (1 cup)

1   medium green sweet
    pepper, chopped (¾ cup)

½   teaspoon bottled minced
    garlic (1 clove)

2   8-ounce cans no salt added
    tomato sauce

1   10-ounce can diced
    tomatoes and green chile
    peppers, undrained

¾   cup water

1   tablespoon snipped fresh
    oregano or 1 teaspoon dried
    oregano, crushed

¼   teaspoon ground black
    pepper

1   cup dried rotini pasta

4   small zucchini, sliced
    (4 cups)

½   cup shredded mozzarella
    cheese (2 ounces)

1 In a 12-inch skillet cook sausage, onion, sweet pepper, and
garlic over medium heat until meat is brown and vegetables are
tender. Drain off fat.

2 Stir tomato sauce, undrained tomatoes and green chile peppers,
water, oregano, and black pepper into meat mixture in skillet.
Bring to boiling; stir in uncooked pasta. Return to boiling; reduce
heat. Cover and simmer about 10 minutes or until pasta is almost
tender. Add zucchini. Return to boiling; reduce heat. Cover and
simmer about 5 minutes more more or just until pasta and zucchini
are tender.

3 Remove skillet from heat. Sprinkle with cheese. Cover and let
stand for 1 to 2 minutes or until cheese is melted.

Makes 5 servings

Nutrition Facts per serving: 448 cal., 27 g total fat (10 g sat. fat), 71 mg chol., 842 mg sodium, 30 g carbo.,
5 g fiber, 22 g pro.

SPICY TURKEY AND BEANS

If your family loves chili, this quick-fixing saucy mixture served over corn muffins will become a weeknight mealtime fixture.

Start to Finish: 30 minutes   **Oven:** per package directions

1   **7- to 8.5-ounce package corn muffin mix**

1   **teaspoon chili powder**

2   **15.5-ounce cans pinto and/ or small red beans, rinsed and drained**

1   **15-ounce can tomato sauce**

1   **10-ounce can diced tomatoes and green chile peppers, undrained**

1   **cup chopped cooked turkey (about 5 ounces)**

½   **cup shredded cheddar or Monterey Jack cheese (2 ounces)**

1 In a medium bowl combine corn muffin mix and ½ teaspoon of the chili powder. Prepare and bake muffins according to package directions, making 6 muffins.

2 Meanwhile, in a medium saucepan combine remaining ½ teaspoon chili powder, the beans, tomato sauce, undrained tomatoes and green chile peppers, and turkey. Cook and stir over medium heat for 8 to 10 minutes or until heated through. Split corn muffins; spoon bean mixture over muffins. Sprinkle individual servings with cheese.

Makes 6 servings

Nutrition Facts per serving: 385 cal., 9 g total fat (2 g sat. fat), 28 mg chol., 1328 mg sodium, 57 g carbo., 8 g fiber, 22 g pro.

TOMATO AND TURKEY SOUP

Fajita seasoning gives a south-of-the-border slant to smoky turkey soup.
If you have it, you can substitute leftover turkey for the smoked variety.

Start to Finish: 20 minutes

3   14-ounce cans reduced-
    sodium chicken broth

1   10-ounce can diced
    tomatoes and green chile
    peppers

2   teaspoons fajita seasoning

¼   teaspoon ground black
    pepper

2   cups chopped smoked
    turkey breast (about
    10 ounces)

1   tablespoon snipped fresh
    cilantro

1 In a large saucepan combine chicken broth, undrained tomatoes and green chile peppers, fajita seasoning, and black pepper. Bring to boiling; reduce heat. Cover and simmer for 10 minutes.

2 Stir in turkey into tomato mixture; heat through. Just before serving, stir in cilantro.

Makes 4 servings

Nutrition Facts per serving: 125 cal., 1 g total fat (0 g sat. fat), 30 mg chol., 2062 mg sodium, 9 g carbo., 0 g fiber, 20 g pro.

SPICY VEGETARIAN CHILI AND POLENTA

This zesty bowl-of-red is a blend of both Tex-Mex and Italian flavors.
Polenta makes a pleasant alternative to traditional corn bread.

Prep: 10 minutes   Cook: 20 minutes

- 1 **tablespoon olive oil**
- 1 **medium onion, chopped (½ cup)**
- 1 **small zucchini, chopped (1 cup)**
- 1 **cup frozen diced hash brown potatoes**
- 1 **10-ounce can diced tomatoes and green chile peppers, undrained**
- 1 **8-ounce can tomato sauce**
- 2 **teaspoons chili powder**
- 1 **15-ounce can kidney beans, rinsed and drained**
- 1 **16-ounce tube refrigerated cooked polenta, cut into 8 slices**
- ½ **cup shredded Monterey Jack cheese (2 ounces)**
- **Dairy sour cream (optional)**

1 For chili, in a large skillet heat oil over medium heat. Add onion; cook until tender, stirring often. Stir in zucchini, hash brown potatoes, undrained tomatoes and green chile peppers, tomato sauce, and chili powder. Bring to boiling; reduce heat. Cover and simmer for 15 minutes. Stir in beans. Simmer, uncovered, about 5 minutes more or until desired consistency.

2 Meanwhile, heat polenta according to package directions. Serve with chili. Sprinkle with cheese. If desired, pass sour cream.

Makes 4 servings

Nutrition Facts per serving: 350 cal., 9 g total fat (3 g sat. fat), 15 mg chol., 1251 mg sodium, 58 g carbo., 12 g fiber, 17 g pro.

RED PEPPER AND STEAK FETTUCCINE

Start the flavorful sauce by giving the roasted peppers and salsa a whirl in the food processor. A little sugar and some chicken broth round out the flavors while sour cream adds its tangy richness.

Start to Finish: 25 minutes

I 9-ounce package refrigerated fettuccine or linguine

I cup fresh pea pods (4 ounces)

6 ounces cooked beef, cut into ¼-inch slices

¼ cup dairy sour cream

1½ teaspoons all-purpose flour

I cup bottled roasted red sweet peppers, drained

2 tablespoons bottled salsa

½ teaspoon sugar

½ cup chicken broth

1 Cook pasta and pea pods according to pasta package directions; drain. Return pasta mixture to pan; cover and keep warm. Meanwhile, cut meat into bite-size pieces. In a small bowl combine sour cream and flour; set aside.

2 For sauce, in a food processor or blender combine roasted peppers, salsa, and sugar. Cover and process or blend until nearly smooth. Transfer mixture to a small saucepan. Stir in broth.

3 Cook and stir over medium heat until bubbly. Stir in sour cream mixture. Cook and stir for 1 minute more. Stir in meat; heat through. Pour sauce over pasta mixture; toss gently to coat.

Makes 3 or 4 servings

Nutrition Facts per serving: 440 cal., 12 g total fat (5 g sat. fat), 111 mg chol., 295 mg sodium, 54 g carbo., 4 g fiber, 29 g pro.

MEDITERRANEAN CHICKEN AND PASTA

The zesty flavors of the Mediterranean dominate this dish. Artichokes, oregano, kalamata olives, and feta cheese mingle with chicken pieces, garlic, and a splash of white wine.

Prep: 15 minutes   Cook: 10 minutes

1	6-ounce jar marinated artichoke hearts
1	tablespoon olive oil
12	ounces skinless, boneless chicken breast halves, cut into bite-size pieces
3	cloves garlic, thinly sliced
¼	cup chicken broth
¼	cup dry white wine
1	tablespoon small fresh oregano leaves or 1 teaspoon dried oregano, crushed
1	cup bottled roasted red sweet peppers, drained and cut into strips
¼	cup pitted kalamata olives
3	cups hot cooked penne pasta
¼	cup crumbled feta cheese (optional)

1 Drain artichokes, reserving marinade. Cut up any large pieces; set aside. In a large skillet heat oil over medium-high heat. Add chicken and garlic. Cook and stir until chicken is brown. Add the reserved artichoke marinade, broth, wine, and, if using, dried oregano.

2 Bring to boiling; reduce heat. Cover and simmer for 10 minutes. Stir in artichokes, roasted peppers, olives, and, if using, fresh oregano. Heat through.

3 To serve, spoon the chicken mixture over pasta. If desired, sprinkle with feta cheese.

Makes 4 servings

Nutrition Facts per serving: 347 cal., 9 g total fat (1 g sat. fat), 49 mg chol., 323 mg sodium, 38 g carbo., 3 g fiber, 26 g pro.

ITALIAN TURKEY SANDWICHES

An aromatic basil-flavored spread boosts these sandwiches from ordinary to extraordinary. Fresh basil is the key here; dried simply doesn't work.

Start to Finish: 20 minutes

⅓ cup fine dry bread crumbs

2 teaspoons dried Italian seasoning, crushed

2 turkey tenderloins (about I pound)

2 teaspoons olive oil

2 tablespoons snipped fresh basil

¼ cup light mayonnaise or salad dressing

8 ½-inch slices Italian bread, toasted

I cup bottled roasted red and/or yellow sweet peppers, cut into thin strips

1 In a large plastic bag combine the bread crumbs and Italian seasoning. Slice each turkey tenderloin in half horizontally to make ½-inch steaks. Place a turkey steak in the bag; seal and shake to coat. Repeat with remaining steaks.

2 In a 12-inch nonstick skillet heat oil over medium heat. Add turkey steaks; cook about 10 minutes or until tender and no longer pink (170°F), turning once halfway through cooking.

3 In a small bowl stir 1 tablespoon of the basil into the mayonnaise. Spread mayonnaise mixture on 1 side of 4 bread slices. Top bread slices with turkey steaks, roasted pepper strips, and the remaining basil. Top with remaining bread slices.

Makes 4 sandwiches

Nutrition Facts per sandwich: 399 cal., II g total fat (2 g sat. fat), 73 mg chol., 671 mg sodium, 40 g carbo., 3 g fiber, 33 g pro.

PASTA WITH PEPPER-CHEESE SAUCE

Roasted sweet peppers and cheese with jalapeños kick up the flavor of a hollandaise sauce mix. Sprinkle the finished dish with grated Parmesan cheese, if you like.

Start to Finish: 25 minutes

8   **ounces dried medium shell macaroni, mostaccioli, or cut ziti pasta**

1   **0.9- to 1.25-ounce package hollandaise sauce mix**

1   **cup bottled roasted red sweet peppers, drained and chopped**

½   **cup shredded Monterey Jack cheese with jalapeño chile peppers (2 ounces)**

1 Cook pasta according to package directions; drain well. Return pasta to pan. Cover and keep warm.

2 Meanwhile, prepare hollandaise sauce according to package directions, except use only 2 tablespoons butter. Stir in roasted peppers. Remove pan from heat. Add cheese to sauce, stirring until cheese melts. Add sauce to pasta in pan; toss to coat.

Makes 4 to 6 servings

Nutrition Facts per serving: 384 cal., 13 g total fat (8 g sat. fat), 36 mg chol., 407 mg sodium, 53 g carbo., 2 g fiber, 13 g pro.

TORTELLINI ALFREDO
WITH ROASTED PEPPERS

Refrigerated tortellini and Alfredo sauce make Italian cooking quick and easy; purchased roasted sweet peppers and a sprinkling of basil make the dish fresh and colorful, too.

Start to Finish: 15 minutes

1 **16-ounce package frozen meat- or cheese-filled tortellini (4 cups)**

1 **10-ounce container refrigerated light Alfredo pasta sauce**

1 **cup bottled roasted red sweet peppers, drained and cut into ½-inch strips**

¼ **cup snipped fresh basil**

Coarsely ground black pepper

1 Cook tortellini according to package directions; drain well. Return tortellini to hot pan.

2 Gently stir Alfredo sauce and roasted peppers into tortellini in pan. Cook over medium heat until hot and bubbly. Stir in basil. Season to taste with black pepper.

Makes 4 servings

Nutrition Facts per serving: 495 cal., 15 g total fat (6 g sat. fat), 98 mg chol., 1150 mg sodium, 65 g carbo., 1 g fiber, 24 g pro.

CHICKEN AND LEMON-BROCCOLI ALFREDO

Fresh lemon offers a pleasant counterpoint to the ultra-rich Alfredo sauce.

Start to Finish: 20 minutes

4   **skinless, boneless chicken breast halves**

    Salt and ground black pepper

1   **tablespoon olive or cooking oil**

8   **ounces mushrooms, halved**

1   **lemon**

3   **cups fresh broccoli florets**

1   **10-ounce container refrigerated Alfredo pasta sauce or light Alfredo pasta sauce**

1 Season chicken with salt and pepper. In large skillet heat oil over medium heat. Add chicken and mushrooms; cook for 4 minutes, turning chicken halfway through.

2 Meanwhile, shred 2 teaspoons lemon peel; set aside. Slice lemon. Add broccoli and lemon slices to skillet. Cover and cook about 8 minutes or until chicken is no longer pink (170°F).

3 Place chicken and vegetables on plates. Add Alfredo sauce to skillet; heat through. Stir in lemon peel. Season to taste with additional pepper. Serve with chicken and vegetables.

Makes 4 servings

Nutrition Facts per serving: 361 cal., 19 g total fat (9 g sat. fat), 107 mg chol., 753 mg sodium, 15 g carbo., 4 g fiber, 34 g pro.

BLACKENED CHICKEN ALFREDO

Too cold to grill outside? You can still serve up this spicy chicken and pasta toss. Cook the chicken on an indoor grill or under the broiler.

Prep: 15 minutes   Grill: 12 minutes

- **3   skinless, boneless chicken breast halves**
- **2   tablespoons olive oil**
- **2   teaspoons blackened seasoning**
- **8   ounces dried mostaccioli (2⅔ cups)**
- **2   cups broccoli florets**
- **1   cup halved packaged peeled baby carrots**
- **1   10-ounce container refrigerated Alfredo pasta sauce or light Alfredo pasta sauce**
- **½   teaspoon blackened seasoning**

1 In a resealable plastic bag place the chicken, oil, and the 2 teaspoons blackened seasoning. Turn bag to coat chicken.

2 For a charcoal grill, place chicken on the rack of an uncovered grill directly over medium coals. Grill for 12 to 15 minutes or until no longer pink (170°F), turning once halfway through grilling. (For a gas grill, preheat grill. Reduce heat to medium. Place chicken on grill rack over heat. Cover and grill as above.) Cut chicken into ½-inch cubes; set aside.

3 Meanwhile, cook pasta according to the package directions, except add the broccoli and carrots for the last 8 minutes of cooking. Drain; return to pan. Stir in grilled chicken, Alfredo sauce, and the ½ teaspoon blackened seasoning. Heat through.

Makes 4 servings

Nutrition Facts per serving: 615 cal., 31 g total fat (1 g sat. fat), 85 mg chol., 567 mg sodium, 52 g carbo., 4 g fiber, 32 g pro.

STOVETOP DIRECTIONS: Prepare as above except do not grill chicken. In a large skillet cook chicken in 1 tablespoon hot olive oil or cooking oil over medium heat for 8 to 10 minutes or until no longer pink (170°F), turning once.

CREAMY CHICKEN-VEGETABLE SOUP

Some creamy soups start with a white sauce. As easy as that is, we've made this recipe even easier by eliminating that step and using a refrigerated Alfredo sauce instead.

Start to Finish: 30 minutes

- 2 **14-ounce cans chicken broth**
- 2 **medium carrots, thinly sliced (1 cup)**
- 2 **stalks celery, thinly sliced (1 cup)**
- 1 **teaspoon dried thyme, crushed**
- 1 **6-ounce package refrigerated cooked chicken breast strips, chopped**
- 1 **small zucchini, halved lengthwise and thinly sliced (1¼ cups)**
- ½ **cup uncooked instant white rice**
- 1 **10-ounce container refrigerated Alfredo pasta sauce or light Alfredo pasta sauce**
- ¼ **cup chopped bottled roasted red sweet peppers or one 4-ounce jar diced pimientos, drained**

1 In a large saucepan combine broth, carrots, celery, and thyme. Bring to boiling; reduce heat. Cover and simmer for 10 minutes.

2 Stir in chicken, zucchini, and rice. Remove from heat. Cover and let stand about 5 minutes or until rice is tender. Stir in Alfredo sauce and roasted peppers; heat through.

Makes 4 servings

Nutrition Facts per serving: 302 cal., 16 g total fat (9 g sat. fat), 71 mg chol., 1729 mg sodium, 22 g carbo., 2 g fiber, 16 g pro.

TUNA AND PASTA ALFREDO

If you have a few extra minutes and a good piece of tuna, cook it up fresh. If not, canned tuna works just fine. Either way, you'll appreciate how the sauce ingredients cook in the same pot for maximum flavor and minimum cleanup.

Start to Finish: 25 minutes

3   **cups dried mini lasagna, broken mafalda, or medium noodles**

1   **tablespoon butter**

2   **cups chopped broccoli rabe or broccoli**

1   **medium red sweet pepper, chopped (¾ cup)**

1   **10-ounce container refrigerated Alfredo pasta sauce or light Alfredo pasta sauce**

2   **teaspoons snipped fresh dill**

1   **to 2 tablespoons milk (optional)**

1   **9.5-ounce can tuna (waterpack), drained and broken into chunks**

½   **cup sliced almonds, toasted (optional)**

1 Cook pasta according to package directions; drain well. Return pasta to hot pan. Cover and keep warm.

2 Meanwhile, in a large saucepan melt butter over medium heat. Add broccoli rabe and sweet pepper; cook until tender. Stir in Alfredo sauce and dill. If necessary, stir in enough of the milk to make sauce desired consistency. Gently stir cooked pasta and tuna into broccoli rabe mixture. Heat through. If desired, top individual servings with almonds.

Makes 6 servings

Nutrition Facts per serving: 387 cal., 12 g total fat (5 g sat. fat), 63 mg chol., 568 mg sodium, 48 g carbo., 3 g fiber, 20 g pro.

ROTINI AND SWEET PEPPER PRIMAVERA

Pasta is so incredibly versatile because it goes well with just about any other ingredient. Here, curly rotini, asparagus spears, red peppers, pattypan squash, and herbs are a winning combination.

Start to Finish: 20 minutes

14 **ounces fresh asparagus spears**

8 **ounces dried rotini or gemelli pasta (about 2½ cups)**

2 **small red and/or yellow sweet peppers, cut into 1-inch pieces**

1 **cup sliced yellow summer squash or zucchini**

1 **10-ounce container refrigerated Alfredo pasta sauce or light Alfredo pasta sauce**

2 **tablespoons snipped fresh tarragon or fresh thyme or 2 teaspoons dried tarragon or thyme, crushed**

¼ **teaspoon crushed red pepper**

1 Snap off and discard woody bases from asparagus spears. Bias-slice asparagus into 1-inch pieces. (You should have about 1½ cups.)

2 Cook pasta according to package directions, adding asparagus, sweet peppers, and squash to the pasta for the last 3 minutes of cooking. Drain. Return the pasta and vegetables to hot pan.

3 Meanwhile, in a small saucepan stir together Alfredo sauce, tarragon, and crushed red pepper. Cook and stir over medium heat about 5 minutes or until mixture is heated through. Pour over pasta and vegetables; toss gently to coat.

Makes 4 servings

Nutrition Facts per serving: 410 cal., 15 g total fat (9 g sat. fat), 41 mg chol., 514 mg sodium, 55 g carbo., 5 g fiber, 13 g pro.

CHICKEN AND LINGUINE WITH PESTO

Pesto has come a long way in the convenience category! The Italian sauce used to be handmade with a mortar and pestle; today, ready-made versions are widely available, and they add an instant windfall of fresh flavor to everything they touch.

Start to Finish: 20 minutes

8   ounces dried linguine

1   10-ounce package frozen broccoli, cauliflower, and carrots

1   10-ounce container refrigerated Alfredo pasta sauce or light Alfredo pasta sauce

⅓   cup purchased basil pesto (refrigerated or bottled)

¼   cup milk

½   of a 2- to 2½-pound deli-roasted chicken

    Milk (optional)

    Grated Parmesan cheese

1 Cook pasta according to package directions, adding frozen vegetables during the last 5 minutes of cooking. Drain. Return to pan.

2 Meanwhile, in a small bowl combine Alfredo sauce, pesto, and ¼ cup milk; set aside. Remove meat from chicken (discard skin and bones); chop or shred meat.

3 Add chicken to pasta and vegetables in pan. Add sauce mixture; toss gently to coat. Heat through over medium-low heat. If desired, stir in additional milk to reach desired consistency. Sprinkle individual servings with cheese.

Makes 4 servings

Nutrition Facts per serving: 801 cal., 48 g total fat (4 g sat. fat), 109 mg chol., 546 mg sodium, 54 g carbo., 3 g fiber, 37 g pro.

PESTO PENNE WITH ROASTED CHICKEN

Purchased pesto and roasted chicken help get this main-dish pasta on the table in a mere 20 minutes. Fresh broccoli cooks with the pasta and lends fresh flavor.

Start to Finish: 20 minutes

8   ounces dried penne, mostaccioli, or bow tie pasta (4 cups)

2   cups broccoli florets

¾   cup purchased basil pesto (refrigerated or bottled)

2½ cups bite-size slices of cooked chicken (about 12 ounces)

1   cup bottled roasted red sweet peppers, drained and cut into strips

¼   cup finely shredded Parmesan cheese (1 ounce)

½   teaspoon coarsely ground black pepper

1 Cook pasta according to package directions, adding broccoli for the last 2 minutes of cooking. Drain, reserving ½ cup of the pasta water. Return drained pasta and broccoli to saucepan.

2 In a small bowl combine pesto and the reserved pasta water. Add chicken, roasted peppers, and pesto mixture to pasta in saucepan. Toss gently to coat. Heat through over medium heat. Add Parmesan cheese to pasta mixture; toss to combine.

3 Divide the cooked pasta among 4 warm pasta bowls. Sprinkle with black pepper. Serve immediately.

Makes 4 servings

Nutrition Facts per serving: 557 cal., 23 g total fat (6 g sat. fat), 49 mg chol., 1228 mg sodium, 56 g carbo., 5 g fiber, 30 g pro.

POACHED CHICKEN
AND PASTA WITH PESTO DRESSING

The chicken cooks in the same pot with the pasta, and a sprightly veggie-studded pesto sauce stirs together in a hurry to create a creamy and colorful version of chicken salad. Pictured on page 142.

Start to Finish: 30 minutes

12   **ounces skinless, boneless chicken breast halves**

6   **ounces dried rotini, penne, or wagon-wheel pasta (2 cups)**

½   **cup light dairy sour cream**

⅓   **cup purchased basil pesto (refrigerated or bottled)**

1   **cup chopped fresh vegetables, such as red, yellow, and/or green sweet pepper; broccoli florets; zucchini; and/or cucumber**

1   **small tomato, chopped (½ cup)**

2   **tablespoons finely shredded Parmesan cheese**

¼   **cup pine nuts or chopped walnuts, toasted (optional)**

1 Cut chicken into 1-inch pieces; set aside.

2 Cook pasta according to package directions, adding chicken for the last 5 to 6 minutes of cooking. Cook until pasta is tender but firm and chicken is no longer pink. Drain pasta and chicken.

3 In a large bowl combine sour cream and pesto. Add pasta mixture, chopped vegetables, and tomato. Toss lightly to coat. Serve warm or chilled. (To chill, cover and chill for up to 4 hours. If necessary, stir in 1 to 2 tablespoons light dairy sour cream before serving.) Sprinkle individual servings with cheese and, if desired, pine nuts.

Makes 4 servings

Nutrition Facts per serving: 452 cal., 18 g total fat (2 g sat. fat), 62 mg chol., 276 mg sodium, 40 g carbo., 2 g fiber, 30 g pro.

SALMON WITH PESTO MAYO

Three ingredients are all it takes to create this tantalizing salmon entrée. Steamed green beans sprinkled with finely shredded lemon peel makes a pleasing side.

Start to Finish: 20 minutes

4 **5- to 6-ounce fresh or frozen skinless salmon fillets**

¼ **cup mayonnaise or salad dressing**

3 **tablespoons purchased basil pesto (refrigerated or bottled)**

Shaved Parmesan cheese (optional)

1 Thaw fish, if frozen. Rinse fish; pat dry with paper towels. Measure thickness of fish.

2 Preheat broiler. Place fish on the greased unheated rack of a broiler pan, tucking under thin edges. Broil 4 inches from heat for 4 to 6 minutes per ½-inch thickness or until fish begins to flake when tested with a fork. (If fillets are 1 inch or more thick, carefully turn once halfway through broiling)

3 Meanwhile, for topping, in a small bowl stir together mayonnaise and pesto. Spoon topping over fillets. Broil for 1 minute or until topping is bubbly. If desired, garnish with shaved Parmesan cheese.

Makes 4 servings

Nutrition Facts per serving: 440 cal., 34 g total fat (5 g sat. fat), 94 mg chol., 256 mg sodium, 2 g carbo., 0 g fiber, 30 g pro.

SHRIMP QUESADILLAS

As you finish cooking the quesadillas on the stovetop, keep them warm in the oven. Be sure to lay them in a single layer on the baking sheet so they stay crisp. If you stack them, they'll steam and get soggy.

Start to Finish: 30 minutes   Oven: 300°F

12   ounces fresh or frozen medium shrimp in shells

8   6- to 7-inch flour tortillas

¼   cup purchased basil pesto (refrigerated or bottled)

1   tablespoon olive oil

1   teaspoon bottled minced garlic (2 cloves)

1   cup red and/or green sweet pepper strips

1   medium onion, sliced and separated into rings

1½   cups shredded Mexican cheese blend (6 ounces)

   Dairy sour cream

   Salsa or habañero pepper sauce

1 Thaw shrimp, if frozen. Peel and devein shrimp. Rinse shrimp; pat dry with paper towels. Set shrimp aside. Spread one side of each tortilla with pesto. Cover; set aside.

2 Preheat oven to 300°F. In a large skillet heat oil over medium heat. Add shrimp and garlic; cook for 1 to 3 minutes or until shrimp turn opaque. Remove from skillet and keep warm. In the same skillet cook sweet pepper strips and onion for 3 to 4 minutes or until vegetables are crisp-tender (add additional oil, if necessary). Remove vegetables from skillet; keep warm.

3 To assemble quesadillas, layer shrimp mixture, vegetables, and cheese onto half of the tortillas. Top with the remaining tortillas, pesto sides down.

4 In large skillet cook one of the quesadillas over medium heat for 2 to 3 minutes or until light brown, turning once. Remove quesadilla from skillet; place on a baking sheet. Keep warm in oven. Repeat with remaining quesadillas.

5 To serve, cut quesadillas into wedges. Serve with sour cream and salsa.

Makes 4 servings

Nutrition Facts per serving: 600 cal., 33 g total fat (12 g sat. fat), 132 mg chol., 986 mg sodium, 47 g carbo., 4 g fiber, 20 g pro.

GREEK BEEF AND PASTA SKILLET

Prepared pasta sauce is one of the most versatile ingredients to keep in stock in the pantry. Here it adds color and a hearty tang to the dish.

Start to Finish: 25 minutes

8	**ounces dried rotini pasta**
1	**tablespoon cooking oil**
12	**ounces packaged beef stir-fry strips**
1	**26- to 28-ounce jar marinara pasta sauce**
¼	**teaspoon salt**
¼	**teaspoon ground cinnamon**
½	**of a 10-ounce package frozen chopped spinach, thawed* and well drained**
⅓	**cup crumbled feta cheese**

1 Cook pasta according to package directions; drain.

2 In a large skillet heat oil over medium-high heat. Add beef strips. Cook and stir for 2 to 3 minutes or until desired doneness. Add marinara sauce, salt, and cinnamon. Cook and stir until sauce is bubbly. Add cooked pasta and spinach. Cook and stir until heated through. Sprinkle individual servings with feta cheese.

Makes 4 servings

Nutrition Facts per serving: 483 cal., 12 g total fat (3 g sat. fat), 63 mg chol., 1063 mg sodium, 60 g carbo., 6 g fiber, 32 g pro.

*NOTE: To cut a package of spinach in half, unwrap the frozen block of spinach and place on a microwave-safe plate. Microwave on 30% power (medium-low) for 2 to 4 minutes or just until soft enough to cut in half with a sharp knife. Put one half in a freezer bag, seal, and return to freezer. Continue to microwave the remaining half on 30% power for 3 to 5 minutes or until thawed.

INDIVIDUAL SICILIAN MEAT LOAVES

If you think meat loaf takes too long to make, this recipe will change your mind. Making mini loaves cuts down considerably on cooking time. Pictured on page 143.

Start to Finish: 30 minutes   Oven: 400°F

1	egg, lightly beaten
1	14-ounce jar marinara pasta sauce (1¾ cups)
¼	cup seasoned fine dry bread crumbs
¼	teaspoon salt
¼	teaspoon ground black pepper
12	ounces lean ground beef
2	ounces mozzarella cheese
4	thin slices proscuitto or cooked ham (about 2 ounces)
1	9-ounce package refrigerated plain or spinach fettuccine
	Finely shredded Parmesan cheese (optional)

1 Preheat oven to 400°F. In a medium bowl combine egg, ¼ cup of the marinara sauce, the bread crumbs, salt, and pepper. Add ground beef; mix well.

2 Cut mozzarella cheese into four logs, each measuring about 2¼×¾×½ inches. Wrap a slice of proscuitto around each cheese log. Shape one-fourth of the meat mixture around each cheese log to form a loaf. Flatten each meat loaf to 1½ inches thick; place in a shallow baking pan.

3 Bake loaves about 20 minutes or until done (160°F).

4 Meanwhile, cook pasta according to package directions. In a small saucepan heat remaining marinara sauce over medium heat until bubbly.

5 Arrange meat loaves over hot cooked pasta. Spoon sauce over all. If desired, sprinkle with Parmesan cheese.

Makes 4 servings

Nutrition Facts per serving: 631 cal., 31 g total fat (12 g sat. fat), 173 mg chol., 1132 mg sodium, 55 g carbo., 3 g fiber, 31 g pro.

SAUSAGE-CAVATELLI SKILLET

Cavatelli are bite-size pasta shells with ruffled edges. They're ideal for capturing every last bite of the zesty, saucy Italian sausage mixture.

Start to Finish: 20 minutes

- **8   ounces dried cavatelli pasta (about 1¾ cups)**
- **1   pound bulk Italian sausage or ground beef**
- **1   medium green sweet pepper, chopped (¾ cup)**
- **1   26- to 28-ounce jar marinara pasta sauce**
- **1   cup shredded mozzarella cheese (4 ounces)**

1 Cook pasta according to package directions; drain well.

2 Meanwhile, in a large skillet cook meat and sweet pepper until meat is brown. Drain off fat. Stir marinara sauce into meat mixture in skillet; cook about 2 minutes or until heated through. Stir in cooked pasta. Sprinkle with cheese. Cover and cook about 2 minutes more or until cheese melts.

Makes 4 servings

Nutrition Facts per serving: 677 cal., 32 g total fat (13 g sat. fat), 93 mg chol., 1469 mg sodium, 60 g carbo., 4 g fiber, 32 g pro.

EASY CHICKEN MARINARA

Use marinara sauce or any of the wide array of pasta sauces available to top the chicken patties.

Start to Finish: 25 minutes

4 **frozen cooked, breaded chicken patties**

2 **cups bottled marinara pasta sauce (1¾ cups)**

½ **to 1 cup shredded mozzarella cheese (2 to 4 ounces)**

Hot cooked spaghetti

1 Place chicken patties on a baking sheet. Bake patties according to package directions. Meanwhile, place marinara sauce in a saucepan and heat through over medium heat.

2 Remove baking sheet from oven; turn chicken patties over. Spoon about ¼ cup sauce over each chicken patty. Top each patty with cheese. Return to oven and bake for 4 to 5 minutes more or until cheese melts.

3 Serve chicken patties over spaghetti with remaining marinara sauce.

Makes 4 servings

Nutrition Facts per serving: 283 cal., 15 g total fat (4 g sat. fat), 36 mg chol., 919 mg sodium, 24 g carbo., 3 g fiber, 14 g pro.

SPICY TURKEY PASTA SAUCE

Squash, red sweet pepper, and red onion add fresh accents to store-bought pasta sauce. Turkey Italian sausage adds delicious flavor.

Start to Finish: 25 minutes

1	**9-ounce package refrigerated fettuccine or linguine**
8	**ounces uncooked turkey Italian sausage (remove casings, if present)**
1	**cup coarsely chopped yellow summer squash**
1	**small red sweet pepper, cut into thin strips**
¼	**cup chopped red onion**
1	**14-ounce jar marinara pasta sauce**
2	**tablespoons shredded Parmesan cheese (optional)**

1 Cook pasta according to package directions. Drain. Return pasta to hot saucepan; cover and keep warm.

2 Meanwhile, in a large skillet cook sausage, squash, sweet pepper, and onion over medium heat until sausage is brown; drain off fat. Stir marinara sauce into sausage mixture in skillet; heat through.

3 Serve sausage mixture over pasta. If desired, sprinkle individual servings with Parmesan cheese.

Makes 4 servings

Nutrition Facts per serving: 350 cal., 10 g total fat (3 g sat. fat), 115 mg chol., 866 mg sodium, 49 g carbo., 5 g fiber, 20 g pro.

TEXAS CHILI MADE EASY

Salsa provides both the tomatoes and sauce. Adjust the spiciness with they type of salsa you choose—mild, medium, or hot.

Start to Finish: 20 minutes

12 **ounces lean ground beef**

1 **15-ounce can pinto beans, undrained**

1 **cup bottled salsa**

½ **cup beef broth**

1 **teaspoon chili powder**

½ **teaspoon ground cumin**

   Sour cream (optional)

1 In a large skillet cook ground beef over medium heat until brown. Drain off fat.

2 Stir undrained beans, salsa, broth, chili powder, and cumin into meat in skillet. Bring to boiling; reduce heat. Cover and simmer for 10 minutes. If desired, serve with sour cream.

Makes 6 servings

Nutrition Facts per serving: 178 cal., 8 g total fat (3 g sat. fat), 36 mg chol., 442 mg sodium, 12 g carbo., 4 g fiber, 15 g pro.

HOT AND SAUCY TORTELLINI

Salsa kicks up the flavor of bottled pasta sauce to make this fast sausage
and tortellini dinner.

Start to Finish: 25 minutes

7 **to 8 ounces dried
cheese-filled tortellini
(about 1¾ cups)**

8 **ounces bulk Italian sausage**

1 **13- to 14-ounce jar tomato-
basil pasta sauce**

1 **16-ounce jar salsa**

2 **tablespoons snipped fresh
cilantro**

1 Cook tortellini according to package directions. Drain and
return to pan.

2 Meanwhile, in a large skillet cook sausage over medium heat
until brown; drain off fat. Stir in pasta sauce and salsa. Bring
to boiling; reduce heat. Cover and simmer for 5 minutes.

3 Stir tortellini and 1 tablespoon of the cilantro into sauce
mixture; heat through. Transfer mixture to a serving bowl or
platter. Sprinkle with remaining 1 tablespoon cilantro.

Makes 4 servings

Nutrition Facts per serving: 450 cal., 20 g total fat (5 g sat. fat), 38 mg chol., 1848 mg sodium, 42 g carbo.,
3 g fiber, 21 g pro.

SIMPLE SALSA SKILLET

Try this Tex-Mex-style combination with a crisp green salad and warm tortillas or corn muffins.

Start to Finish: 25 minutes

1	**tablespoon cooking oil**
1	**medium green sweet pepper, cut into bite-size strips**
1	**medium red sweet pepper, cut into bite-size strips**
1	**16-ounce jar salsa**
1	**15.25-ounce can whole kernel corn, drained**
1	**15-ounce can black beans, rinsed and drained**
1	**9-ounce package frozen chopped cooked chicken, thawed**
	Dairy sour cream (optional)

1 In a large skillet heat oil over medium heat. Add green and red sweet pepper strips; cook for 2 minutes. Add salsa, corn, black beans, and chicken. Stir gently.

2 Cover and cook over medium-low heat about 10 minutes or until heated through, stirring occasionally. If desired, serve with sour cream.

Makes 4 to 6 servings

Nutrition Facts per serving: 302 cal., 7 g total fat (1 g sat. fat), 45 mg chol., 1550 mg sodium, 42 g carbo., 10 g fiber, 27 g pro.

CHUNKY CHICKEN CHILI

Chicken produces a lighter but just as kicky chili, and this one goes together in a snap. Refrigerated corn bread sticks heat nearly as quickly as does a corn bread mix for a crumbly sweet accompaniment.

Start to Finish: 20 minutes

12 **ounces skinless, boneless chicken thighs**

   Nonstick cooking spray

2 **15-ounce cans chili beans with spicy chili gravy, undrained**

1½ **cups frozen pepper stir-fry vegetables (yellow, green, and red sweet peppers and onion)**

¾ **cup bottled salsa**

1 Cut chicken into 1-inch pieces. Coat an unheated large saucepan with nonstick cooking spray. Preheat over medium-high heat. Add chicken; cook and stir until light brown.

2 Stir undrained chili beans, frozen vegetables, and salsa into chicken in skillet. Bring to boiling; reduce heat. Simmer, uncovered, about 7 minutes or until chicken is tender and no longer pink.

Makes 4 servings

Nutrition Facts per serving: 320 cal., 5 g total fat (1 g sat. fat), 70 mg chol., 930 mg sodium, 39 g carbo., 12 g fiber, 29 g pro.

TURKEY TACO SALAD

When you think tacos, you may automatically think of beef. Here, turkey replaces beef with results that are just as tasty. The recipe doubles easily for feeding the family and friends.

Start to Finish: 30 minutes   Oven: 400°F

12 ounces uncooked ground turkey or lean ground beef

1 teaspoon bottled minced garlic (2 cloves)

½ cup bottled salsa

1 cup canned red kidney beans, rinsed and drained

¼ cup water

2 teaspoons chili powder

⅛ teaspoon ground cumin

4 8-inch flour tortillas

2 tablespoons butter, melted

4 cups torn lettuce

2 medium tomatoes, chopped (1 cup)

1 small avocado, seeded, peeled, and chopped

½ cup sliced pitted ripe olives

½ cup shredded cheddar cheese (2 ounces)

   Dairy sour cream (optional)

1 Preheat oven to 400°F. In a large skillet cook ground turkey and garlic over medium heat about 5 minutes or until turkey is no longer pink. Drain off fat. Stir in salsa, kidney beans, water, chili powder, and cumin. Bring to boiling; reduce heat. Cover and simmer for 10 minutes.

2 Meanwhile, lightly brush both sides of the tortillas with melted butter. Place tortillas in a single layer on an ungreased baking sheet. Bake for 7 to 10 minutes or until tortillas are light brown.

3 In a medium bowl combine lettuce, tomatoes, avocado, and olives. Add the hot turkey mixture; toss gently to combine.

4 To serve, transfer the tortillas to dinner plates. Spoon turkey mixture on top of tortillas. Sprinkle with cheese. If desired, serve with sour cream and additional salsa.

Makes 4 servings

Nutrition Facts per serving: 482 cal., 27 g total fat (10 g sat. fat), 97 mg chol., 866 mg sodium, 35 g carbo., 9 g fiber, 26 g pro.

ASIAN BEEF SKILLET

Torn fresh spinach—added just at the end so it doesn't overcook—helps brighten this tasty dish.

Start to Finish: 30 minutes

2   **tablespoons cooking oil**

1   **pound packaged beef stir-fry strips**

2   **stalks celery, bias-sliced (1 cup)**

1   **medium onion, coarsely chopped (½ cup)**

1   **10.75-ounce can condensed cream of mushroom soup**

1   **cup fresh bean sprouts**

⅔   **cup water**

2   **tablespoons soy sauce**

3   **cups torn packaged prewashed fresh spinach**

    Hot cooked rice

    Soy sauce (optional)

1 In a large skillet heat oil over medium heat. Add half of the beef; cook until brown. Remove meat from skillet. Repeat with remaining meat.

2 Add celery and onion to skillet; cook and stir until crisp-tender.

3 Stir in soup, bean sprouts, water, and the 2 tablespoons soy sauce; bring to boiling. Stir in beef and spinach; heat through. Serve over hot cooked rice. If desired, pass additional soy sauce.

Makes 4 servings

Nutrition Facts per serving: 451 cal., 15 g total fat (3 g sat. fat), 50 mg chol., 1100 mg sodium, 43 g carbo., 4 g fiber, 34 g pro.

CREAMY HAM WITH PEAS

This satisfying stew stars the delicious duo of ham and peas—with their contrasting salty/smoky and sweet flavors. The instant mashed potatoes help thicken the mix.

Start to Finish: 25 minutes

3½   **cups milk**

1   **10.75-ounce can condensed cream of mushroom or golden mushroom soup**

¼   **teaspoon dried thyme, crushed**

⅛   **teaspoon ground black pepper**

2   **cups frozen peas or cut broccoli**

½   **cup packaged instant mashed potatoes**

1   **5-ounce can chunk-style ham, drained and broken into pieces**

1 In a large saucepan combine milk, soup, thyme, and pepper. Bring to boiling. Add vegetables; cover and cook about 5 minutes or just until vegetables are tender.

2 Stir instant potatoes into soup mixture. Stir in ham. Heat through.

Makes 4 servings

Nutrition Facts per serving: 349 cal., 13 g total fat (5 g sat. fat), 38 mg chol., 1208 mg sodium, 40 g carbo., 3 g fiber, 17 g pro.

LEMON CHICKEN WITH ASPARAGUS

Remember this recipe when asparagus season rolls around. The vegetable is usually at its freshest, in-season best from February to June.

Start to Finish: 30 minutes

Nonstick cooking spray

4 skinless, boneless chicken breast halves

1 pound fresh asparagus spears, trimmed

1 cup water

1 10.75-ounce can condensed cream of mushroom, cream of chicken, or cream of asparagus soup

¾ cup chicken broth

1 tablespoon lemon juice

Hot cooked couscous

1 Lightly coat a large nonstick skillet with nonstick cooking spray. Preheat skillet over medium heat. Cook chicken in hot skillet for 8 to 10 minutes or until tender and no longer pink (170°F), turning once. Remove chicken from skillet; cover and keep warm.

2 In the same skillet combine asparagus and the water. Bring to boiling; reduce heat. Cover and simmer for 3 to 5 minutes or until asparagus is crisp-tender. Drain.

3 Meanwhile, for sauce, in a small saucepan combine soup, broth, and lemon juice. Cook and stir until heated through. Serve sauce with chicken, asparagus, and hot cooked couscous.

Makes 4 servings

Nutrition Facts per serving: 354 cal., 8 g total fat (3 g sat. fat), 88 mg chol., 844 mg sodium, 27 g carbo., 3 g fiber, 40 g pro.

CHICKEN WITH NOODLES

Chicken with noodles—a classic comfort dish—gets a confetti-like update with olives, red sweet pepper, and peas.

Start to Finish: 20 minutes

8   **ounces dried egg noodles
    (4 cups)**

1   **10.75-ounce can condensed
    cream of mushroom or
    cream of chicken soup**

½   **cup milk**

1   **2.25-ounce can sliced
    pitted ripe olives, drained**

2   **tablespoons chopped
    bottled roasted red sweet
    pepper**

¼   **teaspoon dried marjoram,
    crushed**

⅛   **teaspoon ground black
    pepper**

2   **cups chopped cooked
    chicken (about 10 ounces)**

1   **cup frozen peas**

¼   **cup dry white wine or
    chicken broth**

1 Cook noodles according to package directions. Drain and keep warm.

2 Meanwhile, in a large saucepan combine soup and milk. Stir in olives, roasted pepper, marjoram, and black pepper. Bring to boiling, stirring occasionally. Stir in chicken, peas, and wine; heat through. Stir in hot noodles.

Makes 4 servings

Nutrition Facts per serving: 506 cal., 15 g total fat (4 g sat. fat), 125 mg chol., 827 mg sodium, 55 g carbo., 5 g fiber, 33 g pro.

QUICK THAI CHICKEN PASTA

Thai seasoning varies from brand to brand, but most include a great variety of herbs and spices, such as coriander, ginger, lemon peel, and chile peppers. The product makes it easy to bring a windfall of flavor to a recipe—without a lengthy ingredient list!

Start to Finish: 20 minutes

8 **ounces dried angel hair pasta**

2 **medium carrots, sliced (1 cup)**

1 **cup fresh pea pods, trimmed and cut into halves**

1 **tablespoon cooking oil**

12 **ounces skinless, boneless chicken thighs, cut into bite-size strips**

1 **13.5-ounce can unsweetened coconut milk**

1 **10.75-ounce can condensed cream of mushroom or cream of chicken soup**

1½ **to 2 teaspoons Thai seasoning**

½ **cup chopped peanuts**

1 Cook pasta and carrots according to the pasta package directions, adding pea pods for the last 1 minute of cooking. Drain well. Return pasta mixture to saucepan; cover and keep warm.

2 Meanwhile, in a large skillet heat oil over medium heat. Add chicken; cook and stir until no longer pink. Add coconut milk, soup, and Thai seasoning. Cook over medium heat until heated through, stirring frequently.

3 Pour hot chicken mixture over cooked pasta; toss gently to coat. Transfer to a serving platter or bowl. Sprinkle with peanuts. Serve immediately.

Makes 4 servings

Nutrition Facts per serving: 727 cal., 39 g total fat (21 g sat. fat), 74 mg chol., 858 mg sodium, 60 g carbo., 5 g fiber, 33 g pro.

HULA STIR-FRY

This sweet, crunchy chicken is sure to be a favorite with kids.
And it's simple enough that they pitch in and help make it!

Start to Finish: 25 minutes

1	**pound skinless, boneless chicken breast halves**
1	**tablespoon cooking oil**
1	**16-ounce package frozen stir-fry vegetables**
1	**8-ounce can pineapple chunks (juice pack), undrained**
2	**3-ounce packages ramen noodles (any flavor), broken**
⅔	**cup bottled stir-fry sauce**
½	**cup water**

1 Cut chicken into bite-size pieces. In a large skillet heat oil over medium-high heat. Add chicken; cook and stir about 6 minutes or until no longer pink. Add frozen vegetables to the skillet. Cover and cook for 5 to 7 minutes or until vegetables are crisp-tender.

2 Stir undrained pineapple chunks, ramen noodles (discard seasoning packets), stir-fry sauce, and the water into the chicken mixture in the skillet. Bring to boiling; reduce heat to medium-low. Cover and cook about 3 minutes or until noodles are tender, stirring occasionally.

Makes 4 servings

Nutrition Facts per serving: 471 cal., 14 g total fat (1 g sat. fat), 67 mg chol., 1103 mg sodium, 49 g carbo., 3 g fiber, 37 g pro.

GINGER NOODLE BOWL

Thanks to bottled stir-fry sauce, this is a quick meal you can whip up during the busy work week. Many supermarkets sell mushrooms and other vegetables, already washed and ready for stir-frying. Pictured on page 144.

Start to Finish: 25 minutes

2   cups dried **Chinese egg noodles or fine egg noodles** (4 ounces)

¼   teaspoon ground ginger

⅓   cup bottled stir-fry sauce

2   teaspoons peanut oil or cooking oil

1   cup fresh sugar snap peas or pea pods, tips and stems removed and cut up

1   cup sliced fresh shiitake mushrooms

1   small red sweet pepper, cut into bite-size strips

5   ounces cooked chicken breast, cut into strips (about 1 cup)

¼   cup broken cashews

1   Cook noodles according to package directions. Drain; set aside. Stir ginger into the stir-fry sauce; set aside.

2   In a large skillet heat oil over medium-high heat. Add peas, mushrooms, and sweet pepper; cook and stir for 3 to 5 minutes or until crisp-tender. Add cooked noodles, chicken, stir-fry sauce, and cashews; heat through.

Makes 3 servings

Nutrition Facts per serving: 389 cal., 12 g total fat (2 g sat. fat), 77 mg chol., 739 mg sodium, 44 g carbo., 4 g fiber, 27 g pro.

STACK-IT-UP CHICKEN SALAD

If time is short, skip stacking the salad ingredients and toss them in a large bowl with the peanut dressing.

Start to Finish: 30 minutes

I   **purchased peeled, cored fresh pineapple**

I   **2- to 2½-pound purchased deli-roasted chicken**

½   **of a head napa cabbage, cut crosswise into 1-inch pieces, or 2 romaine hearts, halved crosswise**

I   **cup seedless green and/or red grapes, halved**

I   **Granny Smith apple, cut into chunks**

½   **cup bottled stir-fry sauce**

¼   **cup creamy peanut butter**

¼   **teaspoon crushed red pepper**

  Water

1 Cut pineapple lengthwise into ½-inch-wide spears. Remove skin from chicken and discard. Remove meat from bones; discard bones. Cut chicken into bite-size pieces. On each of 4 dinner plates, build a stack using the cabbage, chicken, grapes, apple, and pineapple.

2 For dressing, in a small bowl whisk together stir-fry sauce, peanut butter, and crushed red pepper. If necessary, whisk in water, 1 teaspoon at a time, until dressing reaches drizzling consistency. Drizzle dressing over arranged salads.

Makes 4 servings

Nutrition Facts per serving: 529 cal., 19 g total fat (5 g sat. fat), 123 mg chol., 998 mg sodium, 44 g carbo., 5 g fiber, 45 g pro.

SWEET-AND-SOUR SHRIMP

Purchased stir-fry sauce and prechopped vegetables from the produce
department make extra-quick work of this already speedy dish. To thaw
the shrimp quickly, place it under cold running water.

Start to Finish: 15 minutes

¾ **pound fresh or frozen
   peeled and deveined shrimp**

⅓ **cup bottled stir-fry sauce**

¼ **cup pineapple-orange juice**

   Nonstick cooking spray

3 **cups assorted fresh stir-fry
   vegetables**

1 Thaw shrimp, if frozen. In a small bowl combine the stir-fry
sauce and pineapple-orange juice; set aside.

2 Coat an unheated nonstick wok or large skillet with cooking
spray. (Add oil, if necessary, during cooking.) Heat wok or skillet
over medium-high heat. Add vegetables; stir-fry for 3 to 5 minutes
or until crisp-tender. Remove from wok. Add shrimp; stir-fry for
2 to 3 minutes or until shrimp turn opaque. Push shrimp to side
of wok.

3 Add sauce mixture to wok. Return vegetables to wok and toss
gently to coat. Cook and stir about 1 minute more or until
heated through.

Makes 4 servings

Nutrition Facts per serving: 119 cal., 1 g total fat (0 g sat. fat), 131 mg chol., 666 mg sodium, 11 g carbo.,
2 g fiber, 17 g pro.

SCALLOP FRIED RICE

Purchased stir-fry sauce doubles as a zippy marinade for the scallops.

Prep: 10 minutes   **Cook:** 5 minutes   **Marinate:** 30 minutes

8   **ounces fresh or frozen bay scallops**

¼   **cup bottled stir-fry sauce**

     Nonstick cooking spray

1   **egg, lightly beaten**

2   **green onions, thinly bias-sliced (¼ cup)**

1   **10-ounce package frozen rice with peas and mushrooms, thawed**

1 Thaw scallops, if frozen. In a small bowl stir together the scallops and stir-fry sauce. Cover and marinate in the refrigerator for 30 minutes.

2 Coat a large skillet with cooking spray. Heat over medium-high heat. Add egg to hot skillet. Stir-fry for 1 minute or until egg is cooked through (should look like scrambled egg). Remove egg from skillet.

3 Add scallops with sauce and green onions to the hot skillet. Stir-fry about 2 minutes or until scallops turn opaque. Add thawed rice mixture and cooked egg to skillet. Stir all ingredients together to coat with sauce. Cook and stir about 2 minutes more or until heated through.

Makes 2 servings

Nutrition Facts per serving: 362 cal., 5 g total fat (1 g sat. fat), 144 mg chol., 1502 mg sodium, 48 g carbo., 2 g fiber, 26 g pro.

CREAMY BARLEY AND BROCCOLI

A little like a creamy risotto, this dish gets its wonderful richness from sweet and nutty Swiss cheese.

Start to Finish: 25 minutes

1	**14-ounce can vegetable broth**
1	**cup quick-cooking barley**
2	**cups packaged fresh broccoli florets**
1	**10.75-ounce can condensed cream of broccoli or cream of celery soup**
½	**cup milk**
½	**teaspoon dried basil, crushed**
¼	**teaspoon ground black pepper**
1	**cup shredded Swiss cheese (4 ounces)**

1 In a medium saucepan bring broth to boiling. Stir in barley. Return to boiling; reduce heat. Cover and simmer for 10 to 12 minutes or until barley is tender and most of the liquid is absorbed, adding broccoli for the last 5 minutes of cooking. Do not drain.

2 Stir soup, milk, basil, and pepper into broccoli mixture in saucepan. Heat through. Add ½ cup of the cheese; stir until melted.

3 Sprinkle individual servings with the remaining ½ cup cheese.

Makes 4 servings

Nutrition Facts per serving: 331 cal., 13 g total fat (7 g sat. fat), 30 mg chol., 1005 mg sodium, 40 g carbo., 6 g fiber, 16 g pro.

SPICY PASTA AND BROCCOLI

Orecchiette is Italian for "little ears" and refers to the disk shape of the pasta. Your family is sure to enjoy it as it is a nice change from spaghetti and other more common pasta shapes.

Start to Finish: 25 minutes

12 **ounces dried orecchiette or medium shell pasta (about 4 cups)**

2 **tablespoons olive oil**

3 **cups packaged fresh broccoli florets, chopped**

1 **cup chicken broth with Italian herbs**

¼ **to ½ teaspoon crushed red pepper**

1 Cook pasta according to package directions. Drain and return pasta to pan. Drizzle 1 tablespoon of the olive oil over pasta; toss to coat. Cover and keep warm.

2 Meanwhile, heat the remaining 1 tablespoon oil in a large skillet. Add broccoli; cook and stir over medium-high heat for 3 minutes. Add broth and crushed red pepper. Bring to boiling; reduce heat. Cover and simmer for 2 to 3 minutes more or until broccoli is crisp-tender. Combine pasta and broccoli mixture; toss to mix.

Makes 4 servings

Nutrition Facts per serving: 404 cal., 9 g total fat (1 g sat. fat), 0 mg chol., 214 mg sodium, 67 g carbo., 4 g fiber, 14 g pro.

LEMON-ALMOND BROCCOLI

Toasted nuts and green vegetables are an appealing combination that is quick and easy to put together. A dash of lemon peel makes the broccoli even better while the nuts add some satisfying crunch.

Start to Finish: 20 minutes

2	**cups packaged fresh broccoli florets**
1	**tablespoon butter**
¾	**cup sliced fresh mushrooms**
1	**green onion, thinly sliced (2 tablespoons)**
2	**tablespoons slivered almonds or chopped pecans, toasted**
½	**teaspoon finely shredded lemon peel**

1 In a covered medium saucepan cook broccoli in a small amount of boiling lightly salted water about 8 minutes or until crisp-tender. Drain.

2 Meanwhile, for sauce, in a small saucepan melt butter over medium heat. Add mushrooms and green onion; cook until tender, stirring occasionally. Remove from heat. Stir in nuts and lemon peel. Toss with hot cooked broccoli.

Makes 4 servings

Nutrition Facts per serving: 69 cal., 6 g total fat (2 g sat. fat), 8 mg chol., 34 mg sodium, 4 g carbo., 2 g fiber, 3 g pro.

ORANGE-SAUCED BROCCOLI AND PEPPERS

Prepare this garden-fresh veggie combo next time you grill pork or chicken. For extra color, use half of a red and half of a yellow sweet pepper.

Start to Finish: 20 minutes

3½	**cups packaged fresh broccoli florets**
1	**medium sweet red or yellow pepper, cut into bite-size strips**
1	**tablespoon butter**
2	**tablespoons finely chopped onion**
½	**teaspoon bottled minced garlic (1 clove)**
1½	**teaspoons cornstarch**
⅔	**cup orange juice**

1 In a medium saucepan cook broccoli and sweet pepper, covered, in a small amount of boiling water about 8 minutes or until broccoli is crisp-tender; drain. Cover and keep warm.

2 For sauce, in a small saucepan melt butter over medium heat. Add onion and garlic; cook for 5 minutes or until onion is tender. Stir in cornstarch. Add orange juice. Cook and stir until mixture is thickened and bubbly. Cook and stir for 2 minutes more. To serve, pour sauce over broccoli mixture. Toss gently to coat.

Makes 6 servings

Nutrition Facts per serving: 57 cal., 2 g total fat (1 g sat. fat), 5 mg chol., 32 mg sodium, 9 g carbo., 2 g fiber, 2 g pro.

BROCCOLI-SWISS SOUP

Cubed ham, cream, and shredded Swiss and broccoli mingle in broth for a satisfying soup. Roasted minced garlic adds a nice flavor depth.

Prep: 15 minutes   Cook: 10 minutes

2   **14-ounce cans chicken broth**

1   **1-pound package fresh broccoli florets**

1   **medium onion, chopped (½ cup)**

2   **teaspoons bottled roasted garlic**

1   **cup shredded Swiss cheese (4 ounces)**

1   **cup half-and-half or light cream**

½   **cup cubed cooked ham**

    Salt and ground black pepper

1 In a large saucepan combine broth, broccoli, onion, and garlic. Bring to boiling; reduce heat. Cover and simmer about 10 minutes or until broccoli is very tender. In a food processor or blender process or blend the broccoli mixture, in 2 or 3 batches, until smooth.

2 Return broccoli mixture to saucepan. Return to a simmer. Add cheese; cook, stirring constantly, until melted. Stir in half-and-half and ham. Season to taste with salt and pepper.

Makes 4 servings

Nutrition Facts per serving: 283 cal., 18 g total fat (10 g sat. fat), 58 mg chol., 1213 mg sodium, 14 g carbo., 4 g fiber, 18 g pro.

CARROTS with CREAMY PARMESAN DIP

To cut a few calories and some fat, use light cream cheese and sour cream products in this dip. Serve the dip with additional fresh vegetable dippers such as packaged fresh broccoli or cauliflower florets.

Prep: 10 minutes   **Chill:** 1 to 24 hours

- 1 **8-ounce package cream cheese, softened**
- 1 **8-ounce carton dairy sour cream**
- 1 **green onion, finely chopped (2 tablespoons)**
- ⅓ **cup grated Parmesan cheese (2 ounces)**
- 2 **teaspoons Italian seasoning**
  Milk (optional)
- 1 **2-pound package peeled baby carrots**

1 In a medium bowl beat cream cheese, sour cream, green onion, Parmesan cheese, and Italian seasoning with an electric mixer on low speed until fluffy. Cover and chill for 1 to 24 hours.

2 If dip is too thick after chilling, stir in 1 to 2 tablespoons milk. Spoon into serving bowl. Serve with carrots.

Makes about 2 cups dip

Nutrition Facts per tablespoon dip: 40 cal., 4 g total fat (2 g sat. fat), 11 mg chol., 49 mg sodium, 1 g carbo., 0 g fiber, 1 g pro.

CUMIN-SCENTED CARROTS

Cumin adds an intriguing Southwest flavor to these carrots.

Start to Finish: 15 minutes

- 2 **cups packaged peeled baby carrots**
- 1 **tablespoon butter**
- ½ **teaspoon ground cumin**
  Salt and ground black pepper

1 In a medium saucepan cook carrots, covered, in a small amount of boiling water for 7 to 9 minutes or until carrots are crisp-tender; drain.

2 Meanwhile, in a medium skillet melt butter over medium heat. Add cumin; cook and stir for 30 seconds. Add the cooked carrots, stirring to coat. Sprinkle lightly with salt and pepper.

Makes 4 servings

Nutrition Facts per serving: 53 cal., 3 g total fat (2 g sat. fat), 8 mg chol., 88 mg sodium, 6 g carbo., 2 g fiber, 1 g pro.

HONEY-GLAZED CARROTS

Honey and a hint of ginger perk up these microwaved carrots.

Start to Finish: 15 minutes

- 1 **1-pound package peeled baby carrots**
- 2 **tablespoons water**
- 2 **tablespoons honey**
- 1 **tablespoon butter**
- ⅛ **teaspoon ground ginger**

1 In a microwave-safe baking dish or casserole combine carrots and water. Microwave, covered, on 100% power (high) for 7 to 9 minutes or until carrots are crisp-tender, stirring once after 4 minutes. Drain off water.

2 Add honey, butter, and ginger to the carrots in baking dish or casserole. Microwave, covered, on 100% power (high) for 1 to 2 minutes more or until butter is melted. Stir until combined.

Makes 4 servings

Nutrition Facts per serving: 102 cal., 3 g total fat (2 g sat. fat), 8 mg chol., 65 mg sodium, 19 g carbo., 3 g fiber, 1 g pro.

BROWN SUGAR–GLAZED CARROTS

If you like, substitute a 1-pound package of crinkle-cut fresh carrots for the baby carrots.

Start to Finish: 25 minutes

1 **1-pound package peeled baby carrots, halved lengthwise**

1 **tablespoon butter**

1 **tablespoon packed brown sugar**

   Dash salt

   Ground black pepper

1 In a medium saucepan cook carrots, covered, in a small amount of boiling salted water for 8 to 10 minutes or until crisp-tender. Drain; remove carrots from pan.

2 In the same saucepan combine butter, brown sugar, and salt. Cook and stir over medium heat until combined. Add carrots. Cook and stir about 2 minutes or until glazed. Season to taste with pepper.

Makes 4 servings

Nutrition Facts per serving: 83 cal., 3 g total fat (2 g sat. fat), 8 mg chol., III mg sodium, I4 g carbo., 2 g fiber, I g pro.

SAUCY CARROTS AND PECANS

Orange marmalade, butter, and salt meld on the stove to glaze a quickly cooked bag of baby carrots that you'll top with chopped pecans. Elegant, luscious, and delicious.

Start to Finish: 20 minutes

1 1-pound package peeled baby carrots

2 tablespoons orange marmalade

1 tablespoon butter

½ teaspoon salt

2 tablespoons pecan pieces, toasted

1 In a covered large saucepan cook the carrots in a small amount of boiling water for 8 to 10 minutes or until crisp-tender. Drain.

2 Return carrots to pan. Add orange marmalade, butter, and salt. Stir until carrots are coated. Top with the pecans.

Makes 4 servings

Nutrition Facts per serving: 124 cal., 6 g total fat (2 g sat. fat), 8 mg chol., 365 mg sodium, 19 g carbo., 4 g fiber, 2 g pro.

STEAMED SPINACH

This recipe is easy to prepare in a microwave oven; microwave the spinach and herbs on 100 percent power (high) for 3 minutes.

Start to Finish: 20 minutes

3	**6-ounce packages prewashed fresh baby spinach or two 10-packages prewashed fresh spinach**
1	**cup snipped fresh parsley, basil, cilantro, or watercress**
¼	**cup sherry vinegar or herb vinegar**
	Salt and freshly ground black pepper
	Lemon wedges (optional)

1 In a large Dutch oven or very large skillet with steamer basket insert bring 1 inch of water to boiling. Combine spinach and herbs or watercress in basket; place over boiling water. Cover and steam for 2 to 3 minutes or until wilted, stirring once. Remove basket carefully; drain. Transfer spinach to a serving bowl. Drizzle with some of the vinegar. Season to taste with salt and pepper.

2 Pass remaining vinegar. If desired, garnish with lemon wedges.

Makes 4 servings

Nutrition Facts per serving: 40 cal., 1 g total fat (0 g sat. fat), 0 mg chol., 256 mg sodium, 6 g carbo., 3 g fiber, 4 g pro.

SAUTEED SPINACH with BACON and MUSTARD

Splurge on a specialty bacon such as applewood smoked or honey-basted hickory smoked.

Start to Finish: 15 minutes

4	**slices bacon, cut into 1-inch pieces**
2	**10-ounce packages prewashed fresh spinach**
1	**tablespoon butter**
1	**tablespoon Dijon-style mustard**
¼	**teaspoon crushed red pepper**

1 In a 12-inch skillet cook bacon over medium heat until crisp. Remove bacon to drain on paper towels, reserving 1 tablespoon drippings in skillet. Gradually add spinach to skillet, stirring frequently with metal tongs. Cook for 2 to 3 minutes or just until spinach is wilted. Remove spinach from skillet to a colander; press lightly to drain. (If using large leaf spinach, use kitchen scissors to snip.)

2 In the same skillet melt butter over medium heat; stir in mustard and crushed red pepper. Add drained spinach; toss to coat and reheat spinach if necessary. Top with cooked bacon. Serve immediately.

Makes 4 to 6 servings

Nutrition Facts per serving: 135 cal., 11 g total fat (4 g sat. fat), 18 mg chol., 340 mg sodium, 5 g carbo., 3 g fiber, 7 g pro.

CREAMED SPINACH

To remove excess liquid, use the back of a wooden spoon to press the cooked or frozen spinach in a fine-mesh sieve.

Start to Finish: 30 minutes

- **2 10-ounce packages prewashed fresh spinach (large stems removed) or two 10-ounce packages frozen chopped spinach, thawed**
- **2 tablespoons butter**
- **1 medium onion, chopped (½ cup)**
- **1 to 1½ teaspoons bottled minced garlic (2 to 3 cloves)**
- **1 cup whipping cream**
- **½ teaspoon ground black pepper**
- **¼ teaspoon salt**
- **¼ teaspoon ground nutmeg**

1 In a Dutch oven or large stockpot cook fresh spinach (if using) in rapidly boiling salted water for 1 minute. Drain well, squeezing out liquid. Pat dry with paper towels. Snip spinach with kitchen shears to coarsely chop; set aside. If using frozen spinach, drain well, squeezing out liquid.

2 In a large skillet melt butter over medium heat. Add onion and garlic; cook about 5 minutes or until onion is tender, stirring occasionally. Stir in cream, pepper, salt, and nutmeg. Bring onion mixture to boiling. Boil gently, uncovered, until cream begins to thicken. Add spinach. Simmer, uncovered, about 2 minutes or until thickened. Season to taste with additional salt and pepper.

Makes 4 servings

Nutrition Facts per serving: 312 cal., 29 g total fat (17 g sat. fat), 98 mg chol., 347 mg sodium, 11 g carbo., 4 g fiber, 6 g pro.

WILTED SPINACH SALAD

Fresh strawberries add colorful sweetness to this all-time favorite wilted salad.

Start to Finish: 25 minutes

6   **cups torn packaged prewashed fresh spinach or romaine**

1   **cup sliced fresh mushrooms**

2   **green onions, thinly sliced (¼ cup)**

    Dash ground black pepper (optional)

3   **slices bacon**

3   **tablespoons vinegar**

1   **teaspoon sugar**

¼   **teaspoon dry mustard**

1   **cup sliced strawberries and/or drained mandarin orange sections**

1   **hard-cooked egg, chopped**

1 In a large bowl combine spinach, mushrooms, and green onions. If desired, sprinkle with pepper; set aside.

2 For dressing, in a 12-inch skillet cook bacon until crisp. Remove bacon, reserving 2 tablespoons drippings in skillet. (Or, if desired, substitute 2 tablespoons salad oil for bacon drippings.) Crumble bacon; set aside. Stir vinegar, sugar, and dry mustard into drippings. Bring to boiling; remove from heat. Add the spinach mixture. Toss mixture in skillet for 30 to 60 seconds or just until spinach is wilted.

3 Transfer mixture to a serving dish. Add the strawberries and/or orange sections. Top salad with chopped egg and crumbled bacon. Serve salad immediately.

Makes 4 servings

Nutrition Facts per serving: 86 cal., 4 g total fat (1 g sat. fat), 57 mg chol., 159 mg sodium, 8 g carbo., 3 g fiber, 6 g pro.

SPINACH SALAD WITH GLAZED ALMONDS

If you're short on time, skip the glazed almonds and toss in a handful of flavored sliced almonds.

Start to Finish: 35 minutes

Nonstick cooking spray

⅓ **cup sliced almonds**

2 **teaspoons sugar**

1 **10-ounce package prewashed spinach**

1 **cup sliced fresh strawberries**

⅔ **cup sliced celery**

2 **green onions, sliced (¼ cup)**

¼ **cup olive oil**

¼ **cup red wine vinegar**

1 **teaspoon sugar**

¼ **teaspoon salt**

2 **drops bottled hot pepper sauce**

1 For glazed almonds: Line a baking sheet with foil. Coat foil with nonstick cooking spray. In a heavy, small skillet combine almonds and the 2 teaspoons sugar. Cook over medium-high heat until sugar begins to melt, shaking skillet occasionally. Do not stir. Reduce heat to low. Continue cooking until sugar is golden brown, stirring occasionally. Remove skillet from heat. Pour nut mixture onto the prepared baking sheet. Cool completely. Break into clusters.

2 Meanwhile, in an extra large bowl combine spinach, strawberries, celery, and green onions.

3 For dressing, in a small bowl whisk together oil, vinegar, the 1 teaspoon sugar, the salt, and hot pepper sauce. Drizzle dressing over spinach mixture. Toss to coat. Divide spinach mixture among 8 salad plates. Sprinkle with glazed almonds.

Makes 8 servings

Nutrition Facts per serving: 113 cal., 10 g total fat (1 g sat. fat), 0 mg chol., 110 mg sodium, 6 g carbo., 2 g fiber, 2 g pro.

ENOKI MUSHROOM AND VEGETABLE CUPS

Green onions, coleslaw mix, sweet pepper, and enoki mushrooms make an
appetizing filling for napa cabbage or flour tortillas.

Start to Finish: 25 minutes

2   **teaspoons olive oil**

1   **teaspoon toasted sesame oil**

1   **cup fresh pea pods, trimmed
    and halved crosswise**

1   **medium red sweet pepper,
    cut into thin strips**

6   **green onions, cut into
    1-inch pieces**

2   **3.2-ounce packages fresh
    enoki mushrooms**

3   **cups packaged shredded
    cabbage with carrot
    (coleslaw mix)**

¼   **cup bottled hoisin sauce**

4   **napa cabbage cups or
    8-inch flour tortillas,
    warmed**

1 In a large skillet combine olive oil and sesame oil; heat over
medium heat. Add pea pods, sweet pepper, and green onions;
cook and stir for 2 to 3 minutes or until vegetables are crisp-tender.
Stir in enoki mushrooms, coleslaw mix, and hoisin sauce. Heat
through.

2 Divide mushroom mixture among cabbage cups or tortillas.
Insert wooden skewers through cabbage cups to hold their
shape, or roll up tortillas. Serve immediately.

Makes 4 servings

Nutrition Facts per serving: 240 cal., 4 g total fat (1 g sat. fat), 0 mg chol., 677 mg sodium, 45 g carbo.,
6 g fiber, 5 g pro.

COLESLAW CRUNCH SALAD

Want a coleslaw with an abundance of crunch? Ramen noodles, toasted almonds, and sunflower seeds provide plenty in this anytime salad.

Start to Finish: 20 minutes

¾ **cup salad oil**

⅓ **cup sugar**

⅓ **cup white vinegar**

2 **2.8-ounce packages beef-flavor ramen noodles**

1 **1-pound package shredded cabbage with carrot (coleslaw mix) (about 8 cups)**

1 **cup slivered almonds, toasted**

2 **medium carrots, chopped or shredded (1 cup)**

4 **green onions, sliced (½ cup)**

½ **cup shelled sunflower seeds**

1 For dressing, in a medium bowl whisk together oil, sugar, vinegar, and the seasoning packets from the ramen noodles. Set aside.

2 In an extra-large bowl combine dry ramen noodles, coleslaw mix, almonds, carrots, green onions, and sunflower seeds. Drizzle dressing over cabbage mixture; toss to coat.

Makes 8 servings

Nutrition Facts per serving: 486 cal., 38 g total fat (4 g sat. fat), 0 mg chol., 395 mg sodium, 32 g carbo., 5 g fiber, 9 g pro.

DUTCH TREAT COLESLAW

This quick-to-prepare slaw serves a bunch and is a perfect addition to summer picnics or backyard barbecues.

Start to Finish: 15 minutes

¼ **to ⅓ cup sugar**

¼ **cup vinegar**

2 **tablespoons water**

¼ **cup salad oil**

1 **teaspoon celery seeds**

⅛ **teaspoon salt**

⅛ **teaspoon ground black pepper**

¼ **cup dairy sour cream**

8 **cups shredded cabbage with carrot (coleslaw mix)**

1 **small green sweet pepper, chopped**

1 For dressing, in a small saucepan combine sugar, vinegar, and the water; heat and stir until sugar dissolves.

2 In a blender combine sugar mixture, oil, celery seeds, salt, and black pepper; cover and blend until well mixed. Add sour cream; cover and blend just until combined.

3 In a large bowl combine coleslaw mix and sweet pepper; add dressing. Toss to combine. Serve immediately or cover and chill in the refrigerator for up to 4 hours. Stir before serving.

Makes 8 to 10 servings

Nutrition Facts per serving: 122 cal., 9 g total fat (2 g sat. fat), 3 mg chol., 56 mg sodium, 12 g carbo., 2 g fiber, 1 g pro.

CRANBERRY COLESLAW

This tangy red-and-green coleslaw makes a pleasant counterpoint to turkey or roast beef. The fresh cranberries give a tart, fresh taste and slight pink tint to the dressing.

Prep: 15 minutes

¼ **cup low-fat mayonnaise or mayonnaise**

1 **to 2 tablespoons honey**

1 **tablespoon cider vinegar**

¼ **cup chopped fresh cranberries or snipped dried cranberries**

5 **cups packaged shredded cabbage with carrot (coleslaw mix)**

Cabbage leaves (optional)

1 For dressing, in a small bowl stir together mayonnaise, honey, and vinegar. Stir in cranberries.

2 Place cabbage in a large bowl. Pour dressing over cabbage; toss to combine. Serve immediately or cover and chill for up to 45 minutes.

Makes 6 servings

Nutrition Facts per serving: 44 cal., 1 g total fat (0 g sat. fat), 2 mg chol., 103 mg sodium, 10 g carbo., 2 g fiber, 1 g pro.

PINEAPPLE COLESLAW

Crisp packaged coleslaw mix and juicy canned pineapple bits make this as fast to make as it is good.

Start to Finish: 10 minutes

1½ **cups packaged shredded cabbage with carrot (coleslaw mix)**

¼ **cup well-drained canned pineapple tidbits (juice pack)**

2 **tablespoons low-fat vanilla yogurt**

2 **tablespoons light mayonnaise dressing or salad dressing**

¼ **cup honey-roasted peanuts, chopped**

In a small bowl combine coleslaw mix, pineapple, yogurt, and mayonnaise dressing; toss to mix. Sprinkle with peanuts.

Makes 4 servings

Nutrition Facts per serving: 75 cal., 4 g total fat (1 g sat. fat), 2 mg chol., 109 mg sodium, 9 g carbo., 1 g fiber, 2 g pro.

BACON AND SPINACH MASHED POTATOES

This colorful side dish has flavors to please the whole family. It's a good way to introduce spinach to your kids.

Start to Finish: 15 minutes

1 **24-ounce package refrigerated mashed potatoes or 3 cups prepared instant mashed potatoes**

¾ **cup shredded cheddar cheese (3 ounces)**

3 **slices bacon, crisp-cooked and crumbled**

2 **cups packaged prewashed fresh baby spinach leaves, shredded**

Crisp-cooked bacon, crumbled (optional)

Heat refrigerated potatoes according to package directions. Transfer potatoes to a serving bowl. Stir in cheese, the 3 slices bacon, and the spinach. If desired, top with additional bacon.

Makes 4 to 6 servings

Nutrition Facts per serving: 255 cal., 12 g total fat (5 g sat. fat), 29 mg chol., 538 mg sodium, 24 g carbo., 2 g fiber, 12 g pro.

CREAMY CHEESY POTATOES

These flavorful mashed potatoes are ready in a fraction of the time it would take from scratch and so rich, they don't need gravy.

Prep: 10 minutes   Bake: 15 minutes   Oven: 375°F

1 **24-ounce package refrigerated mashed potatoes**

¼ **cup whipping cream**

¼ **cup shredded Gruyère, Havarti, or American cheese (1 ounce)**

⅛ **teaspoon cracked black pepper**

1 Preheat oven to 375°F. Spoon potatoes into a 1-quart casserole. Cover with waxed paper or vented plastic wrap. Microwave on 100% power (high) for 3 minutes.

2 Meanwhile, in a small bowl beat cream with an electric mixer on medium speed or a wire whisk until soft peaks form; fold in cheese.

3 Remove casserole from microwave. Uncover potatoes. With a large spoon make a hole in the center of the potatoes by pushing from the center to the sides of the casserole. Spoon the whipping cream mixture into the hole. Sprinkle top with cracked black pepper.

4 Bake, uncovered, for 15 to 20 minutes or until top is golden. If desired, stir before serving.

Makes 4 to 6 servings

Nutrition Facts per serving: 215 cal., 10 g total fat (5 g sat. fat), 28 mg chol., 285 mg sodium, 24 g carbo., 1 g fiber, 6 g pro.

PESTO AND RED PEPPER POTATOES

Pesto, roasted peppers, and Parmesan cheese give these potatoes an Italian flair. Try them with baked or broiled fish.

Start to Finish: 10 minutes

1 **24-ounce package refrigerated mashed potatoes or 3 cups prepared instant mashed potatoes**

½ **cup bottled roasted red sweet peppers, cut into strips**

¼ **cup purchased basil pesto (refrigerated or bottled)**

   Shredded Parmesan cheese

Heat refrigerated potatoes according to package directions. Transfer warm potatoes to a serving bowl. Stir in half of the roasted pepper strips. Gently swirl in the pesto. Top with remaining roasted pepper strips and the Parmesan cheese.

Makes 4 to 6 servings

Nutrition Facts per serving: 268 cal., 14 g total fat (1 g sat. fat), 6 mg chol., 456 mg sodium, 27 g carbo., 2 g fiber, 8 g pro.

BOURSIN MASHED POTATOES

Boursin is a soft triple-cream cheese seasoned with herbs and garlic. It melts to a creamy texture with the mashed potatoes.

Start to Finish: 10 minutes

1 **24-ounce package refrigerated mashed potatoes or 3 cups prepared instant mashed potatoes**

1 **5.2-ounce container semisoft cheese with garlic and herbs (Boursin)**

3 **tablespoons snipped fresh parsley**

   Canned french-fried onions

Heat refrigerated potatoes according to package directions. Transfer warm potatoes to a serving bowl. Stir in cheese and parsley. Top with french-fried onions.

Makes 4 to 6 servings

Nutrition Facts per serving: 301 cal., 17 g total fat (8 g sat. fat), 34 mg chol., 287 mg sodium, 27 g carbo., 1 g fiber, 7 g pro.

MASHED POTATO SOUP

Thick, creamy, and topped with a dollop of sour cream, this creative soup is like having a well-dressed baked potato in a bowl!

Start to Finish: 15 minutes

1   **24-ounce package refrigerated mashed potatoes**

1   **14-ounce can chicken broth**

2   **green onions, sliced (¼ cup)**

2   **ounces Swiss, cheddar, or smoked Gouda cheese, shredded (½ cup)**

    Dairy sour cream (optional)

In a medium saucepan combine mashed potatoes, broth, and green onions. Cook over medium-high heat just until mixture reaches boiling, whisking to make nearly smooth. Add cheese; whisk until cheese is melted. If desired, serve with sour cream.

Makes 3 servings

Nutrition Facts per serving: 239 cal., 9 g total fat (4 g sat. fat), 17 mg chol., 917 mg sodium, 27 g carbo., 2 g fiber, 11 g pro.

VEGETABLES with CREAMY WINE SAUCE

Because the vinegar may react with aluminum and cause curdling, use a stainless-steel saucepan and wire whisk.

Start to Finish: 30 minutes

I **16-ounce package desired frozen mixed vegetables**

¼ **cup dry white wine**

2 **tablespoons finely chopped shallot**

I **tablespoon white wine vinegar**

2 **tablespoons whipping cream**

¾ **cups cold unsalted butter, cut into 2-tablespoon pieces**

Salt

Ground white pepper

1 Cook vegetables according to package directions; drain well.

2 Meanwhile, in a small stainless steel saucepan combine wine, shallot, and vinegar. Bring to boiling; reduce heat to medium. Boil gently, uncovered, for 7 to 9 minutes or until almost all of the liquid has evaporated.

3 Using a wire whisk, stir in whipping cream, then the butter, one piece at a time, allowing each piece to melt before adding the next. Allow about 8 minutes for adding butter. If desired, strain sauce. Season to taste with salt and white pepper. Serve immediately over desired cooked vegetables.

Makes 6 servings

Nutrition Facts per 2 tablespoons sauce: 281 cal., 25 g total fat (16 g sat. fat), 68 mg chol., 90 mg sodium, 11 g carbo., 3 g fiber, 3 g pro.

VEGETABLES WITH BLUE CHEESE SAUCE

Add pizzazz to plain cooked vegetables with an intensely flavored blue cheese sauce that takes only minutes to make.

Start to Finish: 10 minutes

1	**16-ounce package desired frozen mixed vegetables**
1	**3-ounce package cream cheese, cut up**
½	**cup milk**
⅛	**teaspoon ground white or black pepper**
⅓	**cup crumbled blue cheese**
2	**teaspoons snipped fresh chives**

1 Cook vegetables according to package directions; drain well.

2 Meanwhile, for sauce, in a small saucepan combine cream cheese, milk, and pepper. Heat over medium-low heat until cream cheese is melted, whisking to make smooth. Stir in blue cheese and chives. Heat through.

3 Serve sauce over vegetables.

Makes 6 servings

Nutrition Facts per serving: 135 cal., 8 g total fat (5 g sat. fat), 23 mg chol., 190 mg sodium, 12 g carbo., 3 g fiber, 6 g pro.

ASIAN VEGETABLES

This is really four different recipes for frozen mixed vegetables. With all the vegetable combinations available, the pairings are numerous. You'll be sure to find one to satisfy the pickiest eater.

Start to Finish: 10 minutes

| 16-ounce package desired frozen mixed vegetables

¼ cup orange marmalade

| tablespoon soy sauce

1 Cook frozen vegetables according to package directions. Drain well; set aside.

2 Add orange marmalade and soy sauce to the same saucepan. Return vegetables to pan. Heat and stir over medium-low heat until hot.

Makes 6 servings

Nutrition Facts per serving: 83 cal., 0 g total fat (0 g sat. fat), 0 mg chol., 196 mg sodium, 19 g carbo., 3 g fiber, 3 g pro.

VEGETABLES with TARRAGON BUTTER

Melted butter and fresh tarragon give an elegant note to a package of frozen veggies.

Start to Finish: 20 minutes

| 16-ounce package desired frozen vegetables

2 teaspoons snipped fresh tarragon or ⅛ teaspoon dried tarragon, crushed

¼ cup butter, softened

1 Cook vegetables according to package directions; drain well.

2 Stir tarragon into softened butter. Toss butter mixture with hot cooked vegetables.

Makes 6 servings

Nutrition Facts per serving: 116 cal., 8 g total fat (5 g sat. fat), 20 mg chol., 90 mg sodium, 10 g carbo., 3 g fiber, 3 g pro.

EASY PASTA PRIMAVERA

Substitute elbow macaroni, rotini, or whatever pasta you have on hand for the wagon wheels.

Start to Finish: 25 minutes

8 ounces dried wagon wheel pasta

1 16-ounce package desired frozen mixed vegetables

½ of an 8-ounce tub cream cheese spread with chive and onion

¼ to ½ cup milk

Salt and ground black pepper

Shredded Parmesan cheese

1 In a Dutch oven heat a large amount of lightly salted water to boiling. Add pasta; cook 4 minutes. Add vegetables; cook about 5 minutes more or until pasta and vegetables are tender. Drain and return to pan.

2 Add cream cheese spread to pasta mixture. Heat through. Add enough milk to thin to desired consistency. Season to taste with salt and pepper. Sprinkle with Parmesan cheese before serving.

Makes 4 servings

Nutrition Facts per serving: 412 cal., 12 g total fat (8 g sat. fat), 32 mg chol., 415 mg sodium, 60 g carbo., 6 g fiber, 14 g pro.

CHEDDAR-GARLIC BISCUITS

These savory biscuits are super easy and super appealing. Invite idle bystanders to prepare this bread and to collect the rave reviews.

Prep: 10 minutes   Bake: 8 minutes   Oven: 425°F

2   **cups packaged biscuit mix**

½   **cup shredded cheddar cheese (2 ounces)**

⅔   **cup milk**

2   **tablespoons butter, melted**

¼   **teaspoon garlic powder**

1 Preheat oven to 425°F. Grease a baking sheet; set aside.

2 In a large bowl combine biscuit mix and cheddar cheese; add milk. Stir to combine. Drop dough from a rounded tablespoon onto the prepared baking sheet.

3 Bake for 8 to 10 minutes or until golden. In a small bowl combine melted butter and garlic powder; brush over hot biscuits. Serve warm.

Makes 10 to 12 biscuits

Nutrition Facts per biscuit: 178 cal., 11 g total fat (5 g sat. fat), 21 mg chol., 402 mg sodium, 16 g carbo., 1 g fiber, 4 g pro.

PESTO BISCUITS

Keep the ingredients on hand and mix up these speedy biscuits for dinner any day of the week.

Prep: 15 minutes   Bake: 10 minutes   Oven: 450°F

2¼ **cups packaged biscuit mix**

½ **cup milk**

¼ **cup purchased basil pesto (refrigerated or bottled)**

2 **teaspoons olive oil**

2 **tablespoons finely shredded Parmesan cheese**

1 Preheat oven to 450°F. In a medium bowl stir together biscuit mix, milk, and pesto until a soft dough forms.

2 Turn dough out onto a lightly floured surface. Lightly knead 10 times or until nearly smooth. Pat dough ½ inch thick. Using a 2½-inch round cookie cutter, cut dough into rounds. Place rounds on an ungreased baking sheet. Brush lightly with olive oil; sprinkle with cheese.

3 Bake about 10 minutes or until golden. Serve warm.

Makes 10 to 12 biscuits

Nutrition Facts per biscuit: 165 cal., 8 g total fat (2 g sat. fat), 4 mg chol., 426 mg sodium, 19 g carbo., 1 g fiber, 4 g pro.

HONEY AND POPPY SEED BISCUITS

Creamy cottage cheese, honey, and poppy seeds make these biscuits irresistible.

Prep: 15 minutes   Bake: 10 minutes   Oven: 450°F

½ **cup cream-style cottage cheese**

¼ **cup milk**

2 **tablespoons honey**

2¼ **cups packaged biscuit mix**

1 **tablespoon poppy seeds**

Water

Poppy seeds

1 Preheat oven to 450°F. In a food processor or blender combine cottage cheese, milk, and honey. Cover and process or blend until nearly smooth.

2 Prepare biscuit mix according to package directions for rolled biscuits, except substitute the pureed mixture and the 1 tablespoon poppy seeds for the liquid called for on the package. Lightly brush tops with water; sprinkle with poppy seeds.

3 Bake about 10 minutes or until bottoms are light brown.

Makes 10 to 12 biscuits

Nutrition Facts per biscuit: 148 cal., 5 g total fat (1 g sat. fat), 3 mg chol., 394 mg sodium, 21 g carbo., 1 g fiber, 4 g pro.

CINNAMON-SUGAR BISCUITS

Don't have time to make cinnamon rolls but still want a sweet breakfast treat? Try these fun biscuits.

Prep: 25 minutes   Bake: 10 minutes   Oven: 400°F

Nonstick cooking spray

2¼ **cups packaged biscuit mix**

⅔ **cup milk**

2 **tablespoons sugar**

1 **teaspoon ground cinnamon**

1 Preheat oven to 400°F. Lightly coat eight 2½-inch muffin cups with cooking spray; set aside. In a medium bowl stir together biscuit mix and milk until a soft dough forms.

2 Turn dough out on a lightly floured surface. Lightly knead 10 times or until nearly smooth. Roll or press dough into an 8-inch square. Sprinkle with sugar and cinnamon. Cut into sixteen 2-inch squares. Gently press 2 squares together, sugar sides up. Place in prepared muffin cups, cut sides down.

3 Bake for 10 to 12 minutes or until golden. Remove from cups; serve warm.

Makes 8 biscuits

Nutrition Facts per biscuit: 159 cal., 6 g total fat (2 g sat. fat), 2 mg chol., 426 mg sodium, 26 g carbo., 0 g fiber, 3 g pro.

PUMPKIN-RAISIN SCONES

Canned pumpkin and biscuit mix make these tender, flaky scones super easy. Stock the biscuit mix and extra cans of pumpkin in your pantry so you can enjoy these fruity scones year-round.

Prep: 15 minutes   Bake: 12 minutes   Oven: 375°F

- **2   cups packaged biscuit mix**
- **⅓   cup raisins or dried cranberries**
- **¼   cup granulated sugar**
- **2   teaspoons pumpkin pie spice**
- **½   cup canned pumpkin**
- **¼   cup milk**
- **1   tablespoon coarse or granulated sugar**
- **1   tablespoon very finely snipped crystallized ginger**

1 Preheat oven to 375°F. Grease a baking sheet; set aside. In a large bowl combine biscuit mix, raisins, the ¼ cup granulated sugar, and the pumpkin pie spice. In a small bowl combine pumpkin and 3 tablespoons of the milk. Add pumpkin mixture all at once to dry mixture; stir until combined.

2 Turn out onto a lightly floured surface. Knead dough by folding and gently pressing dough for 10 to 12 strokes or until dough is nearly smooth.

3 Pat or lightly roll into a ½-inch-thick circle. Cut into 8 wedges. Place wedges 1 inch apart on prepared baking sheet. In a small bowl combine the 1 tablespoon coarse sugar and the crystallized ginger. Brush dough wedges with remaining 1 tablespoon milk; sprinkle with the ginger mixture.

4 Bake for 12 to 15 minutes or until a toothpick inserted near centers comes out clean. Cool slightly on wire rack. Serve warm.

Makes 8 scones

Nutrition Facts per scone: 189 cal., 5 g total fat (1 g sat. fat), 1 mg chol., 377 mg sodium, 34 g carbo., 1 g fiber, 3 g pro.

FRUITY CHEESECAKE CUPS

This cream cheese and ricotta dessert offers all the creamy richness of cheesecake but you make it in a fraction of the time you would need for a conventional cheesecake.

Prep: 20 minutes   Chill: 4 to 24 hours

½   **of an 8-ounce tub cream cheese (about ½ cup)**

½   **cup ricotta cheese**

3   **tablespoons sugar**

½   **teaspoon finely shredded orange peel or lemon peel**

1   **tablespoon orange juice**

3   **cups fresh fruit (such as sliced strawberries; raspberries; blueberries; cut-up melon; and or sliced, peeled peaches)**

4   **gingersnaps or chocolate wafers, broken**

1 In a food processor or blender combine cream cheese, ricotta cheese, sugar, orange peel, and orange juice. Cover and process or blend until smooth. Cover and chill for 4 to 24 hours.

2 To serve, divide fruit among 4 dessert dishes. Top each serving with cream cheese mixture; sprinkle with broken cookies.

Makes 4 servings

Nutrition Facts per serving: 255 cal., 15 g total fat (9 g sat. fat), 47 mg chol., 157 mg sodium, 25 g carbo., 2 g fiber, 7 g pro.

MIXED BERRY TRIFLE CAKES

This elegant fix-up takes advantage of the cut-up fruit in your supermarket's salad bar or containers of mixed fresh fruit from the produce aisle. Just about any fresh fruit will do, so purchase whatever is available. Pictured on page 257.

Start to Finish: 20 minutes

¼ **cup apricot preserves**

¼ **cup orange juice**

2 **4.5-ounce packages individual shortcake cups (8 cakes)**

1 **6-ounce carton vanilla yogurt**

½ **teaspoon vanilla**

¼ **of an 8-ounce container frozen whipped dessert topping, thawed**

1½ **cups fresh fruit (such as sliced strawberries, blueberries, raspberries, blackberries; sliced apples, pears, and/or plums; and/or sliced, peeled peaches)**

1 In a small bowl stir together preserves and orange juice. Spoon some of the mixture over each shortcake cup.

2 In another small bowl stir together yogurt and vanilla. Fold in whipped topping. Spoon yogurt mixture onto cake over preserves mixture. Top with fruit.

Makes 8 cakes

Nutrition Facts per cake: 176 cal., 4 g total fat (2 g sat. fat), 16 mg chol., 16 mg sodium, 31 g carbo., 1 g fiber, 2 g pro.

TOP-YOUR-OWN ANGEL CAKE

Layers of fresh fruit, toasted cake cubes, and ice cream make a refreshing summertime dessert. Purchase a ready-made angel food cake from the store or bake one from a mix.

Prep: 15 minutes   Bake: 20 minutes   Oven: 300°F

2   **cups bite-size angel food cake cubes (about 2 ounces)**

2   **cups vanilla ice cream**

2   **cups fresh fruit (such as blueberries; raspberries; sliced strawberries; sliced kiwifruit; and/or cut-up, peeled peaches)**

1 Preheat oven to 300°F. Place angel cake cubes in a single layer in a shallow baking pan. Bake for 20 to 25 minutes or until golden brown, stirring occasionally. Remove from oven. Cool completely.

2 In 6 parfait glasses or serving dishes layer angel cake cubes, ice cream, and fruit. Serve immediately.

Makes 6 servings

Nutrition Facts per serving: 145 cal., 6 g total fat (3 g sat. fat), 21 mg chol., 87 mg sodium, 23 g carbo., 2 g fiber, 3 g pro.

FRUIT SUNDAE CONES

Instead of high-fat ice cream cones, serve these refreshing, high-nutrient fruit cones. Coconut and strawberry puree make them naturally sweet.

Start to Finish: 5 minutes

¾   **cup cut-up strawberries**

3   **cups fresh fruit (such as cut-up apples; banana chunks; pitted sweet cherries; seedless red grapes; cut-up kiwifruit; and/or sliced, peeled peaches)**

6   **large waffle cones**

¼   **cup finely shredded coconut.**

1 Place strawberries in a blender; cover and blend until smooth; set aside.

2 Place the cut-up fruit in a medium bowl. If necessary, toss gently to combine. Spoon fruit into cones. Drizzle with the strawberry puree. Top with coconut.

Makes 6 cones

Nutrition Facts per serving: 175 cal., 8 g total fat (0 g sat. fat), 0 mg chol., 56 mg sodium, 27 g carbo., 2 g fiber, 2 g pro.

FUN-DAY SUNDAE PARFAIT

Another time substitute chocolate ice cream, and top it with raspberries and light fudge topping, or for a tropical twist, try mangoes and pineapple sprinkled with a little coconut.

Start to Finish: 15 minutes

1½   cups frozen vanilla or fruit-
       flavor yogurt or ice cream

½   cup coarsely crushed
       vanilla wafers or honey or
       cinnamon graham crackers

1   cup fresh fruit (such
       as sliced bananas or
       strawberries; peeled, sliced
       kiwifruit, peaches, or
       mangoes; cut-up pineapple;
       raspberries; and/or
       blueberries)

6   tablespoons strawberry ice
       cream topping

¼   cup frozen whipped dessert
       topping, thawed (optional)

2   maraschino cherries with
       stems (optional)

1 Chill 2 tall parfait glasses.

2 Place ¼ cup frozen yogurt in the bottom of each chilled glass. Top each with 2 tablespoons of the crushed wafers, ¼ cup fruit, and 1 tablespoon strawberry topping. Repeat layers. Top each with ¼ cup frozen yogurt. Drizzle each with remaining strawberry topping. If desired, top with whipped topping and garnish with maraschino cherries. Serve with long-handled spoons.

Makes 2 servings

Nutrition Facts per serving: 498 cal., 9 g total fat (3 g sat. fat), 15 mg chol., 136 mg sodium, 102 g carbo., 2 g fiber, 5 g pro.

Chocolate Sundae: Substitute 1½ cups chocolate ice cream for the vanilla yogurt or ice cream. Substitute 6 tablespoons caramel ice cream topping for the strawberry ice cream topping.

CHOCOLATE-DRIZZLED ANGEL FOOD CAKE

For a kid-friendly version, skip the orange liqueur and increase the orange juice to ¼ cup.

Start to Finish: 15 minutes

1   **purchased angel food cake**

2   **tablespoons orange liqueur**

2   **tablespoons orange juice**

6   **ounces bittersweet or dark chocolate**

½   **cup butter**

1½   **cups powdered sugar**

¼   **cup whipping cream**

1 Using a long wooden skewer, generously poke holes through the top of the cake to the bottom. Stir together orange liqueur and orange juice. Drizzle orange mixture over cake.

2 For the chocolate glaze, in a small saucepan melt chocolate and butter over low heat, stirring frequently. Remove from heat. Whisk in powdered sugar and whipping cream. Spoon evenly over cake.

Makes 10 to 12 servings

Nutrition Facts per serving: 436 cal., 18 g total fat (11 g sat. fat), 33 mg chol., 440 mg sodium, 66 g carbo., 2 g fiber, 5 g pro.

ANGEL FOOD CAKE
WITH LEMON CREAM AND BERRIES

Store any leftover lemon cream in the refrigerator for up to four days.

Start to Finish: 15 minutes

3 **6-ounce cartons lemon yogurt**

1 **4-serving-size package instant vanilla pudding mix**

1 **8-ounce container frozen whipped dessert topping, thawed**

4 **cups fresh blueberries**

1 **purchased angel food cake, cut into bite-size cubes**

   Fresh mint sprigs (optional)

1 In medium bowl whisk together yogurt and one-fourth of the pudding mix until smooth. Gradually add remaining pudding mix to yogurt, whisking until smooth after each addition. Fold in whipped topping, half at a time.

2 Serve lemon cream and berries over cake cubes. If desired, garnish with mint sprigs.

Makes 16 servings

Nutrition Facts per serving with ¼ cup berries: 221 cal., 3 g total fat (3 g sat. fat), 1 mg chol., 341 mg sodium, 44 g carbo., 1 g fiber, 4 g pro.

TROPICAL ANGEL CAKE

To boost the tropical flavor, sprinkle this refreshing, summery cake with toasted shredded coconut.

Start to Finish: 15 minutes

1	**purchased angel food cake**
3	**cups desired fruit-flavor sherbet**
¼	**cup unsweetened pineapple juice**
1	**8-ounce container frozen whipped dessert topping or frozen light whipped dessert topping, thawed**
	Fresh raspberries (optional)

1 Slice cake in half horizontally. Hollow out insides, leaving two 1-inch-thick shells. Spoon sherbet into bottom shell. Set top half, hollow side down, over bottom. Poke holes in top using a long wooden skewer or the tines of a long fork. Drizzle pineapple juice over top of cake.

2 Frost top and sides of cake with whipped topping. Serve immediately or cover loosely with plastic wrap; freeze up to 1 week. If desired, garnish with raspberries.

Makes 12 servings

Nutrition Facts per serving: 222 cal., 4 g total fat (4 g sat. fat), 0 mg chol., 305 mg sodium, 41 g carbo., 2 g fiber, 3 g pro.

CHERRY TRIFLES

Although you can make them in a flash, these cherry trifles also are a great make-ahead choice for days when you know you'll be pressed for time during the dinner hour. Make them up to 4 hours ahead and refrigerate until serving time.

Start to Finish: 10 minutes

1	**8-ounce container plain low-fat yogurt**
2	**tablespoons cherry preserves**
½	**teaspoon vanilla**
2	**cups angel food cake cubes (about 4 ounces purchased cake)**
1	**15-ounce can pitted dark sweet cherries, drained**
¼	**cup purchased glazed walnuts, chopped**

1 In a small bowl stir together yogurt, cherry preserves, and vanilla; set aside.

2 Divide half of the cake cubes among four parfait glasses or dessert dishes. Top cake cubes in parfait glasses or dessert dishes with half of the dark sweet cherries; spoon half of the yogurt mixture over. Sprinkle with half of the nuts. Repeat layers.

Makes 4 servings

Nutrition Facts per serving: 280 cal., 7 g total fat (2 g sat. fat), 5 mg chol., 198 mg sodium, 51 g carbo., 2 g fiber, 7 g pro.

FRENCH-TOASTED ANGEL FOOD CAKE

After frying the egg-coated cake slices to a golden brown, reassemble the cake
by arranging the slices on a cake platter to create an eye-catching dessert.

Start to Finish: 20 minutes

1   **purchased angel food cake**

6   **eggs, lightly beaten**

1½   **cups milk**

3   **tablespoons sugar**

2   **teaspoons vanilla**

1   **tablespoon butter**

     **Whipped cream or creme
     fraiche**

     Maple syrup

     Cut-up fresh strawberries

1 Slice the angel food cake into ten to twelve 1-inch wedges. In a
shallow dish combine eggs, milk, sugar, and vanilla. Soak cake
wedges in egg mixture for 1 minute per side.

2 In a nonstick skillet or on a nonstick griddle melt butter over
medium heat. Cook 4 wedges at a time for 1 to 2 minutes on
each side or until golden brown. To serve, stand slices in cake
formation. Top with whipped cream. Drizzle with maple syrup and
top with strawberries. Serve immediately.

Makes 10 to 12 servings

Nutrition Facts per serving: 275 cal., 12 g total fat (6 g sat. fat), 187 mg chol., 305 mg sodium, 33 g carbo.,
1 g fiber, 8 g pro.

BANANAS SUZETTE OVER POUND CAKE

The "suzette" portion of this dessert refers to the classic combination of orange-butter sauce and orange-flavored liqueur. Here, it gives bananas the royal treatment.

Start to Finish: 15 minutes

2 **tablespoons butter**

½ **of a 10.75-ounce package frozen pound cake, thawed and cut into 4 slices**

2 **medium ripe, firm bananas**

3 **tablespoons sugar**

2 **tablespoons orange liqueur or orange juice**

2 **tablespoons orange juice**

⅛ **teaspoon ground nutmeg**

1 **cup vanilla ice cream**

1 In a medium skillet melt 1 tablespoon of the butter over medium heat. Add pound cake slices; cook for 1 to 2 minutes or until brown, turning once. Remove from skillet; set aside.

2 Peel bananas; bias-slice each banana into 8 pieces. In the same skillet combine sugar, 2 tablespoons liqueur or orange juice, 2 tablespoons orange juice, and the remaining 1 tablespoon butter. Heat about 1 minute or until butter melts and sugar begins to dissolve. Add the bananas; heat for 2 to 4 minutes more or just until bananas are tender, stirring once. Stir in nutmeg.

3 To serve, place a small scoop of vanilla ice cream on each pound cake slice. Spoon bananas and sauce over ice cream and pound cake slices.

Makes 4 servings

Nutrition Facts per serving: 394 cal., 18 g total fat (11 g sat. fat), 74 mg chol., 229 mg sodium, 53 g carbo., 2 g fiber, 4 g pro.

TROPICAL FRUIT SHORTCAKES

You can start with fresh papaya or look for refrigerated jars of papaya in the produce section of your supermarket.

Start to Finish: 15 minutes

1   **cup chopped papaya**

1   **8-ounce can pineapple tidbits (juice pack), drained**

2   **kiwifruit, peeled and coarsely chopped**

2   **tablespoons honey**

1   **10.75-ounce package frozen pound cake, thawed**

¼   **cup orange juice**

1½   **cups frozen whipped dessert topping, thawed**

Toasted macadamia nuts or pecans (optional)

1 In a small bowl stir together papaya, pineapple, kiwifruit, and honey.

2 Cut 6 slices from the pound cake. (Reserve remaining pound cake for another use.) Drizzle orange juice over cake slices. Spoon fruit mixture over cake slices. Top with whipped topping. If desired, sprinkle with nuts.

Makes 6 servings

Nutrition Facts per serving: 428 cal., 19 g total fat (12 g sat. fat), 115 mg chol., 163 mg sodium, 30 g carbo., 2 g fiber, 5 g pro.

CHERRY-BANANAS FOSTER

Dried tart cherries add a lovely burst of color and flavor to this decadent treat.

Start to Finish: 10 minutes

¼ **cup butter**

⅓ **cup packed brown sugar**

3 **ripe bananas, peeled and sliced (about 2 cups)**

⅓ **cup dried tart cherries**

⅓ **cup spiced rum or rum (optional)**

½ **of a 10.75-ounce package frozen pound cake, thawed and cut into 4 slices**

1 In a large skillet melt butter over medium heat; stir in the brown sugar. Add bananas and cherries; cook and gently stir over medium heat for 1 to 2 minutes or until heated through.

2 If using rum, in a small saucepan heat the rum until it almost simmers. Ignite rum with a long match. Pour over bananas and cherries. Serve immediately over pound cake.

Makes 4 servings

Nutrition Facts per serving: 444 cal., 19 g total fat (12 g sat. fat), 115 mg chol., 246 mg sodium, 69 g carbo., 3 g fiber, 3 g pro.

CRUNCHY POUND CAKE SLICES

Broiling pound cake slices makes them warm and toasty, divine with a delicious dollop of cool cinnamon ice cream.

Prep: 15 minutes   Broil: 2 minutes

- 1 **10.75-ounce package frozen pound cake, thawed**
- ¼ **cup chocolate-hazelnut spread**
- ½ **cup roasted mixed nuts, coarsely chopped**
- 1 **pint caramel or cinnamon ice cream**

1 Preheat broiler. Cut four ½-inch slices from pound cake. (Reserve remaining pound cake for another use.) Place the pound cake slices on a baking sheet. Broil 3 to 4 inches from heat about 2 minutes or until light brown, turning once. Cool slightly.

2 Spread 1 side of each slice with 1 tablespoon of the chocolate-hazelnut spread. Sprinkle with nuts; pat gently to form an even layer. Transfer each slice to a dessert plate and top with a scoop of ice cream. Serve at once.

Makes 4 servings

Nutrition Facts per serving: 763 cal., 45 g total fat (22 g sat. fat), 206 mg chol., 421 mg sodium, 82 g carbo., 2 g fiber, 12 g pro.

COFFEE AND ALMOND PARFAITS

If you don't have parfait glasses, use clear glass dessert bowls or short drinking glasses to achieve the lovely layered effect.

Start to Finish: 30 minutes   Oven: 350°F

½ **of a 10.75-ounce package frozen pound cake, cut into ¾-inch cubes**

2 **6-ounce cartons vanilla low-fat yogurt**

½ **of an 8-ounce container frozen whipped dessert topping, thawed**

2 **tablespoons coffee liqueur or strong brewed coffee**

4 **amaretti cookies, coarsely crushed**

1 Preheat oven to 350°F. In a shallow baking pan arrange cake cubes in an even layer. Bake about 15 minutes or until golden, stirring twice. Cool. Meanwhile, in a medium bowl stir together yogurt and whipped topping.

2 Layer ¼ cup of the cake cubes in each of 4 parfait glasses. Top with half of the yogurt mixture and remaining cake cubes. Stir liqueur into the remaining yogurt mixture; spoon over cake cubes. Sprinkle with the crushed cookies. Serve immediately.

Makes 4 servings

Nutrition Facts per serving: 368 cal., 14 g total fat (10 g sat. fat), 47 mg chol., 212 mg sodium, 46 g carbo., 0 g fiber, 8 g pro.

COOKIES AND CREAM

If no oatmeal cookies are available, use your favorite kind as long as they are soft enough to be cut with a fork.

Start to Finish: 15 minutes

½   **cup whipping cream**

2   **tablespoons honey**

½   **cup dairy sour cream**

18   **to 24 purchased soft-style oatmeal or other soft-style cookies**

Honey

1 In a chilled small bowl combine whipping cream and the 2 tablespoons honey. Beat with chilled beaters of an electric mixer on medium speed until soft peaks form (tips curl). Fold in sour cream.

2 To serve, lay 1 oatmeal cookie on each of 6 dessert plates. Top each with a spoonful of the whipped cream mixture. Top each with another cookie and another spoonful of the whipped cream mixture. Top each stack with a third cookie and more whipped cream mixture. Drizzle with additional honey.

Makes 6 to 8 servings

Nutrition Facts per serving: 456 cal., 21 g total fat (10 g sat. fat), 43 mg chol., 310 mg sodium, 61 g carbo., 2 g fiber, 5 g pro.

MAKE-AHEAD TIP: Prepare whipped cream mixture; cover and chill for up to 1 hour before serving. Assemble individual desserts just before serving.

WHOOPIE PIES

Appropriately named, these small pies have been known to conjure hoots and hollers from kids and adults alike.

Start to Finish: 15 minutes

¼ **cup butter, softened**

½ **of an 8-ounce package reduced-fat cream cheese (Neufchatel), softened**

½ **of a 7-ounce jar marshmallow creme**

12 **purchased soft-style chocolate or other soft-style cookies**

1 For filling, in a medium bowl beat butter and cream cheese with an electric mixer on medium to high speed until smooth and fluffy. Fold in marshmallow creme until combined.

2 Spread the filling evenly on the flat side of half of the cookies. Top with remaining cookies, flat sides down, to make sandwiches. For firmer filling, wrap and chill in refrigerator for 2 hours before serving.

Makes 6 pies

Nutrition Facts per pie: 710 cal., 36 g total fat (16 g sat. fat), 55 mg chol., 353 mg sodium, 90 g carbo., 4 g fiber, 6 g pro.

Peanut Butter Whoopie Pies: Substitute ¼ cup creamy peanut butter for the butter, use purchased soft-style peanut butter or sugar cookies.

MINT SANDWICH COOKIES

Three chocolate-flavored ingredients add up to a chocolate lover's delight.

Start to Finish: 15 minutes

⅓ **cup canned whipped chocolate or vanilla frosting**

8 **layered chocolate-mint candies, chopped**

8 **purchased soft-style chocolate or sugar cookies**

In a small bowl stir together frosting and chopped candies. Spread frosting mixture on the flat side of half of the cookies. Top with the remaining cookies, flat sides down.

Makes 4 sandwich cookies

Nutrition Facts per cookie sandwich: 420 cal., 23 g total fat (11 g sat. fat), 1 mg chol., 195 mg sodium, 56 g carbo., 2 g fiber, 3 g pro.

MINIATURE FRUIT TARTS

A few minutes assembly time is all it takes to transform purchased cookies into a special dessert. Let the kids help you "decorate" the tarts with coconut and sliced fresh fruit.

Start to Finish: 15 minutes

4   **purchased soft-style sugar or chocolate cookies**

¼   **cup tub-style cream cheese with strawberries, chocolate-hazelnut spread, or fudge ice cream topping**

2   **tablespoons coconut**

1   **cup sliced fresh fruit (such as kiwifruit, bananas, and/ or strawberries)**

Spread flat side of each cookie with cream cheese, chocolate-hazelnut spread, or ice cream topping; sprinkle with coconut. Top with fruit.

Makes 4 tarts

Nutrition Facts per tart: 187 cal., 9 g total fat (5 g sat. fat), 23 mg chol., 116 mg sodium, 26 g carbo., 2 g fiber, 2 g pro.

BANANA SPLIT TRIFLES

Talk about tempting! Every delicious layer of this dessert is on display in parfait glasses.

Prep: 15 minutes   Freeze: up to 1 hour

4   **purchased soft-style chocolate chip or oatmeal cookies, crumbled**

2   **ripe bananas, peeled and cut into chunks**

1   **quart tin roof sundae, chocolate chunk, or vanilla ice cream**

1   **12-ounce jar hot fudge sauce or strawberry preserves**

Whipped cream

In each of 4 parfait glasses layer cookies, banana, scoops of ice cream, and sauce (you may not use all of the ice cream or sauce). Top with whipped cream and additional crumbled cookies. If desired, cover and freeze for up to 1 hour.

Makes 4 servings

Nutrition Facts per serving: 524 cal., 23 g total fat (12 g sat. fat), 48 mg chol., 161 mg sodium, 73 g carbo., 3 g fiber, 6 g pro.

PRALINE CRUNCH BARS

Toffee bits and pecans give basic cookie dough a tasty twist. Let the chocolate pieces melt from the heat of the bars then spread them for an easy topping.

Prep: 10 minutes   Bake: 12 minutes   Chill: 10 minutes   Oven: 350°F

1	**18-ounce roll refrigerated sugar cookie dough**
½	**cup toffee pieces**
½	**cup finely chopped pecans**
1	**12-ounce package miniature semisweet chocolate pieces**
⅓	**cup toffee pieces**

1 Preheat oven to 350°F. Place cookie dough, the ½ cup toffee pieces, and the pecans in a large resealable plastic bag and knead to combine. Press dough evenly over the bottom of an ungreased 13×9×2-inch baking pan.

2 Bake for 12 to 15 minutes or until golden brown. Immediately sprinkle with chocolate pieces; let stand for 5 to 10 minutes or until softened, then spread evenly over the bars. Sprinkle with the ⅓ cup toffee bits.

3 Chill in the refrigerator for 10 to 15 minutes to set chocolate.

Makes 28 bars

Nutrition Facts per bar: 191 cal., 11 g total fat (4 g sat. fat), 8 mg chol., 105 mg sodium, 19 g carbo., 2 g fiber, 1 g pro.

TO STORE: Cover and chill for up to 3 days or freeze for up to 1 month.

MAPLE-CINNAMON WEDGES

Purchased sugar cookie dough joins maple syrup, cinnamon, and nuts for a cookie that makes a great after-school snack. Pictured on page 258.

Prep: 15 minutes   **Bake:** 20 minutes   **Oven:** 350°F

1	**18-ounce roll refrigerated sugar cookie dough**
¼	**cup all-purpose flour**
3	**tablespoons butter, melted**
2	**tablespoons pure maple syrup or maple-flavored syrup**
¼	**cup packed brown sugar**
¼	**cup finely chopped pecans**
½	**teaspoon ground cinnamon**

1 Preheat oven to 350°F. Line a 13×9×2-inch baking pan with foil. Lightly grease the foil; set aside. In a large bowl combine cookie dough and flour; stir or knead until well mixed. Press dough evenly into the prepared pan.

2 In a small bowl combine melted butter and maple syrup. Drizzle syrup mixture over dough, spreading evenly. In another small bowl combine brown sugar, pecans, and cinnamon. Sprinkle over syrup layer in pan.

3 Bake about 20 minutes or until edges are firm (center will be soft). Cool on a wire rack. When cool, use foil to lift from pan. Cut into 15 bars; cut each bar in half diagonally to make wedges. Store in a tightly covered container up to 3 days.

Makes 30 wedges

Nutrition Facts per wedge: 105 cal., 5 g total fat (2 g sat. fat), 8 mg chol., 81 mg sodium, 14 g carbo., 0 g fiber, 1 g pro.

SURPRISE CHOCOLATE BITES

A creamy peanut butter center is the surprise inside these chocolatey cookies.

Prep: 30 minutes   Bake: 10 minutes per batch   Oven: 350°F

I **18-ounce roll refrigerated
   sugar cookie dough**

⅓ **cup unsweetened cocoa
   powder**

⅔ **cup creamy peanut butter**

⅔ **cup powdered sugar**

   Granulated sugar

1 Preheat oven to 350°F. Place cookie dough and cocoa in a large resealable plastic bag and knead to combine. In a medium bowl stir together the peanut butter and powdered sugar until combined. With floured hands, roll the peanut butter mixture into thirty 1-inch balls*.

2 To shape cookies, take 1 tablespoon of cookie dough and make an indentation in the center. Press a peanut butter ball into indentation and form dough around ball to enclose it; roll ball gently in your hands to smooth it out. Repeat with remaining dough and peanut butter balls.

3 Place balls 2 inches apart on ungreased cookie sheets. Flatten the balls slightly with the bottom of a glass that has been dipped in granulated sugar.

4 Bake for 10 to 12 minutes or until set. Transfer cookies to wire rack; let cool.

Makes 30 cookies

Nutrition Facts per cookie: 118 cal., 6 g total fat (1 g sat. fat), 5 mg chol., 87 mg sodium, 15 g carbo., 0 g fiber, 2 g pro.

***NOTE:** For easier handling, freeze the peanut butter balls for 30 minutes. Flatten the balls slightly to form disks, then press cookie dough around them.

TO STORE: Layer cookies between waxed paper in an airtight container; cover. Store at room temperature for up to 3 days or freeze for up to 3 months.

MOCHA COOKIES

You'll put sugar in your coffee break and coffee in your sweet when you combine cocoa and espresso powder with sugar cookie dough.

Prep: 10 minutes   Bake: 10 minutes per batch   Oven: 350°F

3   **tablespoons sugar**

2   **tablespoons unsweetened cocoa powder**

1   **tablespoon instant espresso coffee powder or 2 tablespoons instant coffee crystals, crushed**

1   **18-ounce package refrigerated portioned sugar cookie dough**

2   **tablespoons milk**

1 Preheat oven to 350°F. In a small bowl stir together sugar, cocoa powder, and espresso powder. Break cookie dough into portions. Roll each cookie dough portion in milk, then in the sugar mixture. Place cookie dough portions on an ungreased large cookie sheet.

2 Bake for 10 to 12 minutes or until edges are set. Transfer to a wire rack; cool.

Makes 20 cookies

Nutrition Facts per cookie: 123 cal., 5 g total fat (1 g sat. fat), 10 mg chol., 82 mg sodium, 18 g carbo., 1 g fiber, 1 g pro.

LEMON CURD TART

Four wisely chosen ingredients add up to a luscious lemon tart that you can make in about a half an hour and let cool for dessert.

Prep: 10 minutes   Bake: 20 minutes   Cool: 1 hour   Oven: 350°F

½ **of an 18-ounce roll refrigerated sugar cookie dough**

2 **teaspoons finely shredded lemon peel**

½ **cup purchased lemon curd**

2 **to 3 cups fresh raspberries, blueberries, or sliced strawberries (optional)**

1 Preheat oven to 350°F. Lightly grease a 9-inch springform pan with removable bottom.

2 Place cookie dough and lemon peel in a large resealable plastic bag and knead to combine. Press dough evenly over bottom and ½ inch up sides of prepared pan.

3 Bake about 20 minutes or until golden brown and center springs back when lightly touched with finger. Place on a wire rack. Using a thin metal spatula, carefully loosen crust from side of pan. Remove side of pan; cool crust completely on wire rack.

4 Place crust on a serving platter. Spread lemon curd over crust. Top with berries and serve immediately.

Makes 8 servings

Nutrition Facts per serving: 204 cal., 8 g total fat (2 g sat. fat), 24 mg chol., 150 mg sodium, 34 g carbo., 2 g fiber, 1 g pro.

Lime Curd Tart: Substitute 2 teaspoons finely shredded lime peel for the finely shredded lemon peel. Substitute ½ cup purchased lime curd for the lemon curd, and substitute 2 to 3 cups sliced fresh mango, pineapple, and orange segments for the fresh berries.

FRUIT CRISP

This dessert is right-sized—just enough for tonight. Crumbly oats and coconut add crunch to gently spiced luscious fruit.

Prep: 15 minutes   Bake: 20 minutes   Cool: 10 minutes   Oven: 350°F

1	**21-ounce can blueberry, apple, or cherry pie filling**
1	**tablespoon lemon juice**
¼	**teaspoon ground nutmeg**
1	**cup quick-cooking rolled oats**
¼	**cup shredded coconut or chopped nuts**
2	**tablespoons packed brown sugar**
¼	**cup butter**
	Half-and-half or light cream (optional)

1 Preheat oven to 350°F. For filling, in a medium bowl stir together pie filling, lemon juice, and nutmeg. Spoon into six 6-ounce custard cups set in a shallow baking pan or into a 9-inch pie plate. Set aside.

2 For topping, in another medium bowl stir together oats, coconut, and brown sugar. Using a pastry blender, cut in butter until crumbly. Sprinkle topping over filling.

3 Bake for 20 to 25 minutes or until edges are bubbly and topping is golden brown. Serve warm. If desired, pass half-and-half to pour over crisp.

Makes 6 servings

Nutrition Facts per serving: 294 cal., 11 g total fat (6 g sat. fat), 22 mg chol., 139 mg sodium, 47 g carbo., 4 g fiber, 3 g pro.

POLENTA-PECAN APPLE COBBLER

Cobbler is well known as warm cooked fruit with a buttery biscuit topper, typically. In this version the grain role goes to polenta, a.k.a. cooked cornmeal. So it's cobbler, the same, but different.

Prep: 15 minutes   **Bake:** 25 minutes   **Cool:** 30 minutes   **Oven:** 375°F

½ **cup all-purpose flour**

⅓ **cup quick-cooking polenta mix or yellow cornmeal**

2 **tablespoons granulated sugar**

1 **teaspoon baking powder**

½ **teaspoon salt**

3 **tablespoons butter**

½ **cup chopped pecans**

2 **tablespoons packed brown sugar**

½ **teaspoon ground cinnamon**

2 **21-ounce cans apple pie filling**

⅓ **cup half-and-half or light cream**

Half-and-half or light cream (optional)

1 Preheat oven to 375°F. For topping, in a medium bowl stir together flour, polenta mix, granulated sugar, baking powder, and salt. Using a pastry blender, cut in butter until mixture resembles coarse crumbs; set aside. In a small bowl combine pecans, brown sugar, and cinnamon; set aside.

2 In a medium saucepan heat the apple pie filling until bubbly, stirring frequently. Cover and set aside to keep hot. Stir the ⅓ cup half-and-half into flour mixture, stirring just to moisten.

3 Transfer hot apple pie filling to a 2-quart square baking dish. Immediately drop topping by rounded teaspoons on top of filling. Sprinkle evenly with pecan mixture.

4 Bake about 25 minutes or until topping is light brown. Cool for 30 minutes before serving. If desired, serve with additional half-and-half.

Makes 6 servings

Nutrition Facts per serving: 441 cal., 15 g total fat (6 g sat. fat), 22 mg chol., 498 mg sodium, 77 g carbo., 4 g fiber, 4 g pro.

APRICOT-PEACH COBBLER

Biscuit mix is the key to this sunny cobbler that is ready in only minutes. Chances are it will take less than that for your happy diners to eat it up!

Prep: 10 minutes   Bake: according to package directions

- **15-ounce can unpeeled apricot halves in light syrup**
- **7.75-ounce package cinnamon swirl biscuit mix (Bisquick® complete)**
- **21-ounce can peach pie filling**
- **teaspoon vanilla**
  Vanilla ice cream (optional)

1 Drain apricot halves, reserving syrup. Preheat oven according to package directions for biscuit mix. Prepare and bake biscuit mix according to package directions, except use ½ cup of the reserved apricot syrup in place of the water called for on the package.

2 Meanwhile, in a medium saucepan combine pie filling, the drained apricots, and any remaining apricot syrup. Heat through. Remove from heat; stir in vanilla. Spoon fruit mixture into bowls. Top with warm biscuits. If desired, serve with vanilla ice cream.

Makes 6 servings

Nutrition Facts per serving: 284 cal., 4 g total fat (0 g sat. fat), 0 mg chol., 346 mg sodium, 59 g carbo., 2 g fiber, 3 g pro.

LAYERED APPLE-CRANBERRY PIE

Apple pie filling layers on top of whole cranberry sauce for a collaborative but not commingled flavor sensation. A scoop of vanilla ice cream makes a traditional but ideal complement.

Prep: 10 minutes   **Bake: 40 minutes**   **Stand: 15 minutes**   **Oven: 375°F**

1   **15-ounce package rolled refrigerated unbaked piecrusts (2 crusts)**

1   **21-ounce can apple pie filling**

½   **of a 16-ounce can whole cranberry sauce**

Granulated or coarse sugar (optional)

1 Preheat oven to 375°F. Let piecrusts stand at room temperature for 15 minutes as directed on package.

2 Unroll piecrusts. Line a 9-inch pie plate with 1 of the piecrusts; spoon in apple pie filling. Spoon the cranberry sauce over pie filling.

3 Cut slits in the remaining piecrust; place on filled pie. Fold edge of top pastry under edge of bottom pastry. Crimp edge as desired. If desired, sprinkle with sugar.

4 To prevent overbrowning, cover edge of pie with foil. Bake for 25 minutes. Remove foil. Bake for 15 to 20 minutes more or until top is golden. Cool on wire rack.

Makes 8 servings

Nutrition Facts per serving: 356 cal., 14 g total fat (6 g sat. fat), 10 mg chol., 224 mg sodium, 56 g carbo., 1 g fiber, 1 g pro.

BLUEBERRY AND PEACH PIE

Fresh blueberries enliven prepared peach pie filling to produce a
good-looking pie with the taste of summer. If fresh blueberries aren't
available, use frozen.

Prep: 20 minutes   Bake: 50 minutes   Oven: 375°F

- 1 **15-ounce package rolled refrigerated unbaked piecrusts (2 crusts)**
- 1 **21-ounce can peach pie filling**
- 1½ **cups fresh blueberries**
- ⅓ **cup slivered almonds, toasted**
- 1 **tablespoon milk**
- 2 **teaspoons coarse sugar or granulated sugar**
-    **Sweetened whipped cream or vanilla ice cream (optional)**

1 Preheat oven to 375°F. Let piecrusts stand at room temperature for 15 minutes as directed on package. Meanwhile, in a large bowl stir together pie filling, blueberries, and almonds.

2 Unroll piecrusts. Line a 9-inch pie plate with 1 of the piecrusts; spoon in filling. Using a 1-inch round cutter, cut 3 holes in center of remaining piecrust; place on filled pie. Fold edge of top pastry under edge of bottom pastry. Crimp edge as desired. Brush top with milk; sprinkle with sugar.

3 To prevent overbrowning, cover edge of pie with foil. Bake for 25 minutes. Remove foil; bake for 25 to 30 minutes more or until filling is bubbly and pastry is golden. Cool on a wire rack. If desired, serve pie with sweetened whipped cream.

Makes 8 servings

Nutrition Facts per serving: 355 cal., 17 g total fat (6 g sat. fat), 10 mg chol., 212 mg sodium, 48 g carbo., 2 g fiber, 3 g pro.

ROCKY ROAD PARFAITS

Layer chocolate pudding into these dreamy duotone desserts topped with a rocky road trio of chocolate, peanuts, and marshmallows.

Prep: 15 minutes **Stand: 5 minutes**

1	**4-serving-size package chocolate or chocolate fudge instant pudding mix**
2	**cups milk**
½	**cup frozen whipped dessert topping, thawed**
¼	**cup unsalted peanuts, coarsely chopped**
¼	**cup tiny marshmallows**
	Chocolate curls (see note, page 254) (optional)

1 Prepare pudding mix according to package directions using the milk. Remove ¾ cup of the pudding and place in a small bowl; fold in whipped topping until combined.

2 Divide the remaining chocolate pudding among four 6-ounce glasses or dessert dishes. Top with dessert topping mixture. Let stand for 5 to 10 minutes or until set. Sprinkle with peanuts and marshmallows just before serving. If desired, garnish with chocolate curls.

Makes 4 servings

Nutrition Facts per serving: 246 cal., 9 g total fat (4 g sat. fat), 10 mg chol., 412 mg sodium, 34 g carbo., 1 g fiber, 7 g pro.

MAKE-AHEAD DIRECTIONS: Prepare as directed through step 2. Cover and chill parfaits for up to 24 hours. Serve as directed in step 2.

CHOCOLATE-PEANUT BUTTER-SWIRL DESSERT

For a lighter version, use light cream cheese, fat-free milk, and sugar-free pudding mix.

Prep: 20 minutes   Chill: 2 hours

1   **cup graham cracker crumbs**

½   **cup finely chopped peanuts**

3   **tablespoons butter, melted**

¼   **cup tub-style cream cheese**

2   **tablespoons creamy peanut butter**

2   **tablespoons milk**

2   **cups milk**

1   **4-serving-size package chocolate instant pudding mix**

1 In a medium bowl combine graham cracker crumbs and chopped peanuts. Stir in butter until combined. Reserve 3 tablespoons of the mixture; set aside. Press remaining mixture into the bottom of 2-quart square baking dish. Cover and chill while preparing filling.

2 In a small bowl stir together cream cheese and peanut butter until smooth. Gradually stir in 2 tablespoons milk until smooth. Set aside.

3 In a large bowl whisk together 2 cups milk and pudding mix until combined. Continue whisking for 2 minutes. Spread over graham cracker crust in pan. Drop peanut butter mixture in small mounds on top of pudding. Using a thin metal spatula or table knife, gently swirl peanut butter mixture into pudding. Sprinkle with reserved crumb mixture.

4 Cover and chill about 2 hours or until set. To serve, spoon into dessert dishes.

Makes 12 servings

Nutrition Facts per serving: 180 cal., 11 g total fat (4 g sat. fat), 16 mg chol., 270 mg sodium, 17 g carbo., 1 g fiber, 5 g pro.

GRANOLA-TOPPED PUDDING

For a more elaborate presentation, layer the pudding and cream cheese mixture in parfait glasses before topping with granola and chocolate curls.

Start to Finish: 15 minutes

1	**4-serving-size package chocolate instant pudding mix**
2	**cups milk**
½	**of an 8-ounce package reduced-fat cream cheese (Neufchâtel), softened**
¼	**cup peanut butter**
1	**cup granola cereal**
	Milk chocolate curls* (optional)

1 In a large bowl whisk together the pudding mix and 1¾ cups of the milk for 2 minutes or until thickened; set aside. In a medium bowl whisk together the cream cheese, peanut butter, and the remaining ¼ cup milk until smooth.

2 Spoon pudding mixture evenly into 4 dessert dishes. Top evenly with cream cheese mixture. Sprinkle each serving with granola before serving. If desired, garnish with chocolate curls.

Makes 4 servings

Nutrition Facts per serving: 428 cal., 19 g total fat (8 g sat. fat), 31 mg chol., 661 mg sodium, 53 g carbo., 4 g fiber, 14 g pro.

*NOTE: To make chocolate curls, draw a vegetable peeler across a thick bar of chocolate. Chocolate that is at room temperature will yield the best curls.

CHOCOLATE-MINT CUPS

If you prefer this layered chocolate dessert without mint, leave out the mint extract. If you like, replace it with rum or almond extract.

Prep: 20 minutes   Chill: 2 hours

I   **4-serving-size package chocolate instant pudding mix**

2   **cups milk**

¼   **of an 8-ounce container frozen whipped dessert topping, thawed**

⅛   **to ¼ teaspoon mint extract**

   Green or red food coloring (optional)

   Whipped topping (optional)

   Mint sprig (optional)

1 Prepare pudding mix according to package directions using the 2 cups milk. Set aside. In a small bowl combine dessert topping, mint extract, and, if desired, food coloring to make desired color.

2 In 6 small dessert bowls layer half the pudding, followed by dessert topping and remaining pudding. Cover and chill for 2 hours or until set. If desired, top with whipped topping and mint.

Makes 6 servings

Nutrition Facts per serving: 130 cal., 3 g total fat (3 g sat. fat), 7 mg chol., 272 mg sodium, 21 g carbo., 1 g fiber, 3 g pro.

FRUIT AND PUDDING WAFFLE CONES

Remember this pudding and fruit treat for those times when the neighborhood kids choose your yard for a game of tag or kickball.

Start to Finish: 10 minutes

1   **4-serving-size package lemon, vanilla, or white chocolate instant pudding mix**

1⅓   **cups milk**

1   **cup fresh fruit, such as blueberries, sliced kiwifruit, sliced strawberries, raspberries, or sliced bananas**

4   **waffle ice cream cones or large waffle ice cream bowls**

Prepare pudding according to package directions using the 1⅓ cups milk. Spoon fruit into cones. Top with pudding. Serve immediately.

Makes 4 servings

Nutrition Facts per serving: 226 cal., 2 g total fat (1 g sat. fat), 7 mg chol., 397 mg sodium, 47 g carbo., 2 g fiber, 4 g pro.

MAPLE-CINNAMON WEDGES
page 243

CHINESE CHICKEN SALAD
page 298

BARBECUE SHEPHERD'S PIE
page 307

CHICKEN WALDORF SALAD
page 317

SIZZLING BEEF SALAD
page 323

**BEEF STEAK
IN THAI MARINADE**
page 325

**BEER-GLAZED
PORK CHOPS**
page 329

**BEAN-AND-BEEF
ENCHILADA CASSEROLE**
page 333

**BAKED ROTINI
WITH HAM**
page 334

BAKED PENNE WITH MEAT SAUCE page 343

SHORTCUT LASAGNA
page 344

ROASTED TURKEY CALZONES
page 349

**HALIBUT WITH TOMATOES
AND OLIVES**
page 388

TUSCAN RAVIOLI STEW
page 399

CAJUN BEANS ON CORN BREAD
page 401

PLUMP APPLE DUMPLINGS
WITH CARAMEL SAUCE

Store-bought puff pastry and caramel ice cream topping turn the arduous task
of making apple dumplings into a simple 30-minute project. The baking takes a
little longer, but these juicy desserts are well worth the wait.

Prep: 30 minutes   Bake: 35 minutes   Oven: 400°F

½ of a 17.3-ounce package
   frozen puff pastry sheets
   (1 sheet), thawed

4 medium cooking apples
   (such as Golden Delicious
   or Jonathan)

1 tablespoon sugar

½ teaspoon ground cinnamon

1 egg

1 teaspoon water

½ cup caramel ice cream
   topping

⅓ cup chopped pecans,
   toasted

1 Unfold puff pastry on a lightly floured surface. Roll pastry into
a 14-inch square. Using a fluted pastry cutter or table knife, cut
pastry into four 7-inch squares. Set aside.

2 Preheat oven to 400°F. Core apples; if desired, peel apples.
If necessary, trim bottoms of apples so they stand upright.
Place an apple in the center of each pastry square. In a small bowl
combine sugar and cinnamon; spoon into centers of apples.

3 In another small bowl beat egg and the water with a fork.
Moisten the edges of the pastry squares with egg mixture; fold
corners to center over fruit. Pinch to seal, pleating and folding
pastry along seams as necessary. Place dumplings in an ungreased
13×9×2-inch baking pan. Brush wrapped apples with egg mixture.

4 Bake dumplings about 35 minutes or until fruit is tender and
pastry is brown.

5 Meanwhile, for sauce, in a microwave-safe 2-cup glass measure
combine caramel topping and pecans. Microwave, uncovered, on
100% (high) power for 30 to 60 seconds or until heated through.

6 Serve dumplings warm with sauce.

Makes 4 servings

Nutrition Facts per serving: 571 cal., 27 g total fat (1 g sat. fat), 53 mg chol., 355 mg sodium, 78 g carbo.,
6 g fiber, 5 g pro.

SHORTCUT NAPOLEONS

Pudding made with sour cream is a luscious flavor surprise in this berry dessert. Choose either vanilla or chocolate pudding.

Prep: 30 minutes   Bake: 18 minutes   Cool: 30 minutes   Oven: 400°F

½   **of a 17.3-ounce package frozen puff pastry sheets (1 sheet), thawed**

1   **package 4-serving-size instant vanilla or chocolate pudding mix**

1¼   **cups milk**

1   **8-ounce carton dairy sour cream**

1   **cup raspberries or sliced strawberries**

1   **cup powdered sugar**

3   **to 4 teaspoons milk**

1   **tablespoon chocolate-flavor syrup**

1 Preheat oven to 400°F. On a lightly floured surface unfold pastry and roll into a 10-inch square. Using a sharp knife, cut pastry into eight 5×2½-inch rectangles. Arrange pastry rectangles on an ungreased baking sheet. Prick several times with a fork.

2 Bake for 18 to 20 minutes or until golden. Transfer to a wire rack; cool.

3 Meanwhile, prepare pudding mix according to package directions, except use the 1¼ cups milk and beat in sour cream along with the milk.

4 To assemble, split rectangles in half horizontally. Spoon about ⅓ cup of the pudding mixture onto bottom half of each cooled pastry rectangle; top with raspberries and top halves of pastry rectangles.

5 In a small bowl combine powdered sugar and enough of the 3 to 4 teaspoons milk to make of drizzling consistency. Spoon over pastry rectangles to glaze. Drizzle chocolate-flavor syrup over glaze. If desired, gently draw a knife through the syrup in several places to make a pretty design. Serve immediately or refrigerate for up to 2 hours.

Makes 8 pastries

Nutrition Facts per pastry: 323 cal., 16 g total fat (4 g sat. fat), 16 mg chol., 331 mg sodium, 41 g carbo., 1 g fiber, 4 g pro.

PEACH-RASPBERRY PASTRY STACKS

This recipe makes enough to serve a large dinner party, and the "stacks" are positively beautiful. Toasty colored pastry, sunny lemon curd whipping cream, with a crown of red berry preserves and fresh berry garnish.

Prep: 35 minutes   Bake: 12 minutes   Cool: 30 minutes   Oven: 375°F

½ **of a 17.3-ounce package frozen puff pastry sheets (I sheet), thawed**

2 **cups frozen unsweetened peach slices, thawed**

I **cup whipping cream**

½ **cup purchased lemon curd**

¼ **cup seedless red raspberry preserves or strawberry jelly**

Fresh raspberries (optional)

1 Preheat oven to 375°F. On a lightly floured surface unfold puff pastry. Cut puff pastry into 3 rectangles along the fold lines. Cut each rectangle in half; cut each rectangle in half diagonally to form a total of 12 triangles. Place triangles 1 inch apart on an ungreased baking sheet.

2 Bake for 12 to 15 minutes or until golden. Transfer to a wire rack; cool. (If desired, place cooled baked pastry triangles in an airtight container; cover. Store at room temperature overnight.)

3 Coarsely chop peach slices; drain well in colander. Pat peaches dry with paper towels.

4 In a chilled large mixing bowl beat cream with chilled beaters of an electric mixer on medium speed until soft peaks form (tips curl); fold in lemon curd. Fold in chopped peaches. If desired, cover and chill for up to 4 hours.

5 Spoon preserves into a small saucepan; heat over medium-low heat just until melted, stirring occasionally.

6 Split puff pastry triangles horizontally and place bottom halves on dessert plates; top with lemon curd mixture. Top with remaining puff pastry halves. Lightly drizzle with melted preserves. If desired, garnish with fresh raspberries.

Makes 12 pastry stacks

Nutrition Facts per pastry stack: 232 cal., 14 g total fat (5 g sat. fat), 37 mg chol., 96 mg sodium, 17 g carbo., 2 g fiber, 1 g pro.

NUTTY CARAMEL CLUSTER WEDGES

This sweet creation is part pastry, part candy bar, and practically no work.
What could be better?

Prep: 15 minutes   **Bake:** 20 minutes   **Oven:** 375°F

½ **of a 17.3-ounce package frozen puff pastry sheets (1 sheet), thawed**

2 **cups chopped chocolate-covered caramel and pecan candies**

½ **cup chopped pecans, toasted**

1 Preheat oven to 375°F. Grease a large baking sheet; set aside. On a lightly floured surface roll pastry into a 13×9-inch rectangle. Place pastry on prepared baking sheet. Prick all over with a fork.

2 Bake for 15 to 17 minutes or until golden. Top baked pastry with chopped candies. Bake for 5 minutes more or until candies are softened. Remove from oven and sprinkle with pecans. Cool completely on pan on a wire rack. Cut into triangles. To store, place wedges in layers separated by waxed paper in an airtight container; cover. Store at room temperature for up to 3 days or freeze for up to 3 months.

Makes 18 wedges

Nutrition Facts per wedge: 173 cal., 12 g total fat (2 g sat. fat), 3 mg chol., 75 mg sodium, 17 g carbo., 1 g fiber, 2 g pro.

ALMOND TWISTS

Easy-to-handle frozen puff pastry slashes the preparation time for crisp, pastrylike cookies to weeknight doable.

Prep: 15 minutes   Bake: 15 minutes   Cool: 30 minutes   Oven: 400°F

½ **of a 17.3-ounce package frozen puff pastry sheets (1 sheet), thawed**

⅓ **cup almond paste**

1 **egg yolk**

3 **tablespoons packed brown sugar**

2 **teaspoons water**

1 **recipe Powdered Sugar Icing**

Coarsely chopped sliced almonds

1 Preheat oven to 400°F. On a lightly floured surface unfold the pastry. Roll the pastry into a 14-inch square. Using a fluted pastry wheel or sharp knife, cut the square in half.

2 For filling, in a small mixing bowl crumble almond paste. Add egg yolk and brown sugar. Beat with an electric mixer on medium speed until smooth. Beat in water, 1 teaspoon at a time, until filling is of spreading consistency.

3 Spread filling over 1 pastry half. Place remaining pastry half on top of filling. Cut dough lengthwise into seven 14×1-inch strips; cut each strip crosswise into quarters to make 28 pieces. Twist each piece twice. Place twists about 2 inches apart on an ungreased baking sheet.

4 Bake for 12 to 15 minutes or until golden. Transfer twists to a wire rack and let cool. Drizzle Powdered Sugar Icing over twists. Sprinkle with almonds. To store, place twists in layers separated by waxed paper in an airtight container; cover. Store at room temperature up to 2 days.

Makes 28 twists

Nutrition Facts per twist: 82 cal., 4 g total fat (0 g sat. fat), 7 mg chol., 35 mg sodium, 10 g carbo., 0 g fiber, 1 g pro.

Powdered Sugar Icing: In a small bowl stir together 1 cup powdered sugar, ¼ teaspoon vanilla, and enough milk (1 to 2 tablespoons) to make drizzling consistency.

NEAPOLITAN ICE CREAM SUNDAES

The delicate baked crepe chips fracture easily, so handle them carefully.

Prep: 20 minutes   **Bake:** 6 minutes   **Oven:** 375°F

- 1 **tablespoon sugar**
- ½ **teaspoon ground cinnamon**
- ½   **of a 4- to 5-ounce package refrigerated ready-to-use crepes (5)**
- 2 **tablespoons butter, melted**
- 1 **rectangular half-gallon carton Neapolitan ice cream**
- 1 **recipe Sweetened Whipped Cream (optional)**
   Maraschino cherries (optional)
- 1 **11.75-ounce jar hot fudge ice cream topping, warmed (optional)**

1 Preheat oven to 375°F. Grease 2 large baking sheets; set aside. In a small bowl stir together sugar and cinnamon. Brush both sides of crepes with butter and sprinkle with sugar mixture. Cut each crepe into quarters and arrange on the prepared baking sheets. Bake, one baking sheet at a time, for 3 to 4 minutes or until crepes are light brown. Cool crepes on the baking sheets. Remove and set aside. (Note: you will need to handle these gently as they are delicate and break easily.)

2 Cut ice cream crosswise into 10 slices; halve slices crosswise again.

3 To serve, arrange crepe pieces and ice cream slices in bowls. If desired, top with Sweetened Whipped Cream and cherries; and pass hot fudge ice cream topping.

Makes 10 sundaes

Nutrition Facts per sundae: 254 cal., 13 g total fat (8 g sat. fat), 55 mg chol., 113 mg sodium, 45 g carbo., 0 g fiber, 4 g pro.

Sweetened Whipped Cream: In a chilled large mixing bowl use a large whisk or electric mixer to beat 1 cup whipping cream, 2 tablespoons powdered sugar, and ½ teaspoon vanilla until stiff peaks form. Makes 2 cups.

MINT ICE CREAM WAFFLE SUNDAES

You will have extra Berry Sauce. Place remaining Berry Sauce in an airtight container and store in the refrigerator up to 2 weeks. Use on ice cream, pancakes, or waffles.

Start to Finish: 20 minutes

4   **giant waffle ice cream cones**

1   **pint mint or pistachio ice cream**

½   **cup of the Berry Sauce or ½ cup purchased dark chocolate or fudge ice cream topping**

Fresh raspberries, blackberries and/or blueberries (optional)

Small fresh mint leaves (optional)

1 Place each waffle cone in a tall cup or bowl. Divide scoops of ice cream among the cones. Top with ice cream topping or Berry Sauce.

2 If desired, add several berries and mint leaves to tops of sundaes.

Makes 4 sundaes

Nutrition Facts per sundae: 450 cal., 17 g total fat (9 g sat. fat), 25 mg chol., 135 mg sodium, 69 g carbo., 2 g fiber, 7 g pro.

Berry Sauce: In a medium saucepan combine one 12-ounce package frozen unsweetened raspberries, 1 cup fresh or frozen blackberries, 1 cup fresh or frozen blueberries, and ½ cup sugar. Bring to boiling over medium heat, stirring frequently. Reduce heat; simmer, uncovered, about 15 minutes or until mixture is slightly thickened. Remove from heat; cool slightly. Place berry mixture in a blender or food processor. Cover and blend or process until smooth. Makes 2 cups.

MAPLE-GLAZED BANANAS

Make sure the bananas are ripe but still firm. If they are overripe, they will become mushy during cooking.

Start to Finish: 15 minutes

¼ **cup butter**

¼ **cup packed brown sugar**

¼ **cup pure maple syrup or maple-flavored syrup**

1 **tablespoon lemon juice**

½ **teaspoon ground cinnamon**

3 **ripe bananas, halved lengthwise and cut into 1-inch pieces**

1 **pint vanilla ice cream**

1 In heavy medium skillet melt butter over medium heat. Stir in brown sugar, syrup, lemon juice, and cinnamon. Bring to boiling; reduce heat. Simmer, uncovered, for 2 minutes. Add bananas; spoon some of the syrup mixture over bananas. Cook and stir for 1 to 2 minutes more or until heated through. Remove from heat.

2 Scoop ice cream into dessert dishes. Spoon warm bananas and syrup over ice cream.

Makes 4 servings

Nutrition Facts per serving: 471 cal., 24 g total fat (15 g sat. fat), 99 mg chol., 135 mg sodium, 64 g carbo., 2 g fiber, 4 g pro.

CEREAL-COATED ICE CREAM SUNDAES

Use whatever ice cream and fruit you have on hand for this dessert.
The cereal adds a pleasing crunch.

Start to Finish: 15 minutes

1   **10-ounce package frozen raspberries or strawberries in syrup**

2   **ripe bananas, peeled**

2   **cups wheat cereal flakes, crushed**

½   **teaspoon ground cinnamon**

1   **pint ice cream (any flavor)**

1 Thaw raspberries according to the quick-thaw directions on package; set aside. Meanwhile, cut bananas into ½-inch slices. Divide banana slices among 4 dessert dishes; set aside.

2 Place cereal in a shallow dish; stir in cinnamon. Using an ice cream scoop, place one scoop of ice cream in crumbs; roll the ice cream to coat with crumbs. Transfer to a dessert dish with bananas. Repeat with 3 more scoops of ice cream. Sprinkle any remaining cereal mixture over ice cream in dishes. Spoon raspberries and their syrup over each serving.

Makes 4 servings

Nutrition Facts per serving: 410 cal., 13 g total fat (8 g sat. fat), 68 mg chol., 174 mg sodium, 71 g carbo., 5 g fiber, 5 g pro.

ICE CREAM COOKIE SANDWICHES

Simplify this recipe even further by slicing and baking the cookie dough according to package directions. You'll get round cookies instead of square. Or skip the baking and use purchased peanut butter cookies.

Prep: 40 minutes   Bake: 8 minutes   Freeze: 4 to 48 hours   Oven: 350°F

| 18-ounce roll refrigerated peanut butter cookie dough

¼ cup all-purpose flour

6 tablespoons raspberry, cherry, or strawberry preserves

| pint vanilla ice cream

1 Preheat oven to 350°F. In a large bowl combine cookie dough and flour; stir or knead until well mixed. On a lightly floured surface roll dough into a 13½×9-inch rectangle. Cut into 1½-inch squares. Transfer to ungreased cookie sheets. Bake for 8 to 10 minutes or until edges are firm and tops are light brown. Cool on cookie sheets for 1 minute. Remove and cool completely on a wire rack.

2 Place 1 teaspoon preserves on flat side of 1 cookie. Place a small scoop of ice cream (about 1½ tablespoons) on preserves. Top with another cookie, flat side down, and press lightly. Repeat with remaining cookies, preserves, and ice cream (there will be extra cookies). Wrap and freeze for 4 to 48 hours.

Makes 16 sandwiches and 22 extra cookies

Nutrition Facts per ice cream sandwich: 175 cal., 9 g total fat (3 g sat. fat), 23 mg chol., 104 mg sodium, 22 g carbo., 0 g fiber, 3 g pro.

Pastel Ice Cream Sandwiches: Substitute a 16-ounce roll of refrigerated sugar cookie dough for the peanut butter cookie dough. Substitute 6 tablespoons lemon or lime curd for the preserves, and substitute 1 pint rainbow, orange, or pineapple sherbet for the vanilla ice cream.

ONE GROCERY BAG: FIVE MEALS

What's for dinner? Grab one of our shopping lists, head to the store, and poll the family when you arrive home to let them decide what they want. For each shopping list, they can choose from five recipes. Make it a habit to pick up the items on each shopping list and you'll always have the fixings for a great meal on hand.

SHOPPING LIST:
ITALIAN

Makes: Meatball Skewers with Marinara Dipping Sauce (p.285),
Italian Wedding Soup (p.286), Italian Grinders (p.287),
Penne and Meatballs (p.288), and Meatball and Pasta Casserole (p.289).

2   red and/or yellow sweet peppers

1   6-ounce package fresh baby spinach

1   medium red onion or fennel bulb

1   1-pound package dried mini penne pasta

1   26- to 28-ounce jar marinara pasta sauce

3   14-ounce cans chicken broth with roasted garlic

1   package (6) hoagie buns

1   8-ounce package Italian cheese blend

1   15-ounce carton ricotta pasta

1   16-ounce package frozen cooked Italian-style meatballs
    (32 bite-size meatballs)

SHOPPING LIST:
ITALIAN
(see p.284)

MEATBALL SKEWERS
WITH MARINARA DIPPING SAUCE

You don't need to thaw the meatballs, but microwave them on 100% power (high) for 1 to 1½ minutes or until they are soft enough to push the skewers through them.

Prep: 15 minutes   Grill: 10 minutes

- 1   **16-ounce package frozen cooked Italian-style meatballs (32 bite-size meatballs), thawed**
- 1   **medium red or yellow sweet pepper, cut into 1½-inch pieces**
- 1   **medium red onion or fennel bulb, cut into 1-inch wedges**
- 1   **tablespoon cooking oil**
  Ground black pepper
- 1   **26- to 28-ounce jar marinara pasta sauce**
- 1   **6-ounce package prewashed fresh baby spinach**

1 On eight 10- to 12-inch skewers* alternately thread meatballs, sweet pepper, and onion. Brush meatballs and vegetables with oil. Sprinkle with black pepper.

2 For a charcoal grill, place skewers on the rack of an uncovered grill directly over medium coals. Grill for 10 to 12 minutes or until vegetables are crisp-tender and lightly charred, turning once or twice. (For a gas grill, preheat grill. Reduce heat to medium. Place skewers on a grill rack over heat. Cover and grill as above.)

3 Meanwhile, in a medium saucepan heat marinara sauce just until bubbly. Line dinner plates with spinach. Serve the skewers on spinach-lined plates. Pour marinara sauce into small bowls for dipping.

Makes 4 to 6 servings

Nutrition Facts per serving: 542 cal., 37 g total fat (13 g sat. fat), 40 mg chol., 1816 mg sodium, 35 g carbo., 5 g fiber, 20 g pro.

*NOTE: If using wooden skewers, soak in water at least 30 minutes before grilling or broiling.

BROILING DIRECTIONS: Preheat broiler. Place the skewers on the unheated rack of a broiling pan. Broil 4 to 5 inches from the heat about 10 minutes or until vegetables are crisp-tender and lightly charred, turning once.

ITALIAN WEDDING SOUP

This soup is a natural considering the items on the shopping list. If you purchased the hoagie rolls, split and toast them, sprinkle with the extra shredded cheese and run them under broiler to melt the cheese. Serve with the soup. Pictured on page 259.

Prep: 20 minutes   **Cook:** 12 minutes

1	**tablespoon cooking oil**
2	**medium red and/or yellow sweet peppers, chopped (1½ cups)**
1	**medium red onion or fennel bulb, chopped (½ cup)**
3	**14-ounce cans chicken broth with roasted garlic**
1	**cup bottled marinara pasta sauce**
1	**16-ounce package frozen cooked Italian-style meatballs (32 bite-size meatballs)**
1	**cup dried mini penne pasta**
3	**cups packaged prewashed fresh baby spinach, chopped**
	Shredded Italian cheese blend

1 In a Dutch oven heat oil over medium heat. Add sweet peppers and onion; cook and stir about 5 minutes or until tender.

2 Add chicken broth and marinara sauce to sweet pepper mixture; bring to boiling. Carefully stir in meatballs and pasta. Return to boiling; reduce heat. Simmer, uncovered, for 12 to 15 minutes or until pasta is tender. Stir in spinach. Sprinkle individual servings with shredded cheese.

Makes 6 servings

Nutrition Facts per serving: 387 cal., 23 g total fat (10 g sat. fat), 58 mg chol., 1605 mg sodium, 25 g carbo., 5 g fiber, 19 g pro.

ITALIAN GRINDERS

Serve these meatball sandwiches when your kids ask their friends to stay for dinner. They'll make you the most popular mom on the street!

Start to Finish: 30 minutes

- 1 **package (6) hoagie buns**
- 1 **tablespoon cooking oil**
- 2 **medium red and/or yellow sweet peppers, cut into bite-size strips**
- ½ **of a medium red onion or fennel bulb, cut into thin wedges**
- 1 **16-ounce package frozen cooked Italian-style meatballs (32 bite-size meatballs)**
- 1 **26- to 28-ounce jar marinara pasta sauce**
- 2 **cups packaged prewashed fresh baby spinach**
- 1 **8-ounce package shredded Italian cheese blend (2 cups)**

1 Preheat broiler. Split hoagie buns horizontally, without cutting completely through the buns. Place buns on 2 baking sheets, cut sides up. Broil, 1 sheet at a time, 4 to 5 inches from the heat for 2 to 3 minutes or until lightly toasted. Cool on the baking sheets on wire racks.

2 In a large skillet heat oil over medium heat. Add sweet peppers and onion; cook and stir about 10 minutes or until crisp-tender. Remove peppers and onion from skillet; set aside.

3 Meanwhile, heat the meatballs in the microwave oven according to package directions. Add meatballs and marinara sauce to the hot skillet. Bring to boiling, stirring frequently.

4 Using a slotted spoon, place meatballs on the hoagie buns on the baking sheets. Reserve sauce. Top meatballs with cooked peppers and onion and the spinach. Sprinkle with shredded cheese. Broil, 1 sheet at a time, 4 to 5 inches from heat about 2 minutes or until cheese is melted. Serve with reserved sauce.

Makes 6 sandwiches

Nutrition Facts per sandwich: 740 cal., 38 g total fat (15 g sat. fat), 54 mg chol., 1967 mg sodium, 73 g carbo., 5 g fiber, 30 g pro.

PENNE AND MEATBALLS

For ease and economy, it's hard to top spaghetti and meatballs. But if you're looking for a bit of change, try this meatball dinner. Penne is the pasta of choice and fresh vegetables—sweet peppers, onion (or fennel), and spinach—enhance the bottled sauce.

Start to Finish: 25 minutes

8   ounces dried mini penne
    pasta

1   tablespoon cooking oil

2   medium red and/or yellow
    sweet peppers, cut into
    bite-size strips

1   medium red onion or fennel
    bulb, cut into thin wedges

1   26- to 28-ounce jar
    marinara sauce

1   16-ounce package frozen
    cooked Italian-style
    meatballs (32 bite-size
    meatballs)

3   cups packaged prewashed
    fresh baby spinach

    Shredded Italian cheese
    blend

1 Cook pasta according to package directions. Drain and set aside.

2 Meanwhile, in a large saucepan heat oil over medium heat. Add sweet peppers and onion; cook and stir about 5 minutes or until tender. Add marinara sauce and meatballs. Bring to boiling; reduce heat. Cook about 5 minutes more or until meatballs are heated through, stirring occasionally.

3 Stir spinach into meatball mixture; cook just until spinach is wilted. Serve meatball mixture over pasta. Sprinkle individual servings with shredded cheese.

Makes 4 to 6 servings

Nutrition Facts per serving: 801 cal., 42 g total fat (15 g sat. fat), 50 mg chol., 1905 mg sodium, 79 g carbo., 7 g fiber, 31 g pro.

SHOPPING LIST:
ITALIAN
(see p.284)

MEATBALL AND PASTA CASSEROLE

If you save casseroles for weekends because they require lots of time to assemble, think again. This cheesy meatball and pasta bake goes together in 25 minutes and bakes for another 30, giving you a chance to catch your breath between work and dinner.

Prep: 25 minutes   Bake: 30 minutes   Oven: 350°F

- 8   **ounces dried mini penne pasta**
- 2   **tablespoons cooking oil**
- 1   **6-ounce package prewashed fresh baby spinach**
- 2   **medium red and/or yellow sweet peppers, coarsely chopped (1½ cups)**
- 1   **medium red onion or fennel bulb, coarsely chopped (½ cup)**
- 1   **26- to 28-ounce jar marinara sauce**
- 1   **16-ounce package frozen cooked Italian-style meatballs (32 bite-size meatballs)**
- 1   **15-ounce carton ricotta cheese**
- 1   **8-ounce package shredded Italian cheese blend (2 cups)**

1 Preheat oven to 350°F. Cook pasta according to package directions. Drain and set aside.

2 In a large skillet heat 1 tablespoon of the oil over medium heat. Add spinach, in batches if necessary, and cook just until it wilts. Drain well; set aside.

3 In the same skillet heat the remaining 1 tablespoon of oil over medium heat. Add sweet peppers and onion; cook and stir about 5 minutes or until tender. Stir in marinara sauce. Bring to boiling; remove from heat. Stir in pasta and meatballs.

4 Transfer meatball mixture to a 3-quart baking dish; spread the meatball mixture into an even layer. Top with spinach. Drop spoonfuls of ricotta cheese evenly over the spinach layer. Sprinkle with shredded cheese.

5 Bake for 30 to 35 minutes or until cheese is melted and sauce is bubbly.

Makes 6 servings

Nutrition Facts per serving: 750 cal., 44 g total fat (21 g sat. fat), 112 mg chol., 1452 mg sodium, 51 g carbo., 8 g fiber, 38 g pro.

SHOPPING LIST: MEXICAN

Makes: Chicken Nachos (p.291), Chicken Quesadillas (p.292),
Soft Shell Chicken Tacos (p.293), Taco Salad (p.294),
and Chicken Enchiladas (p.295).

1   large tomato

1   10-ounce package shredded iceberg lettuce

1   16-ounce can refried beans

1   16-ounce jar salsa

1   10-ounce can enchilada sauce

1   13.5-ounce package tortilla chips

1   10.5-ounce package 6-inch flour tortillas (10)

1   8-ounce carton dairy sour cream

1   8-ounce package shredded Mexican-style four-cheese blend

2   6-ounce packages refrigerated cooked chicken breast strips

CHICKEN NACHOS

A couple packages of cooked chicken strips turn this popular appetizer into a star attraction. Keep the meal casual by placing the nachos in the center of the table and letting everyone help themselves.

Prep: 20 minutes   Bake: 5 minutes per pan   Oven: 450°F

1 **16-ounce can refried beans**

2 **6-ounce packages refrigerated cooked chicken breast strips**

1 **13.5-ounce package tortilla chips**

1 **8-ounce package shredded Mexican-style four-cheese blend (2 cups)**

1 **large tomato, chopped (¾ cup)**

1 **cup bottled salsa**

1 **8-ounce carton dairy sour cream**

1 Preheat oven to 450°F. In a small saucepan cook refried beans over medium heat until heated through, stirring occasionally.

2 Meanwhile, heat chicken breast strips according to package directions; coarsely chop chicken.

3 Divide tortilla chips between 2 foil-lined baking sheets. Top tortilla chips with spoonfuls of refried beans, chicken, and cheese.

4 Bake, one sheet at a time, about 5 minutes or until cheese is melted. Top with tomato, salsa, and sour cream.

Makes 8 servings

Nutrition Facts per serving: 515 cal., 28 g total fat (11 g sat. fat), 72 mg chol., 1216 mg sodium, 46 g carbo., 6 g fiber, 24 g pro.

SHOPPING LIST:
MEXICAN
(see p.290)

CHICKEN QUESADILLAS

The tortillas are generously stuffed with chicken, beans, and cheese and cooked until crisp making a satisfying entrée or substantial appetizer.

Prep: 20 minutes   Cook: 2 minutes per batch   Oven: 300°F

1   cup canned refried beans

2   6-ounce packages refrigerated cooked chicken breast strips

1   10.5-ounce package 6-inch flour tortillas (10)

½   of an 8-ounce package shredded Mexican-style four-cheese blend (1 cup)

1   16-ounce jar salsa

    Nonstick cooking spray

½   cup dairy sour cream

1 In a small saucepan cook refried beans over medium heat until heated through, stirring occasionally.

2 Meanwhile, heat chicken breast strips according to package directions; chop chicken.

3 To assemble quesadillas, spread refried beans over 5 of the flour tortillas. Divide the chicken and the cheese among the bean-topped tortillas; top each with 1 tablespoon salsa. Place remaining tortillas on top. Spray quesadillas with nonstick cooking spray.

4 Heat a very large skillet over medium heat for 1 minute. Place 2 of the quesadillas in skillet; cook for 2 to 3 minutes or until light brown, turning once. Transfer quesadillas to a baking sheet. Keep warm in a 300°F oven. Repeat with remaining quesadillas.

5 Cut quesadillas into wedges. Serve with remaining salsa and sour cream.

Makes 5 quesadillas

Nutrition Facts per quesadilla: 459 cal., 18 g total fat (9 g sat. fat), 81 mg chol., 1881 mg sodium, 47 g carbo., 6 g fiber, 29 g pro.

SOFT SHELL CHICKEN TACOS

Try tacos tonight! You can have these cheesy chicken tacos on the table in less time than it takes to drive to the neighborhood taco stand.

Start to Finish: 20 minutes

1	**16-ounce can refried beans**
2	**6-ounce packages refrigerated cooked chicken breast strips**
1	**10.5-ounce package 6-inch flour tortillas (10)**
1	**8-ounce package shredded Mexican-style four-cheese blend (2 cups)**
2	**cups packaged shredded iceberg lettuce**
1	**large tomato, chopped (¾ cup)**
½	**cup bottled salsa**
½	**cup dairy sour cream**

1 In a small saucepan cook refried beans over medium heat until heated through, stirring occasionally.

2 Meanwhile, heat chicken breast strips according to package directions.

3 Spread about 2 tablespoons of refried beans on each tortilla. Top with chicken, cheese, lettuce, and tomato. Fold tortillas over filling. Serve with salsa and sour cream.

Makes 10 tacos

Nutrition Facts per taco: 289 cal., 13 g total fat (7 g sat. fat), 52 mg chol., 889 mg sodium, 26 g carbo., 4 g fiber, 18 g pro.

TACO SALAD

Broken tortilla chips stand in for the tortilla bowls in this super quick taco salad. They offer the same crunch factor for a fraction of the time commitment.

Start to Finish: 15 minutes

2   **6-ounce packages refrigerated cooked chicken breast strips**

1   **10-ounce package shredded iceberg lettuce**

4   **cups tortilla chips, coarsely broken**

½   **of an 8-ounce package shredded Mexican-style four-cheese blend (1 cup)**

1   **large tomato, coarsely chopped (¾ cup)**

1   **16-ounce jar salsa**

1   **8-ounce carton dairy sour cream**

1 Heat chicken breast strips according to package directions.

2 Line a large serving platter with lettuce. Top with tortilla chips, chicken, cheese, and tomato.

3 In small bowl stir together salsa and sour cream. Serve salsa mixture with salad.

Makes 6 to 8 servings

Nutrition Facts per serving: 315 cal., 18 g total fat (10 g sat. fat), 73 mg chol., 1203 mg sodium, 19 g carbo., 3 g fiber, 21 g pro.

CHICKEN ENCHILADAS

You'll impress your family with this dish. These saucy enchiladas look like you spent all afternoon in the kitchen.

Prep: 20 minutes   Bake: 15 minutes   Oven: 400°F

- 1 **16-ounce can refried beans**
- 2 **6-ounce packages refrigerated cooked chicken breast strips**
- 1 **8-ounce package shredded Mexican-style four-cheese blend (2 cups)**
- 1 **10-ounce can enchilada sauce**
- 1 **10.5-ounce package 6-inch flour tortillas (10)**
- 1 **large tomato, chopped (¾ cup)**
- ½ **cup dairy sour cream**

1 Preheat oven to 400°F. In a small saucepan cook refried beans over medium heat until heated through, stirring occasionally.

2 Meanwhile, heat chicken breast strips according to package directions; chop chicken. In a large bowl combine the chopped chicken, refried beans, and 1 cup of the cheese. Set chicken mixture aside.

3 Place enchilada sauce in a shallow dish. Dip each tortilla into the sauce to coat, letting excess drip off. Fill each tortilla with some of the chicken mixture and roll up. Place filled tortillas in a 2-quart rectangular baking dish. Pour any remaining sauce over the enchiladas. Sprinkle with the remaining 1 cup cheese.

4 Bake, uncovered, about 15 minutes or until heated through. Sprinkle with chopped tomato. Serve with sour cream.

Makes 5 servings

Nutrition Facts per serving: 587 cal., 26 g total fat (14 g sat. fat), 104 mg chol., 1995 mg sodium, 51 g carbo., 7 g fiber, 36 g pro.

SHOPPING LIST:
CHINESE

Makes: Undone Wonton Soup (p.297), Chinese Chicken Salad (p.298), Chicken Egg Roll Turnovers (p.299), Chicken Stir-Fry (p.300), and Asian Noodles (p.301).

1   5- to 8-ounce package mixed greens

1   16-ounce package egg roll wrappers

8   ounces dried fettuccine or Chinese egg noodles

3   14-ounce cans chicken broth

1   12-ounce bottle rice vinegar

1   11.5-ounce jar stir-fry sauce

1   2.25-ounce package sliced almonds

1   dozen eggs

12   ounces skinless, boneless chicken breast halves

1   16-ounce package frozen pepper stir-fry vegetables (yellow, green, and red sweet peppers and onion)

SHOPPING LIST:
CHINESE
(see p.296)

UNDONE WONTON SOUP

Wonton soup is a snap when you skip the step of stuffing the wontons. Just stir strips of egg roll wrappers and the wonton filling ingredients directly into the soup.

Prep: 15 minutes   Cook: 15 minutes

- 1 **tablespoon cooking oil**
- 12 **ounces skinless, boneless chicken breast halves, chopped**
- 3 **14-ounce cans chicken broth**
- ¼ **cup bottled stir-fry sauce**
- 1 **tablespoon rice vinegar**
- 1 **16-ounce package frozen pepper stir-fry vegetables (yellow, green, and red sweet peppers and onion)**
- 6 **egg roll wrappers, cut into ½-inch strips**
- 2 **eggs, lightly beaten**

1 In a 4-quart Dutch oven heat oil over medium-high heat. Add chicken; cook and stir for 3 to 4 minutes or until no longer pink.

2 Stir chicken broth, stir-fry sauce, and rice vinegar into chicken in Dutch oven. Bring to boiling. Add stir-fry vegetables and egg roll wrapper strips; return to boiling. Reduce heat and simmer about 3 minutes or until egg roll strips are tender, stirring often to prevent the egg roll wrappers from sticking together. Pour eggs into the soup in a steady stream, stirring a few times to create shreds.

Makes 6 to 8 servings

Nutrition Facts per serving: 248 cal., 6 g total fat (1 g sat. fat), 108 mg chol., 1388 mg sodium, 27 g carbo., 1 g fiber, 20 g pro.

CHINESE CHICKEN SALAD

Baked strips of egg roll wrappers and sliced almonds add crunch to this fresh and colorful salad. Pictured on page 260.

Prep: 20 minutes   **Bake: 6 minutes**   **Cook: 7 minutes**   **Oven: 400°F**

4   **egg roll wrappers, cut into bite-size strips**

Nonstick cooking spray

¼   **cup bottled stir-fry sauce**

2   **tablespoons rice vinegar**

1   **tablespoon cooking oil**

12   **ounces skinless, boneless chicken breast halves, cut into bite-size strips**

1   **16-ounce package frozen pepper stir-fry vegetables (yellow, green, and red sweet peppers and onion)**

1   **5- to 8-ounce package mixed greens**

2   **tablespoons sliced almonds, toasted**

1 Preheat oven to 400°F. Place egg roll wrapper strips on a large baking sheet. Lightly coat strips with cooking spray. Bake for 6 to 7 minutes or until crisp and brown. Set aside.

2 For dressing, in a small bowl stir together stir-fry sauce and rice vinegar.

3 In a large skillet heat oil over medium-high heat. Add chicken; cook and stir for 3 to 4 minutes or until no longer pink. Remove chicken from skillet. Add stir-fry vegetables to skillet (if necessary, add additional oil). Cook and stir for 4 to 5 minutes or until vegetables are hot. Drain off any excess liquid.

4 In a large bowl combine chicken and vegetables. Add dressing; toss to coat. Arrange greens on a platter or divide greens among 4 individual plates. Top greens with chicken mixture. Sprinkle with egg roll wrapper strips and toasted almonds.

Makes 4 servings

Nutrition Facts per serving: 297 cal., 6 g total fat (1 g sat. fat), 52 mg chol., 772 mg sodium, 31 g carbo., 3 g fiber, 25 g pro.

CHICKEN EGG ROLL TURNOVERS

Egg roll wrappers make a handy crust for these baked turnovers filled with chicken and peppers.

Prep: 25 minutes   Bake: 10 minutes   Oven: 400°F

1 **tablespoon cooking oil**

12 **ounces skinless, boneless chicken breast halves, cut into thin strips**

1 **16-ounce package frozen pepper stir-fry vegetables (yellow, green, and red sweet peppers and onion)**

¼ **cup bottled stir-fry sauce**

4 **egg roll wrappers**

Nonstick cooking spray

1 Preheat oven to 400°F. For filling, in a large skillet heat oil over medium-high heat. Add chicken; cook and stir for 3 to 4 minutes or until no longer pink. Remove chicken from skillet. Add stir-fry vegetables to skillet (if necessary, add additional oil). Cook and stir for 4 to 5 minutes or until hot. Drain off any excess liquid. Return chicken to skillet. Add stir-fry sauce; toss to coat. Cool for 5 minutes. Place filling in a food processor, half at a time if necessary; cover and process until chopped.*

2 To assemble turnovers, place egg roll wrappers on flat surface; brush edges with water. Spoon one-fourth of the chicken mixture onto each wrapper. Fold wrappers in half over filling to make triangles. Press edges to seal. Place on a lightly greased baking sheet. Lightly coat turnovers with nonstick cooking spray.

3 Bake about 10 minutes or until light brown. Serve warm.

Makes 4 turnovers

Nutrition Facts per turnover: 270 cal., 5 g total fat (1 g sat. fat), 52 mg chol., 765 mg sodium, 29 g carbo., 2 g fiber, 24 g pro.

*NOTE: If you do not have a food processor, chop the filling by hand, or, if you like, skip the chopping step.

CHICKEN STIR-FRY

Stir-fry sauces are available in several flavors and any will work in this simple stir-fry.

Start to Finish: 20 minutes

1	**tablespoon cooking oil**
12	**ounces skinless, boneless chicken breast halves, cut into bite-size strips**
1	**16-ounce package frozen pepper stir-fry vegetables (yellow, green, and red sweet peppers and onion)**
½	**cup bottled stir-fry sauce**
2	**tablespoons sliced almonds, toasted**

1 In a large skillet heat oil over medium-high heat. Add chicken; cook and stir for 2 to 3 minutes or until no longer pink. Remove chicken from skillet.

2 Add stir-fry vegetables to skillet (if necessary, add additional oil); cook and stir for 4 to 5 minutes or until hot. Drain off any excess liquid. Return chicken to skillet. Add stir-fry sauce; cook and stir until mixture is coated and heated through. Sprinkle with toasted almonds.

Makes 4 servings

Nutrition Facts per serving: 213 cal., 6 g total fat (1 g sat. fat), 49 mg chol., 1102 mg sodium, 15 g carbo., 2 g fiber, 22 g pro.

SERVING SUGGESTION: Look for packaged precooked rice that can be reheated in the microwave oven to serve with this stir-fry.

ASIAN NOODLES

If you're a fan of the noodle bowls served in Asian restaurants, you'll be wowed with this 20-minute version you can make in your own kitchen any day of the week.

Start to Finish: 20 minutes

8   **ounces dried fettuccine or Chinese egg noodles, broken**

1   **tablespoon cooking oil**

12 **ounces skinless, boneless chicken breast halves, cut into bite-size strips**

1   **16-ounce package frozen pepper stir-fry vegetables (yellow, green, and red sweet peppers and onion)**

½   **of an 11.5-ounce bottle stir-fry sauce (½ cup)**

2   **tablespoons sliced almonds, toasted**

1 Prepare pasta according to package directions; drain and set aside.

2 Heat oil in a large skillet over medium-high heat. Add chicken to skillet; cook and stir for 2 to 3 minutes or until no longer pink. Remove from skillet. Add stir-fry vegetables to skillet (if necessary, add additional oil). Cook and stir about 5 minutes or until vegetables are hot. Drain any excess liquid from skillet. Return chicken to skillet. Add stir-fry sauce. Cook and stir until mixture is coated and heated through. Add drained pasta; toss to coat. Sprinkle with almonds.

Makes 4 to 6 servings

Nutrition Facts per serving: 429 cal., 7 g total fat (1 g sat. fat), 49` mg chol., 1243 mg sodium, 59 g carbo., 3 g fiber, 30 g pro.

SHOPPING LIST: BBQ

Makes: Barbecue Melts (p.303), Shredded Pork Pizza (p.304), Barbecue Pork Turnovers (p.305), Cowboy Haystacks (p.306), and Barbecue Shepherd's Pie (p.307).

2 red and/or yellow sweet peppers

1 onion

1 11-ounce can whole kernel corn with sweet peppers

1 17- to 18-ounce package refrigerated BBQ sauce with cooked shredded pork

1 8-ounce package shredded Monterey Jack cheese

1 24-ounce package refrigerated mashed potatoes

1 15-ounce package rolled refrigerated unbaked pie crust (2 crusts)

1 12-inch Italian bread shell (Boboli®)

1 loaf Texas toast

BARBECUE MELTS

Warning: These extra-saucy sandwiches may drip barbecue sauce on your shirt. For those who insist on wearing white, serve them with a knife and fork. If you like, skip the second slice of bread and serve open-face.

Start to Finish: 20 minutes

1	**17- to 18-ounce package refrigerated BBQ sauce with cooked shredded pork**
1	**tablespoon cooking oil**
2	**medium red and/or yellow sweet peppers, cut into thin strips**
1	**medium onion, cut into thin wedges**
12	**slices Texas toast, toasted**
½	**of an 8-ounce package shredded Monterey Jack cheese (1 cup)**

1 Preheat broiler. Heat shredded pork according to package directions. In a large skillet heat oil over medium heat. Add sweet peppers and onion; cook about 5 minutes or until crisp-tender.

2 Place 6 slices of Texas toast on a baking sheet. Top with the shredded pork, then with sweet peppers and onion. Top with shredded cheese.

3 Broil 4 inches from the heat for 1 to 2 minutes or until cheese is melted. Top with remaining Texas toast.

Makes 6 sandwiches

Nutrition Facts per sandwich: 463 cal., 16 g total fat (5 g sat. fat), 138 mg chol., 1215 mg sodium, 59 g carbo., 1 g fiber, 26 g pro.

SHREDDED PORK PIZZA

Today's pizzerias serve all kinds of pizzas beyond the typical tomato and cheese pie. Here's an American version with a Southern-style barbecue topping. Pictured on page 138.

Prep: 15 minutes   Bake: 12 minutes   Oven: 425°F

1	**17- to 18-ounce package refrigerated BBQ sauce with cooked shredded pork**
1	**tablespoon cooking oil**
2	**medium red and/or yellow sweet peppers, cut into thin strips**
1	**medium onion, cut into thin wedges**
1	**12-inch Italian bread shell (Boboli®)**
½	**of an 8-ounce package shredded Monterey Jack cheese (1 cup)**

1 Preheat oven to 425°F. Heat shredded pork according to package directions.

2 In a large skillet heat oil over medium heat. Add sweet peppers and onion; cook about 5 minutes or until crisp-tender.

3 Place the Italian bread shell on a large baking sheet. Spoon shredded pork over the bread shell, spreading evenly to the edges. Top with sweet peppers and onion. Sprinkle with cheese.

4 Bake about 12 minutes or until cheese is melted and the edge of the crust is light brown.

Makes 8 servings

Nutrition Facts per serving: 318 cal., 11 g total fat (3 g sat. fat), 33 mg chol., 862 mg sodium, 39 g carbo., 1 g fiber, 17 g pro.

SHOPPING LIST:
BBQ
(see p.302)

BARBECUE PORK TURNOVERS

A package of barbecued pork makes an easy yet zesty filling for these two-fisted turnovers. Let them cool a few minutes before biting into them—the filling is hot when served straight from the oven.

Prep: 15 minutes   Bake: 15 minutes   Oven: 425°F

- 1 **tablespoon cooking oil**
- 1 **medium red or yellow sweet pepper, chopped (¾ cup)**
- 1 **medium onion, chopped (½ cup)**
- 1 **17- to 18-ounce package refrigerated BBQ sauce with cooked shredded pork**
- 1 **11-ounce can whole kernel corn with sweet peppers, drained**
- 1 **15-ounce package rolled refrigerated unbaked piecrusts (2 crusts)**

1 Preheat oven to 425°F. In a large skillet heat oil over medium heat. Add sweet pepper and onion; cook about 5 minutes or until crisp-tender. Stir in shredded pork and drained corn; heat through.

2 Unroll piecrusts, cut each piecrust in half. Spoon one-fourth of the pork mixture onto half of each crust portion, at least ½-inch from edges. Fold crust over and seal edges with the tines of a fork. Use the fork to prick the top of each turnover several times to allow steam to escape. Place turnovers on a greased baking sheet.

3 Bake for 15 to 20 minutes or until golden brown.

Makes 4 turnovers

Nutrition Facts per turnover: 753 cal., 34 g total fat (11 g sat. fat), 42 mg chol., 1812 mg sodium, 91 g carbo., 3 g fiber, 17 g pro.

COWBOY HAYSTACKS

To serve these fun stacks family-style, set out bowls of mashed potatoes, vegetables, pork mixture, and cheese and let everyone construct their own serving.

Start to Finish: 20 minutes

1 **24-ounce package refrigerated mashed potatoes**

1 **17- to 18-ounce package refrigerated BBQ sauce with cooked shredded pork**

1 **tablespoon cooking oil**

2 **medium red and/or yellow sweet peppers, cut in thin strips**

1 **medium onion, cut in thin wedges**

1 **11-ounce can whole kernel corn with sweet peppers, drained**

1½ **cups shredded Monterey Jack cheese (6 ounces)**

1 Prepare mashed potatoes according to package directions. Heat shredded pork according to package directions.

2 In a large skillet heat oil over medium heat. Add sweet peppers and onion; cook about 5 minutes or until crisp-tender. Stir in drained corn; heat through.

3 For each serving plate, make a mound of mashed potatoes. Top potato mounds with shredded pork, the sweet pepper mixture, and the cheese.

Makes 6 servings

Nutrition Facts per serving: 387 cal., 15 g total fat (6 g sat. fat), 47 mg chol., 1242 mg sodium, 43 g carbo., 3 g fiber, 20 g pro.

BARBECUE SHEPHERD'S PIE

The ingredients give a barbecue spin to this favorite comfort food. If you like, make it with the garlic-flavored mashed potatoes instead of the plain ones. Pictured on page 261.

Prep: 20 minutes   Bake: 20 minutes   Oven: 375°F

1	**24-ounce package refrigerated mashed potatoes**
1	**tablespoon cooking oil**
2	**medium red and/or yellow sweet peppers, chopped (1½ cups)**
1	**medium onion, chopped (½ cup)**
1	**17- to 18-ounce package refrigerated BBQ sauce with cooked shredded pork**
1	**11-ounce can whole kernel corn with sweet peppers, drained**
½	**of an 8-ounce package shredded Monterey Jack cheese (1 cup)**

1 Preheat oven to 375°F. Prepare mashed potatoes according to the package directions.

2 In a large skillet heat oil over medium heat. Add sweet peppers and onion; cook about 5 minutes or until tender. Add shredded pork and drained corn; heat through.

3 Spread the mashed potatoes into the bottom and up the sides of a 2-quart rectangular baking dish. Spoon pork mixture into the center and spread evenly. Top with shredded cheese.

4 Bake about 20 minutes or until heated through.

Makes 6 servings

Nutrition Facts per serving: 352 cal., 12 g total fat (5 g sat. fat), 38 mg chol., 1191 mg sodium, 43 g carbo., 3 g fiber, 18 g pro.

SHOPPING LIST: DELI COUNTER

Makes: Antipasto Platter (p.309), Panzanella (p.310), Italian Muffaletta (p.311), Italian Panini (p.312), and Stromboli (p.313).

2 medium tomatoes

1 5- to 8-ounce package mixed greens

1 16-ounce jar pickled mixed vegetables (giardiniera)

1 9-ounce jar pitted kalamata olives

1 16-ounce bottle Italian salad dressing

4 ounces sliced salami

4 ounces sliced deli ham

4 ounces provolone cheese

1 10- to 12-inch Italian flat bread (focaccia)

1 3-pound package frozen pizza dough

ANTIPASTO PLATTER

You'll need a large platter, at least 12 inches in diameter, for this awesome appetizer. It's full of deli meats and cheese, so your guests won't leave hungry.

Start to Finish: 20 minutes

1   **10- to 12-inch Italian flat bread (focaccia)**

4   **ounces sliced salami**

4   **ounces sliced deli ham**

2   **medium tomatoes, cut into wedges**

     Salt and ground black pepper

½   **cup bottled Italian salad dressing**

4   **ounces provolone cheese, cut into bite-size cubes**

1   **16-ounce jar pickled mixed vegetables (giardiniera), drained**

⅔   **cup pitted kalamata olives**

1 Cut focaccia into small wedges or sticks. Roll the salami and ham into tube or horn shapes. Sprinkle tomato wedges with salt and pepper.

2 Pour salad dressing into a small serving bowl; place bowl in the center of a large platter. Arrange the focaccia, salami, ham, tomato wedges, provolone cheese, pickled vegetables, and olives around the bowl on the platter.

Makes 12 servings

Nutrition Facts per serving: 204 cal., 12 g total fat (4 g sat. fat), 22 mg chol., 1279 mg sodium, 17 g carbo., 1 g fiber, 9 g pro.

PANZANELLA

Half of the focaccia goes into the salad while the remaining half is cut into wedges and served on the side.

Prep: 20 minutes   Stand: 15 minutes   Oven: 425°F

½   **of a 10- to 12-inch Italian flat bread (focaccia)**

2   **tablespoons butter, melted**
    Ground black pepper

2   **medium tomatoes, coarsely chopped (1 cup)**

⅓   **cup bottled Italian salad dressing**

6   **cups packaged mixed greens**

4   **ounces sliced salami and/or sliced deli ham, cut into thin strips**

4   **ounces provolone cheese, cut into bite-size cubes**

⅓   **cup pitted kalamata olives, halved**

1 Preheat oven to 425°F. Cut half of the bread into 6 wedges; wrap wedges in plastic wrap and set aside.

2 For the croutons, cut the remaining half of the bread into 1-inch cubes. Place bread cubes in a 15×10×1-inch baking pan. Drizzle with melted butter and sprinkle with pepper; toss to coat. Bake about 8 minutes or until golden brown. Cool.

3 To assemble salad, in a very large bowl toss together croutons and tomatoes. Drizzle with salad dressing; toss to coat. Let stand for 15 minutes. Add mixed greens, salami, provolone cheese, and olives. Toss to combine. Serve salad with reserved bread wedges.

Makes 6 servings

Nutrition Facts per serving: 307 cal., 22 g total fat (9 g sat. fat), 41 mg chol., 971 mg sodium, 18 g carbo., 2 g fiber, 13 g pro.

ITALIAN MUFFALETTA

If you're a fan of this New Orleans specialty and want to stick to the traditional method, when chilling the sandwich, place a skillet filled with several cans of vegetables or fruit on top of it. Pictured on page 262.

Prep: 20 minutes   Chill: 1 to 8 hours

- 1 **16-ounce jar pickled mixed vegetables (giardiniera), drained**
- 1 **cup pitted kalamata olives**
- 1 **medium tomato, coarsely chopped (½ cup)**
- ¼ **cup bottled Italian salad dressing**
- 1 **10- to 12-inch Italian flat bread (focaccia), split in half horizontally**
- 4 **ounces sliced salami**
- 4 **ounces sliced deli ham**
- 4 **ounces provolone cheese, sliced**

1 In a food processor combine pickled vegetables, olives, and tomato. Cover and pulse with several off/on turns until finely chopped. Transfer mixture to a small bowl. Stir in salad dressing.

2 Place the bottom half of the focaccia on a work surface. Spread the vegetable mixture over the focaccia. Top with salami, ham, and provolone cheese. Top with the top half of the focaccia. Wrap the sandwich tightly with plastic wrap. Weight the sandwich with a cast iron pan. Chill for 1 to 8 hours before serving.

Makes 6 servings

Nutrition Facts per serving: 386 cal., 21 g total fat (7 g sat. fat), 44 mg chol., 2381 mg sodium, 33 g carbo., 2 g fiber, 18 g pro.

ITALIAN PANINI

An indoor electric grill is a handy appliance to have and makes quick work of this meaty sandwich.

Prep: 20 minutes   Cook: 5 minutes

- 1   **10- to 12-inch Italian flat bread (focaccia)**
- ⅓   **cup bottled Italian salad dressing**
- 4   **ounces provolone cheese, sliced**
- 4   **ounces sliced salami**
- 4   **ounces sliced deli ham**
- 1   **medium tomato, sliced**

1 Slice focaccia in half horizontally. Drizzle cut sides of focaccia with salad dressing. Top bottom half of focaccia with half of the cheese. Top with salami, ham, tomato, and remaining cheese. Top with top half of the focaccia. Cut sandwich into 6 wedges.

2 Preheat a covered indoor electric grill to medium heat. Place 2 or 3 sandwich wedges on grill rack; close the lid. Grill for 5 to 10 minutes or until focaccia is toasted and cheese is melted. Repeat with remaining sandwich wedges. (Or, lightly grease a large heavy skillet or grill pan. Heat skillet or grill pan over medium heat. Place sandwiches, half at a time if necessary, in skillet; top with a heavy cast-iron skillet. Cook for 5 to 10 minutes or until focaccia is toasted and cheese is melted, turning once halfway through cooking time.)

Makes 6 sandwiches

Nutrition Facts per sandwich: 349 cal., 19 g total fat (7 g sat. fat), 44 mg chol., 1216 mg sodium, 29 g carbo., 1 g fiber, 18 g pro.

STROMBOLI

This loaf stuffed with deli meats and cheese is perfect to serve on paper plates in front of the TV whether you're watching a football game or a favorite movie.

Prep: 20 minutes   Bake: 30 minutes   Stand: 10 minutes   Oven: 375°F

1	**16-ounce portion frozen pizza dough, thawed**
4	**ounces sliced salami**
4	**ounces sliced deli ham**
4	**ounces provolone cheese, sliced**
¼	**cup pitted kalamata olives, halved**
1	**tablespoon butter, melted**

1 Preheat oven to 375°F. Line a 15×10×1-inch baking pan with foil; grease foil. Set pan aside.

2 On a lightly floured surface roll pizza dough into a 13×10-inch rectangle. (If dough is difficult to roll out, cover and let rest a few minutes.) Top dough rectangle with salami and ham to within ½ inch of the edges. Top with cheese and olives. Brush edges with a little water.

3 Starting from a long side, roll up into a spiral; pinch edge to seal. Pinch ends and tuck under spiral. Place, seam side down, in prepared baking pan. Brush with melted butter. Using a sharp knife, make shallow diagonal cuts at 2-inch intervals along the top to allow steam to escape.

4 Bake for 30 to 35 minutes or until golden brown. (If necessary, cover loosely with foil after 20 minutes of baking to prevent overbrowning.) Let stand for 10 minutes before slicing.

Makes 8 servings

Nutrition Facts per serving: 270 cal., 15 g total fat (6 g sat. fat), 33 mg chol., 815 mg sodium, 22 g carbo., 1 g fiber, 12 g pro.

A Month of Menus

Compile the five shopping lists into one, add the fixings for simple side dishes and desserts, and you'll be good-to-go for dinner Monday through Friday. Follow the plan for all four weeks and rest assured that dinner is in the bag every weekday night for an entire month. Mix and match menus from one week to the next. Or, for those days when dinner truly is impossible, snatch your favorite takeout and save your shopping list meal for the weekend. (Boldface type indicates recipes in this chapter.)

MONDAY	TUESDAY	WEDNESDAY	THURSDAY	FRIDAY
Cowboy Haystacks (p.306) Steamed broccoli spears Sourdough bread Cherry pie	**Chinese Chicken Salad** (p.298) Whole wheat rolls Fresh pineapple slices	**Penne and Meatballs** (p.288) Country Italian bread Mixed greens with desired dressing Gelato	**Soft Shell Chicken Tacos** (p.293) Fresh fruit salad Lemon squares (from a mix)	**Italian Panini** (p.312) Multigrain chips Relish tray (olives, pickles, raw vegetables) Chocolate cake
Italian Wedding Soup (p.286) Crusty Italian bread Rice pudding with cookies	**Barbecue Pork Turnovers** (p.305) Potato salad (from deli) Corn chips Apple and pear wedges with caramel dipping sauce	**Chicken Stir-Fry** (p.300) Crab Rangoon (frozen or takeout) Fried rice (from a packaged mix) Orange sherbet	**Panzanella** (p.310) Red and green grapes Cheesecake	**Chicken Nachos** (p.291) Fresh mango and papaya slices Cupcakes
Italian Muffaletta (p.311) Pasta salad (from deli) Spumoni ice cream	**Chicken Enchiladas** (p.295) Fruit salad Corn bread squares Chocolate pudding with sugar cookies	**Barbecue Melts** (p.303) Spinach and tomato salad with desired dressing Angel food cake with strawberries and whipped cream	**Asian Noodles** (p.301) Steamed snow peas Assorted bakery cookies	**Meatball Skewers with Marinara Dipping Sauce** (p.285) Baguette Grilled zucchini Lemon meringue pie
Taco Salad (p.294) Fresh fruit plate Hot fudge sundaes	**Undone Wonton Soup** (p.297) Eggrolls (frozen or takeout) Sliced kiwifruit and strawberries Fortune cookies	**Antipasto Platter** (p.309) Cheese sticks (frozen) with marinara sauce Fudge brownies with ice cream	**Italian Grinders** (p.287) Kettle cooked potato chips Coleslaw (from deli) Fruit crisp (frozen or from a mix)	**Shredded Pork Pizza** (p.304) Caesar salad Apple turnovers

MAKE NOW, SERVE LATER

A little strategic planning makes for fuss-free meals. Assemble salads and sandwiches that wait in the fridge until you're ready to eat. Marinate meats while you're at work and cook them when you arrive home. Other dishes are prepared, and then refrigerated or frozen until you need them. With these recipes and a little advance effort, dinner is in the bag.

PORK AND NOODLE SALAD

It's amazing how much nutty flavor just 2 teaspoons of sesame oil bring to this salad. Look for sesame oil in the Asian ingredients aisle of the supermarket.

Prep: 30 minutes   Chill: 2 to 24 hours

8   ounces dried **Chinese egg noodles** or fine dried noodles

1½ pounds fresh **asparagus** spears, trimmed and cut into 2-inch pieces, or one 16-ounce package frozen cut asparagus

4   medium **carrots**, cut into thin ribbons or bite-size strips (2 cups)

1   pound cooked lean **pork**, cut into thin strips

1   recipe **Soy-Sesame Vinaigrette**

     Sesame seeds (optional)

     Sliced green onion (optional)

1 Cook noodles according to package directions; drain. Rinse with cold water until cool; drain.

2 If using fresh asparagus, cook in a covered saucepan in a small amount of lightly salted boiling water for 4 to 6 minutes or until crisp-tender. (Or, if using frozen asparagus, cook according to package directions.) Drain well.

3 In a large bowl combine noodles, asparagus, carrots, and pork. Cover and chill in the refrigerator for 2 to 24 hours.

4 To serve, drizzle Soy-Sesame Vinaigrette over salad; toss gently to coat. If desired, sprinkle with sesame seeds and green onion.

Makes 8 (1½-cup) servings

Nutrition Facts per serving: 338 cal., 12 g total fat (3 g sat. fat), 71 mg chol., 654 mg sodium, 35 g carbo., 3 g fiber, 23 g pro.

Soy-Sesame Vinaigrette: In a screw-top jar combine ½ cup reduced-sodium soy sauce, ¼ cup rice vinegar or vinegar, ¼ cup honey, 2 tablespoons salad oil, and 2 teaspoons toasted sesame oil. Cover and shake well to mix. Chill for 2 to 24 hours. Shake again before using.

CHICKEN WALDORF SALAD

The original Waldorf Salad dates to the late 1800s, and consists of apples, walnuts, and celery in a mayonnaise dressing. This updated version adds dried cherries and substitutes pecans for the walnuts. Pictured on page 263.

Chill: up to 24 hours   Start to Finish: 20 minutes

- **2   cups shredded or cubed cooked chicken (10 ounces)**
- **2   medium red and/or green apples, cored and coarsely chopped (2 cups)**
- **⅓   cup dried tart cherries**
- **⅓   cup coarsely chopped toasted pecans or peanuts**
- **¼   cup thinly sliced celery**
- **⅓   cup mayonnaise or salad dressing**
- **⅓   cup dairy sour cream**
- **1   tablespoon lemon juice**
- **1   tablespoon honey**
- **½   teaspoon dried rosemary, crushed**
- **Lettuce leaves**

1 In a large bowl combine chicken, apples, dried cherries, pecans, and celery.

2 For dressing, in a small bowl stir together mayonnaise, sour cream, lemon juice, honey, and rosemary. Pour the dressing over chicken mixture; toss gently to coat. Cover and chill for up to 24 hours. Serve the salad on lettuce leaves.

Makes 4 servings

Nutrition Facts per serving: 466 cal., 30 g total fat (6 g sat. fat), 76 mg chol., 191 mg sodium, 30 g carbo., 4 g fiber, 22 g pro.

CHICKEN AND PASTA SALAD

Chicken teamed with fresh fruit, water chestnuts, and bottled dressing is an easy, ready-when-you-are salad.

Prep: 30 minutes   Chill: 4 to 24 hours

1½	**cups dried radiatore, mostaccioli, tirali, and/or medium shell pasta**
3	**cups chopped cooked chicken (15 ounces)**
3	**cups seedless grapes, halved**
1½	**cups halved small strawberries**
1	**8-ounce can sliced water chestnuts, drained**
⅔	**cup bottled cucumber ranch salad dressing**
⅛	**teaspoon cayenne pepper**
1	**to 2 tablespoons milk (optional)**
	Leaf lettuce
	Sliced almonds, toasted (optional)

1 Cook pasta according to package directions. Drain pasta. Rinse with cold water. Drain again.

2 In a large bowl combine chicken, pasta, grapes, strawberries, and water chestnuts; toss to mix.

3 For dressing, in a small bowl stir together salad dressing and pepper. Pour dressing over chicken mixture. Toss lightly to coat. Cover and chill in the refrigerator for 4 to 24 hours.

4 Before serving, if necessary, stir in enough milk (1 to 2 tablespoons) to moisten. Serve salad on lettuce. If desired, sprinkle with almonds.

Makes 6 servings

Nutrition Facts per serving: 455 cal., 20 g total fat (3 g sat. fat), 67 mg chol., 269 mg sodium, 43 g carbo., 3 g fiber, 27 g pro.

TURKEY PAELLA SALAD

This colorful salad starts with a package of saffron-flavored yellow rice mix.

Prep: 40 minutes   Chill: 2 to 24 hours

I	**8-ounce package saffron-flavored yellow rice mix**
2	**to 3 cups chopped cooked turkey (10 to 15 ounces)**
I	**cup chopped tomatoes (2 medium)**
I	**cup packaged fresh broccoli florets or frozen baby sweet peas**
I	**medium red or yellow sweet pepper, chopped (¾ cup)**
⅓	**cup dried cranberries or golden raisins**
2	**green onions, sliced (¼ cup)**
2	**ounces prosciutto, crisp-cooked,* or cooked ham, cut into thin strips**
¾	**cup bottled vinaigrette salad dressing**
⅓	**cup sliced almonds, toasted**
2	**tablespoons snipped fresh basil or tiny fresh basil leaves**

1 Prepare rice according to package directions. Spread cooked rice on a baking sheet. Cover and chill in the refrigerator about 20 minutes or until cool.

2 In an extra-large bowl combine turkey, tomatoes, broccoli, sweet pepper, cranberries, green onions, and prosciutto. Add rice and salad dressing; toss to mix. Cover and chill in the refrigerator for 2 to 24 hours. Sprinkle individual servings with almonds and basil.

Makes 6 (1 ½-cup) servings

Nutrition Facts per serving: 433 cal., 24 g total fat (4 g sat. fat), 25 mg chol., 846 mg sodium, 42 g carbo., 6 g fiber, 15 g pro.

*__NOTE:__ To crisp-cook prosciutto, arrange slices in a single layer on a parchment paper–lined baking sheet. Bake in a 450°F oven for 6 to 8 minutes or until brown and crisp. Remove and cool on the baking sheet.

CABBAGE AND CHICKEN SALAD

Try this refreshing salad as a take-along lunch. The night before, stir-fry cut-up chicken and toss with coleslaw mix, a few other crisp veggies, and Asian salad dressing. Pack in individual containers for toting.

Chill: up to 24 hours   Start to Finish: 25 minutes

- 1 **pound skinless, boneless chicken breast halves**
- 1 **tablespoon cooking oil**
- 1 **16-ounce package shredded cabbage with carrot (coleslaw mix)**
- 1 **medium red or yellow sweet pepper, chopped (¾ cup)**
- 4 **green onions, thinly sliced (½ cup)**
- ½ **cup bottled Chinese chicken salad dressing or Asian salad dressing**
- 1 **tablespoon finely shredded lemon peel**
- ¼ **teaspoon ground black pepper**
- ⅓ **cup sliced almonds, toasted, or chow mein noodles**

1 Cut chicken into thin bite-size strips. In a wok or a very large skillet heat oil over medium-high heat. Add chicken. Stir-fry for 2 to 3 minutes or until no pink remains. Remove from wok. Cool chicken slightly.

2 In an extra-large bowl combine chicken, cabbage, sweet pepper, and green onions. In a small bowl combine salad dressing, lemon peel, and pepper. Pour dressing mixture over cabbage mixture; toss to coat. Cover and chill for up to 24 hours. Sprinkle with almonds before serving.

Makes 6 servings

Nutrition Facts per serving: 248 cal., 12 g total fat (2 g sat. fat), 44 mg chol., 175 mg sodium, 13 g carbo., 3 g fiber, 21 g pro.

CHILI-CHEESE HOAGIES

For the bold among us, serve these crowd-pleasing hoagies with pickled jalapeño peppers on the side.

Prep: 35 minutes   **Bake:** 35 minutes   **Cool:** 30 minutes   **Chill:** 2 to 24 hours   **Oven:** 375°F

- 1   pound lean ground beef
- 1   large onion, chopped (1 cup)
- 2   small green and/or red sweet peppers, chopped (1 cup)
- 1   teaspoon bottled minced garlic (2 cloves)
- 1   14.5-ounce can diced tomatoes for chili, undrained
- ½   teaspoon ground cumin (optional)
- ¼   teaspoon ground black pepper
- 8   hoagie buns or French-style rolls
- 8   thin slices Monterey Jack cheese or Monterey Jack cheese with jalapeño peppers (8 ounces)
- 8   thin slices cheddar cheese (8 ounces)
     Pickled jalapeño chile peppers (optional)

1 In a large skillet cook ground beef, onion, sweet peppers, and garlic over medium heat until meat is brown. Drain off fat. Add undrained tomatoes, cumin (if desired), and black pepper. Bring to boiling; reduce heat. Simmer, uncovered, about 15 minutes or until thick, stirring occasionally. Cool the mixture for 30 minutes or chill in the refrigerator until ready to assemble the sandwiches.

2 Split buns lengthwise. Hollow out bun bottoms leaving a ¼-inch-thick shell. Place a slice of Monterey Jack cheese, cut to fit, on bottom half of bun. Spoon meat mixture on top of cheese. Place a slice of cheddar cheese on top of meat. If desired, sprinkle with pickled jalapeño peppers. Top with bun top. Repeat with remaining buns. Wrap each bun in parchment paper, then in foil. Chill in the refrigerator for 2 to 24 hours.

3 To serve, preheat oven to 375°F. Place wrapped sandwiches on a baking sheet. Bake for 35 to 40 minutes or until cheese is melted and filling is hot.

Makes 8 sandwiches

Nutrition Facts per sandwich: 738 cal., 31 g total fat (15 g sat. fat), 91 mg chol., 1274 mg sodium, 79 g carbo., 5 g fiber, 36 g pro.

LAHVOSH ROLL

Lahvosh, which looks like a giant crisp cracker, is softened before using.
You may be able to find the presoftened variety and skip a step.

Prep: 20 minutes   **Stand:** 1 hour   **Chill:** 2 to 24 hours

1   **15-inch sesame seed Armenian cracker bread (lahvosh) or two 10-inch flour tortillas**

½   **of an 8-ounce tub cream cheese with chives and onion**

2   **marinated artichoke hearts, drained and chopped (¼ cup)**

2   **tablespoons diced pimiento**

1   **teaspoon dried oregano, crushed**

6   **ounces thinly sliced prosciutto or cooked ham**

4   **ounces sliced provolone cheese**

1   **large romaine lettuce leaf, rib removed**

1 If using lahvosh, dampen both sides of lahvosh by holding it briefly under gently running cold water. Place lahvosh, sesame side down, between two damp clean kitchen towels. Let stand about 1 hour or until soft.

2 In a small bowl stir together cream cheese, artichoke hearts, pimiento, and oregano. Remove top towel from lahvosh. Spread lahvosh with cream cheese mixture. Arrange prosciutto over cream cheese. Place provolone cheese slices in center and lettuce leaf next to cheese. Roll from lettuce edge, using the towel to lift and roll the bread. (Or, if using tortillas, spread tortillas with cream cheese mixture. Divide remaining ingredients between the tortillas. Roll up tortillas.)

3 Wrap roll(s) in plastic wrap. Chill in the refrigerator, seam side(s) down, for 2 to 24 hours. To serve, cut into 1-inch slices.

Makes 6 servings

Nutrition Facts per serving: 299 cal., 16 g total fat (9 g sat. fat), 51 mg chol., 1202 mg sodium, 21 g carbo., 0 g fiber, 16 g pro.

SIZZLING BEEF SALAD

Pungent red chile paste and hoisin sauce add an Asian accent to beef. Look for both products in the Asian foods section of your supermarket. Pictured on page 263.

Prep: 20 minutes   **Grill:** 14 minutes   **Marinate:** 4 to 24 hours

12   **ounces boneless beef top sirloin steak, cut 1 inch thick**

      Salt

1   **tablespoon purchased red chile paste (sambal)**

⅓   **cup lime juice**

3   **tablespoons cooking oil**

2   **tablespoons bottled hoisin sauce**

6   **cups shredded romaine**

1   **medium fresh papaya, seeded, peeled, and sliced**

2   **tablespoons chopped honey-roasted peanuts**

1 Sprinkle both sides of meat lightly with salt. Spread one or both sides of steak with chile paste. Place steak in a resealable plastic bag set in a shallow dish. Seal bag. Marinate in the refrigerator for 4 to 24 hours.

2 For a charcoal grill, grill steak on the rack of an uncovered grill directly over medium coals until desired doneness, turning once halfway through grilling. Allow 14 to 18 minutes for medium-rare doneness (145°F) or 18 to 22 minutes for medium doneness (160°F). (For a gas grill, preheat grill. Reduce heat to medium. Place steaks on grill rack over heat. Cover and grill as above.)

3 Meanwhile, for dressing, in a screw-top jar combine lime juice, oil, and hoisin sauce. Cover and shake well. Arrange romaine on 4 dinner plates. Thinly slice steak. Arrange steak slices on romaine; add papaya. Drizzle with dressing; sprinkle with peanuts.

Makes 4 servings

Nutrition Facts per serving: 287 cal., 16 g total fat (3 g sat. fat), 36 mg chol., 366 mg sodium, 16 g carbo., 4 g fiber, 21 g pro.

FAJITA-STYLE FLANK STEAK

A good long soak in this lime-salsa marinade will make a semitough cut of beef, such as flank steak, tender and terrific.

Prep: 15 minutes   Broil: 15 minutes   Marinate: 8 to 24 hours

1   1½-pound beef flank steak
¼   cup bottled Italian salad dressing
¼   cup bottled salsa
½   teaspoon finely shredded lime peel
1   tablespoon lime juice
1   tablespoon snipped fresh cilantro or parsley
⅛   teaspoon bottled hot pepper sauce

1 Trim fat from steak. Place steak in a resealable plastic bag set in a shallow dish. For marinade, in a small bowl stir together salad dressing, salsa, lime peel, lime juice, cilantro, and hot pepper sauce. Pour over steak; seal bag. Marinate in the refrigerator for 8 to 24 hours, turning the bag occasionally.

2 Preheat broiler. Drain steak, reserving marinade. Place steak on the unheated rack of a broiler pan. Broil 3 to 4 inches from the heat for 15 to 18 minutes for medium doneness (160°F), turning once and brushing occasionally with marinade up to the last 5 minutes of broiling.

3 Pour any remaining marinade into a small saucepan; bring to boiling. Boil for 1 minute. Thinly slice steak across the grain. Serve steak with hot marinade.

Makes 6 servings

Nutrition Facts per serving: 208 cal., 11 g total fat (4 g sat. fat), 40 mg chol., 288 mg sodium, 2 g carbo., 0 g fiber, 24 g pro.

BEEF STEAK IN THAI MARINADE

Thai red curry paste, unsweetened coconut milk, and fish sauce are available in the Asian foods section of most grocery stores. The curry paste and fish sauce will keep for months in the refrigerator. Pictured on page 264.

Prep: 15 minutes   Grill: 14 minutes   Marinate: 4 to 24 hours

1¼ **pounds boneless beef top sirloin steak, cut 1 inch thick**

¼ **cup unsweetened coconut milk**

4 **teaspoons lime juice**

1 **to 2 tablespoons red curry paste**

1 **tablespoon soy sauce**

1 **teaspoon sugar**

¼ **of a stalk lemongrass, trimmed and coarsely chopped, or ⅛ teaspoon finely shredded lemon peel**

Hot cooked rice (optional)

1 Trim fat from steak. Place steak in a resealable plastic bag set in a shallow dish.

2 For marinade, in a food processor or blender combine coconut milk, lime juice, red curry paste, soy sauce, sugar, and lemongrass. Cover and process or blend until smooth. Pour over meat; seal bag. Marinate in the refrigerator for 4 to 24 hours, turning bag occasionally. Drain steak, reserving marinade.

3 For a charcoal grill, grill steak on the rack of an uncovered grill directly over medium coals until desired doneness, turning and brushing once with reserved marinade halfway through grilling. Allow 14 to 18 minutes for medium-rare doneness (145°F) or 18 to 22 minutes for medium doneness (160°F). (For a gas grill, preheat grill. Reduce heat to medium. Place steak on grill rack over heat. Cover and grill as above.) Discard any remaining marinade. Thinly slice steak across the grain. If desired, serve steak with hot cooked rice.

Makes 4 servings

Nutrition Facts per serving: 209 cal., 8 g total fat (3 g sat. fat), 86 mg chol., 339 mg sodium, 2 g carbo., 0 g fiber, 30 g pro.

STEAKS WITH PINEAPPLE-TERIYAKI SAUCE

Japanese teriyaki sauce is a natural partner for sweet pineapple. Try the Pineapple-Teriyaki Sauce with chicken and pork, too.

Prep: 15 minutes   Broil: 12 minutes   Marinate: 6 to 24 hours

1½ **to 2 pounds boneless beef top loin steaks, cut 1 inch thick**

¼   **cup bottled teriyaki sauce**

¼   **cup water**

1   **green onion, finely chopped (2 tablespoons)**

1   **teaspoon bottled minced garlic (2 cloves)**

1   **teaspoon grated fresh ginger**

1   **recipe Pineapple-Teriyaki Sauce**

1 Trim fat from steaks. Please steaks in a resealable plastic bag set in a shallow dish.

2 For marinade, in a small bowl stir together teriyaki sauce, water, green onion, garlic, and ginger. Pour marinade over steak; seal bag. Marinate in the refrigerator for 6 to 24 hours, turning bag occasionally.

3 Preheat broiler. Drain steaks, discarding the marinade. Place steaks on the unheated rack of a broiler pan. Broil 4 to 5 inches from heat for 12 to 14 minutes for medium-rare (145°F) or 15 to 18 minutes total for medium (160°F), turning once halfway through broiling. Cut steaks into serving-size pieces. Serve with Pineapple-Teriyaki Sauce.

Makes 6 to 8 servings

Nutrition Facts per serving: 202 cal., 6 g total fat (2 g sat. fat), 60 mg chol., 757 mg sodium, 10 g carbo., 1 g fiber, 28 g pro.

Pineapple-Teriyaki Sauce: In a small saucepan combine one 8-ounce can crushed pineapple (juice pack); ¼ cup finely chopped red sweet pepper; 1 green onion, chopped (2 tablespoons); 2 tablespoons bottled teriyaki sauce; 1 teaspoon bottled minced garlic (2 cloves); and 1 teaspoon grated fresh ginger. Heat through.

ASIAN-MARINATED PORK TENDERLOIN

Keep pork tenderloin in mind when you have the yen for roasted meat.
This tender cut needs only about a half-hour to roast.

Prep: 15 minutes   Roast: 25 minutes   Stand: 10 minutes   Marinate: 2 to 24 hours   Oven: 425°F

- 1 **1-pound pork tenderloin**
- ¼ **cup chicken broth**
- 2 **tablespoons rice vinegar**
- 2 **tablespoons reduced-sodium soy sauce**
- 2 **green onions, sliced (¼ cup)**
- 2 **teaspoons sugar**
- 2 **teaspoons sesame seeds**
- 2 **teaspoons grated fresh ginger**
- 1½ **teaspoons bottled minced garlic (3 cloves)**
- ½ **teaspoon ground black pepper**

1 Trim fat from meat. Place meat in a large resealable plastic bag set in a shallow dish. For marinade, in a small bowl stir together chicken broth, vinegar, soy sauce, green onions, sugar, sesame seeds, ginger, garlic, and pepper. Pour over meat; seal bag. Turn to coat meat. Marinate in the refrigerator for 2 to 24 hours, turning bag occasionally.

2 Preheat oven to 425°F. Drain meat, discard marinade. Place meat on a rack in a shallow roasting pan. Roast for 25 to 35 minutes or until an instant read thermometer registers 155°F. Cover meat with foil and let stand for 10 minutes. The temperature of the meat after standing should be 160°F. Cut meat into thin slices.

Makes 4 servings

Nutrition Facts per serving: 157 cal., 3 g total fat (1 g sat. fat), 74 mg chol., 410 mg sodium, 5 g carbo., 1 g fiber, 25 g pro.

CURRIED MUSTARD PORK CHOPS

The pork chops marinate in a spunky combo of brown mustard, curry powder, and crushed red pepper.

Prep: 15 minutes   Grill: 30 minutes   Marinate: 6 to 24 hours

- **4   boneless pork loin chops, cut 1 inch thick (about 2 pounds)**
- **½   cup spicy brown mustard**
- **¼   cup chicken broth**
- **1   green onion, sliced (2 tablespoons)**
- **1   tablespoon curry powder**
- **1   tablespoon olive oil**
- **1   tablespoon honey**
- **½   teaspoon bottled minced garlic (1 clove)**
- **¼   to ½ teaspoon crushed red pepper**
- **Snipped fresh parsley (optional)**

1 Trim fat from chops. Place chops in a resealable plastic bag set in a shallow dish. For marinade, in a small bowl combine mustard, chicken broth, green onion, curry powder, oil, honey, garlic, and crushed red pepper. Pour marinade over chops; seal bag. Turn to coat. Marinate in the refrigerator for 6 to 24 hours, turning occasionally.

2 Drain pork, discarding marinade. For a charcoal grill, arrange medium-high coals around a drip pan. Test for medium heat above the pan. Place chops on a grill rack over the drip pan. Cover and grill for 30 to 35 minutes or until chops are slightly pink in center and juices run clear (160°F), turning once halfway through grilling. (For a gas grill, preheat grill. Reduce heat to medium. Adjust heat for indirect cooking. Place meat on grill rack. Grill as above.) If desired, sprinkle chops with parsley.

Makes 4 servings

Nutrition Facts per serving: 330 cal., 10 g total fat (3 g sat. fat), 150 mg chol., 382 mg sodium, 3 g carbo., 0 g fiber, 51 g pro.

BEER-GLAZED PORK CHOPS

The German-style seasonings call for hot potato salad or grilled potatoes as an accompaniment. Pictured on page 264.

Prep: 15 minutes   Grill: 30 minutes   Marinate: 6 to 24 hours

4   boneless pork top loin
     chops, cut 1¼ inches thick

1   12-ounce bottle stout
     (dark beer)

¼   cup honey mustard

1½   teaspoons bottled minced
     garlic (3 cloves)

1   teaspoon caraway seeds

1 Trim fat from chops. Place chops in a resealable plastic bag set in a shallow dish. For marinade, in a medium bowl stir together stout, mustard, garlic, and caraway seeds. Pour over chops in bag; seal bag. Turn to coat. Marinate in the refrigerator for 6 to 24 hours, turning bag occasionally.

2 Drain chops; pour marinade into a small saucepan. Bring to boiling; reduce heat. Simmer, uncovered, about 15 minutes or until marinade is reduced by about half.

3 For a charcoal grill, arrange medium-hot coals around a drip pan. Test for medium heat above the pan. Place chops on a grill rack over pan. Cover and grill for 30 to 35 minutes or until chops are slightly pink in center and juices run clear (160°F), turning once halfway through grilling and brushing frequently with marinade during the last 10 minutes of grilling. (For a gas grill, preheat grill. Reduce heat to medium. Adjust for indirect cooking. Place meat on grill rack. Grill as above.) Discard any remaining marinade.

Makes 4 servings

Nutrition Facts per serving: 194 cal., 3 g total fat (1 g sat. fat), 61 mg chol., 63 mg sodium, 11 g carbo., 0 g fiber, 21 g pro.

ALOHA CHICKEN

The five-ingredient marinade gives island-style flavor to the chicken.
Continue the theme and serve with fresh pineapple slices.

Prep: 15 minutes   Grill: 50 minutes   Marinate: 4 to 24 hours

- **6   chicken breast halves**
- **⅓   cup soy sauce**
- **¼   cup packed brown sugar**
- **2   green onions, sliced (¼ cup)**
- **2   tablespoons grated fresh ginger**
- **2   teaspoons bottled minced garlic (4 cloves)**

1 If desired, remove skin from chicken. Place chicken in a resealable plastic bag set in a shallow dish. For marinade, in a small bowl combine soy sauce, brown sugar, green onions, ginger, and garlic. Pour marinade over chicken. Seal bag; turn to coat chicken. Marinate in the refrigerator for 4 to 24 hours, turning bag occasionally.

2 Drain chicken, discarding marinade. For a charcoal grill, arrange medium-hot coals around a drip pan. Test for medium heat above the pan. Place chicken, bone sides down, on a grill rack over the drip pan. Cover and grill for 50 to 60 minutes or until chicken is no longer pink (170°F). (For a gas grill, preheat grill. Reduce heat to medium. Adjust for indirect cooking. Place chicken on grill rack. Grill as above.)

Makes 6 servings

Nutrition Facts per serving: 466 cal., 22 g total fat (6 g sat. fat), 155 mg chol., 1273 mg sodium, 11 g carbo., 0 g fiber, 52 g pro.

BAKED ZITI

To complete your meal, open a bag of mixed salad greens and warm a loaf of crusty bread in the oven.

Prep: 30 minutes   Bake: 60 minutes   Stand: 10 minutes   Oven: 375°F

- 1   **pound package dried ziti**
- 1   **large red or green sweet pepper, chopped (1 cup)**
- 1   **15-ounce carton low-fat ricotta cheese**
- 1   **8-ounce package shredded mozzarella cheese (2 cups)**
- 1   **3.5-ounce package sliced pepperoni, quartered**
- ½   **teaspoon salt**
- ½   **teaspoon dried basil, crushed**
- ¼   **teaspoon ground black pepper**
- ¼   **cup grated Parmesan cheese**
- 1   **24- to 26-ounce jar marinara sauce**
- 1   **28-ounce can whole peeled tomatoes in puree**
-     **Nonstick cooking spray**

1 Bring a large pot of salted water to boiling. Add ziti; cook for 5 minutes. Add sweet pepper; cook for 4 minutes. Drain; rinse with cool water. Transfer to a very large bowl.

2 In medium bowl mix ricotta cheese, half of the mozzarella cheese, the pepperoni, salt, basil, black pepper, and 3 tablespoons of the Parmesan cheese. Add to ziti mixture; stir to combine. Stir in half of the marinara sauce and half of the tomatoes.

3 Lightly coat a 3- to 3½-quart rectangular or oval baking dish with cooking spray. Transfer pasta mixture to prepared dish. Combine remaining marinara sauce and tomatoes; spoon over ziti mixture. Sprinkle with remaining mozzarella cheese and remaining Parmesan cheese. Cover with plastic wrap. Refrigerate overnight.

4 Preheat oven to 375°F. Remove and discard plastic wrap; cover baking dish with foil. Bake for 45 minutes; uncover and bake for 15 to 20 minutes more or until heated through. Let stand 10 minutes before serving.

Makes 8 servings

Nutrition Facts per serving: 530 cal., 19 g total fat (9 g sat. fat), 49 mg chol., 1093 mg sodium, 64 g carbo., 4 g fiber, 27 g pro.

TO SERVE RIGHT AWAY: Preheat oven to 375°F. Cover baking dish with foil. Bake for 30 minutes. Uncover and bake for 10 to 15 minutes or until heated through. Let stand for 10 minutes before serving.

BAKED BEEF RAVIOLI

Tomato soup yields a pleasing sweetness to this dish, made extra lush with mozzarella and Parmesan cheeses.

Prep: 20 minutes   Bake: 40 minutes   Chill: up to 24 hours   Oven: 350°F

2	**9-ounce packages refrigerated cheese-filled ravioli**
1½	**pounds lean ground beef**
1	**large onion, chopped (1 cup)**
1	**tablespoon bottled minced garlic (6 cloves)**
1	**14-ounce can no-salt-added diced tomatoes, undrained**
1	**10.75-ounce can reduced-fat and reduced-sodium condensed tomato soup**
1½	**teaspoons dried Italian seasoning, crushed**
	Nonstick cooking spray
1	**cup shredded mozzarella cheese (4 ounces)**
½	**cup finely shredded Parmesan cheese (2 ounces)**

1 Cook ravioli according to package directions; drain and return to pan.

2 Meanwhile, in a large skillet cook ground beef, onion, and garlic until meat is brown and onion is tender. Drain off fat. Stir undrained tomatoes, tomato soup, and Italian seasoning into meat mixture in skillet. Gently stir into cooked ravioli. Lightly coat a 3-quart rectangular baking dish with cooking spray. Spread mixture in the prepared dish. Sprinkle with mozzarella cheese and Parmesan cheese. Cover with plastic wrap. Chill in the refrigerator up to 24 hours.

3 To serve, preheat oven to 350°F. Remove and discard plastic wrap; cover baking dish with foil. Bake for 25 minutes. Uncover and bake for 15 to 20 minutes more or until heated through.

Makes 8 to 10 servings

Nutrition Facts per serving: 524 cal., 30 g total fat (13 g sat. fat), 111 mg chol., 533 mg sodium, 35 g carbo., 3 g fiber, 29 g pro.

TO SERVE RIGHT AWAY: Preheat oven to 375°F. Bake, uncovered, about 20 minutes or until heated through.

BEAN-AND-BEEF ENCHILADA CASSEROLE

This hearty casserole is the perfect dish to gather the family around the table. Consider it comfort food with a south-of-the-border twist. Pictured on page 265.

Prep: 25 minutes   Bake: 40 minutes   Chill: up to 24 hours   Oven: 350°F

8   **ounces lean ground beef**

1   **medium onion, chopped (½ cup)**

1   **teaspoon chili powder**

½   **teaspoon ground cumin**

1   **15-ounce can pinto beans, rinsed and drained**

1   **4-ounce can diced green chile peppers, undrained**

1   **8-ounce carton dairy sour cream or light dairy sour cream**

2   **tablespoons all-purpose flour**

¼   **teaspoon garlic powder**

8   **6-inch corn tortillas**

1   **10-ounce can enchilada sauce or one 10.5-ounce can tomato puree**

1   **cup shredded cheddar cheese (4 ounces)**

1 In a large skillet cook ground beef, onion, chili powder, and cumin over medium heat until onion is tender and meat is no longer pink. Drain off fat. Stir in pinto beans and undrained chile peppers; set aside.

2 In a small mixing bowl stir together sour cream, flour, and garlic powder; set aside.

3 Place half of the tortillas in the bottom of a lightly greased 2-quart rectangular baking dish, cutting to fit if necessary. Top with half of the meat mixture, half of the sour cream mixture, half of the enchilada sauce, and ½ cup cheese. Repeat layers, except reserve remaining ½ cup cheese. Cover dish with plastic wrap; chill in refrigerator for up to 24 hours.

4 To serve, preheat oven to 350°F. Remove and discard plastic wrap. Cover dish with foil. Bake for 35 to 40 minutes or until bubbly. Sprinkle with remaining ½ cup cheese. Bake, uncovered, about 5 minutes more or until cheese melts.

Makes 6 servings

Nutrition Facts per serving: 429 cal., 24 g total fat (12 g sat. fat), 64 mg chol., 632 mg sodium, 36 g carbo., 6 g fiber, 19 g pro.

TO SERVE RIGHT AWAY: Preheat oven to 350°F. Bake as directed.

BAKED ROTINI WITH HAM

This creamy, colorful dish goes together so easily that you may choose to make it and serve right away instead of later. Either way, it's guaranteed good eating. Pictured on page 265.

Prep: 25 minutes   Bake: 25 minutes   Stand: 10 minutes   Chill: up to 24 hours   Oven: 350°F

8   **ounces dried tri-color rotini (3 cups)**

1   **16- to 17-ounce jar Alfredo pasta sauce**

½   **cup milk**

½   **cup shredded mozzarella cheese (2 ounces)**

½   **cup chopped cooked ham (2 ounces)**

1   **teaspoon dried Italian seasoning, crushed**

⅛   **teaspoon ground black pepper**

¼   **cup grated Parmesan cheese**

1 Cook rotini according to package directions; drain and return to pan. Stir in Alfredo sauce, milk, mozzarella cheese, ham, Italian seasoning, and pepper.

2 Transfer rotini mixture to four 7- to 8-ounce individual au gratin dishes or ramekins or a 1½-quart au gratin dish. Sprinkle with Parmesan cheese. Cover with plastic wrap and chill for up to 24 hours.

3 To serve, preheat oven to 350°F. Remove and discard plastic wrap. Cover with foil. Bake for 25 to 30 minutes for the individual dishes, or about 45 minutes for the large dish, or until mixture is heated through. Let stand for 10 minutes. Stir before serving.

Makes 4 servings

Nutrition Facts per serving: 503 cal., 28 g total fat (13 g sat. fat), 121 mg chol., 1084 mg sodium, 51 g carbo., 2 g fiber, 20 g pro.

TO SERVE RIGHT AWAY: After assembling casserole(s), cover with foil. Preheat oven to 350°F. Bake as directed.

MUSTARD CRISP CHICKEN

Coat the chicken in the delicious mustard-thyme mixture in the morning, then pop it in the oven as soon as you get home.

Prep: 15 minutes   Bake: 40 minutes   Chill: up to 24 hours   Oven: 375°F

2½   **to 2¾ pounds meaty chicken pieces**

¼   **cup Dijon-style mustard**

2   **tablespoons water**

2   **teaspoons snipped fresh thyme or ¾ teaspoon dried thyme, crushed**

½   **teaspoon bottled minced garlic (1 clove)**

¼   **teaspoon ground black pepper**

¼   **teaspoon paprika**

¾   **cup fine dry bread crumbs**

2   **tablespoons butter, melted**

1 Remove skin from chicken; set chicken aside. In a large bowl or shallow dish combine mustard, water, thyme, garlic, pepper, and paprika. Place bread crumbs in another bowl. Coat chicken with mustard mixture, allowing excess to drip off, then roll in the bread crumbs.

2 Place chicken in a baking dish; cover with plastic wrap. Chill in the refrigerator for up to 24 hours.

3 To bake, preheat oven to 375°F. Arrange chicken in a foil-lined 15×10×1-inch baking pan so pieces do not touch. Drizzle with melted butter. Bake chicken, uncovered, for 40 to 50 minutes or until golden and an instant-read thermometer inserted in chicken registers 170°F for breasts or 180°F for drumsticks or thighs. Do not turn chicken.

Makes 4 to 6 servings

Nutrition Facts per serving: 466 cal., 16 g total fat (4 g sat. fat), 198 mg chol., 725 mg sodium, 13 g carbo., 1 g fiber, 63 g pro.

TO SERVE RIGHT AWAY: Preheat oven to 375°F. Prepare as directed through step 1. Arrange crumb-coated chicken pieces on foil-lined 15×10×1-inch baking pan so the pieces do not touch. Drizzle chicken with melted butter. Bake chicken, uncovered, for 40 to 50 minutes or until golden and an instant-read thermometer inserted in chicken registers 170°F for breasts or 180°F for drumsticks or thighs. Do not turn chicken.

TEX-MEX CHICKEN 'N' RICE CASSEROLE

A package of rice and vermicelli mix gets the flavors hopping in this crowd pleaser. The supportive cast of ingredients, including chile peppers, chili powder, and cumin, contribute to the potent Tex-Mex flavor.

Prep: 30 minutes   Bake: 40 minutes   Stand: 5 minutes   Chill: up to 24 hours   Oven: 425°F

- 1 **tablespoon olive oil**
- 1 **medium onion, chopped (½ cup)**
- 1 **6.9-ounce package chicken-flavor rice and vermicelli mix**
- 1 **14-ounce can chicken broth**
- 2 **cups water**
- 2 **cups chopped cooked chicken (10 ounces)**
- 2 **medium tomatoes, seeded and chopped (1 cup)**
- 3 **tablespoons canned diced green chile peppers, drained**
- 1 **teaspoon dried basil, crushed**
- 1½ **teaspoons chili powder**
- ⅛ **teaspoon ground cumin**
- ⅛ **teaspoon ground black pepper**
- ½ **cup shredded cheddar cheese (2 ounces)**

1 In a medium saucepan heat oil over medium heat. Add onion and cook until tender. Stir in rice and vermicelli mix (including seasoning packet). Cook and stir for 2 minutes. Stir in chicken broth and water. Bring to boiling; reduce heat. Cover and simmer for 20 minutes (liquid will not be fully absorbed).

2 Transfer the rice mixture to a large bowl. Stir in chicken, tomatoes, chile peppers, basil, chili powder, cumin, and black pepper. Transfer to an ungreased 2-quart casserole; cover with plastic wrap. Chill casserole in the refrigerator for up to 24 hours.

3 To serve, preheat oven to 425°F. Remove and discard plastic wrap. Bake casserole, covered with lid or foil, about 40 minutes or until heated through. Uncover and sprinkle with cheese. Let stand for 5 minutes before serving.

Makes 6 servings

Nutrition Facts per serving: 323 cal., 14 g total fat (4 g sat. fat), 53 mg chol., 971 mg sodium, 30 g carbo., 2 g fiber, 21 g pro.

TO SERVE RIGHT AWAY: Preheat oven to 425°F. Cover casserole with lid or foil and bake for 25 minutes. Sprinkle with cheese. Let stand for 5 minutes before serving.

CHICKEN, WILD RICE, AND VEGETABLE CASSEROLE

This stick-to-the-ribs casserole makes perfect potluck fare. Serving chicken in chunks rather than whole breasts makes it easy for diners to take just a spoonful. Don't be surprised, however, if they come back for more.

Prep: 25 minutes   **Bake:** 1 hour   **Cook:** 25 minutes   **Chill:** up to 24 hours   **Oven:** 350°F

- 1 **6-ounce package long grain and wild rice mix**
- 3 **cups bite-size pieces cooked chicken (about 1 pound)**
- 2 **cups frozen French-cut green beans, thawed**
- 1 **10.75-ounce can condensed cream of celery soup**
- 1 **8-ounce can sliced water chestnuts, drained**
- ½ **cup mayonnaise or salad dressing**
- 1 **medium onion, chopped (½ cup)**
- 3 **tablespoons sliced almonds**
- 1 **2-ounce jar sliced pimientos, drained**
- 1 **tablespoon lemon juice**
- 1 **cup shredded cheddar cheese (4 ounces)**

1 Cook rice mix according to package directions.

2 Meanwhile, in an extra-large bowl combine chicken, green beans, soup, drained water chestnuts, mayonnaise, onion, almonds, pimientos, and lemon juice. Stir in cooked rice mixture. Transfer to an ungreased 3-quart rectangular baking dish. Cover baking dish with foil. Chill casserole in the refrigerator for up to 24 hours.

3 To serve, preheat oven to 350°F. Bake, covered, for 55 minutes. Sprinkle with cheese. Bake, uncovered, about 5 minutes more or until heated through and cheese is melted.

Makes 8 servings

Nutrition Facts per serving: 422 cal., 24 g total fat (7 g sat. fat), 68 mg chol., 773 mg sodium, 30 g carbo., 3 g fiber, 23 g pro.

TO SERVE RIGHT AWAY: Preheat oven to 350°F. Cover baking dish with foil. Bake for 30 minutes. Sprinkle with cheese. Bake, uncovered, about 5 minutes more or until heated through and cheese is melted.

ARTICHOKE-TURKEY CASSEROLE

A poultry-rice bake is a handy way to use leftover chicken or turkey. This recipe adds a few flavor flourishes with artichokes and crisp, crumbled bacon.

Prep: 20 minutes   Bake: 50 minutes   Stand: 10 minutes   Chill: up to 24 hours   Oven: 350°F

  1 medium carrot, chopped (½ cup)

  1 small red sweet pepper, seeded and chopped (½ cup)

  2 green onions, sliced (¼ cup)

  1 tablespoon butter

  1 10.75-ounce can condensed cream of chicken soup

  1 8- to 9-ounce package frozen artichoke hearts, thawed and cut up

  1½ cups chopped cooked turkey or chicken (about 8 ounces)

  1 cup cooked white rice or wild rice

  ⅔ cup milk

  ½ cup shredded mozzarella cheese (2 ounces)

  2 slices bacon, crisp-cooked, drained, and crumbled

  ½ teaspoon dried thyme, crushed

  3 tablespoons grated Parmesan cheese

1 In a large skillet cook carrot, sweet pepper, and green onions in hot butter over medium heat until carrot is crisp-tender. Remove from heat and stir in soup, artichoke hearts, turkey, rice, milk, mozzarella cheese, bacon, and thyme. Transfer to an ungreased 2-quart rectangular baking dish. Sprinkle with Parmesan cheese.

2 Cover casserole with plastic wrap. Chill in the refrigerator for up 24 hours.

3 To serve, preheat oven to 350°F. Remove and discard plastic wrap. Cover casserole with foil. Bake, covered, for 30 minutes. Uncover and bake about 20 minutes more or until bubbly. Let stand 10 minutes before serving.

Makes 6 servings

Nutrition Facts per serving: 248 cal., 11 g total fat (5 g sat. fat), 47 mg chol., 611 mg sodium, 18 g carbo., 3 g fiber, 18 g pro.

TO SERVE RIGHT AWAY: Preheat oven to 350°F. Cover casserole with foil. Bake for 20 minutes. Uncover and bake about 20 minutes more or until bubbly. Let stand for 10 minutes before serving.

TURKEY MANICOTTI
WITH CHIVE CREAM SAUCE

A simple cream cheese sauce makes this dish—large pasta shells stuffed with a blend of chopped cooked turkey and broccoli—elegant enough to serve to visitors.

Prep: 30 minutes **Bake: 35 minutes** **Chill: up to 24 hours** **Oven: 350°F**

12 **dried manicotti shells**

1 **8-ounce tub cream cheese spread with chive and onion**

⅔ **cup milk**

¼ **cup grated Romano or Parmesan cheese**

2 **cups chopped cooked turkey (10 ounces)**

1 **10-ounce package frozen chopped broccoli, thawed and drained**

1 **4-ounce jar diced pimientos, drained**

¼ **teaspoon ground black pepper**

Grated Romano or Parmesan cheese (optional)

1 Cook manicotti shells according to package directions; drain. Rinse with cold water; drain again. Meanwhile, for sauce, in a heavy, small saucepan heat cream cheese over medium-low heat until melted, stirring constantly. Slowly stir in milk until smooth. Stir in the ¼ cup Romano cheese.

2 For filling, in a medium bowl combine ¾ cup of the sauce, the turkey, broccoli, pimientos, and pepper.

3 Using a small spoon, carefully fill each manicotti shell with about ⅓ cup filling. Arrange filled shells in a 3-quart rectangular baking dish. Pour remaining sauce over shells. Cover casserole with plastic wrap. Chill in the refrigerator for up to 24 hours.

4 To serve, preheat oven to 350°F. Remove and discard plastic wrap. Cover casserole with foil. Bake for 35 to 40 minutes or until heated through. If desired, sprinkle with additional Romano cheese.

Makes 6 servings

Nutrition Facts per serving: 381 cal., 17 g total fat (10 g sat. fat), 78 mg chol., 256 mg sodium, 32 g carbo., 3 g fiber, 22 g pro.

TO SERVE RIGHT AWAY: Preheat oven to 350°F. Cover baking dish with foil. Bake for 25 to 30 minutes or until heated through. If desired, sprinkle with additional Romano cheese.

MEDITERRANEAN TUNA CASSEROLE

This is not your mother's tuna casserole. Italian-style ingredients—artichoke hearts, dried tomatoes, olives, and mozzarella cheese—give it a worldly update.

Prep: 25 minutes   Bake: 50 minutes   Stand: 10 minutes   Chill: up to 24 hours   Oven: 350°F

4   **ounces dried fettuccine, broken**

1   **tablespoon butter**

¼   **cup chopped onion**

1   **10.75-ounce can condensed cream of chicken soup**

1   **9- to 12-ounce can solid white tuna (water pack), drained and broken into chunks**

1   **8- to 9-ounce package frozen artichoke hearts, thawed and cut up**

⅔   **cup milk**

½   **cup shredded mozzarella cheese (2 ounces)**

3   **tablespoons oil-packed dried tomatoes, drained and snipped**

3   **tablespoons sliced, pitted ripe olives**

½   **teaspoon dried thyme, crushed**

3   **tablespoons grated Parmesan cheese**

1 Cook fettuccine according to package directions; drain.

2 Meanwhile, in a large skillet melt butter over medium heat. Add onion; cook until tender. Remove from heat. Stir in soup, tuna, artichoke hearts, milk, mozzarella cheese, dried tomatoes, olives, and thyme. Stir in cooked fettuccine. Transfer to a lightly greased 2-quart rectangular baking dish. Sprinkle with Parmesan cheese. Cover with plastic wrap. Chill in the refrigerator for up to 24 hours.

3 To serve, preheat oven to 350°F. Remove and discard plastic wrap. Cover casserole with foil. Bake for 35 minutes. Uncover and bake about 15 minutes more or until casserole is bubbly. Let stand for 10 minutes before serving.

Makes 6 servings

Nutrition Facts per serving: 280 cal., 11 g total fat (5 g sat. fat), 37 mg chol., 732 mg sodium, 25 g carbo., 4 g fiber, 19 g pro.

TO SERVE RIGHT AWAY: Preheat oven to 350°F. Cover casserole with foil. Bake for 20 minutes. Uncover and bake about 20 minutes more or until casserole is bubbly. Let stand for 10 minutes before serving.

FLORENTINE LASAGNA

A traditional lasagna in most respects—except for the colorful addition of spinach—this classic Italian casserole will taste great alongside a salad of cooked and chilled green beans tossed with a vinaigrette.

Prep: 25 minutes   Bake: I hour   Stand: 10 minutes   Chill: up to 24 hours   Oven: 375°F

12 **ounces Italian sausage or uncooked turkey Italian sausage**

1 **medium onion, chopped (½ cup)**

1 **14.5-ounce can diced tomatoes, drained**

1 **8-ounce can tomato sauce**

2 **teaspoons dried Italian seasoning, crushed**

6 **dried lasagna noodles (6 ounces)**

1 **egg, lightly beaten**

1 **15-ounce carton ricotta cheese**

⅓ **cup grated Parmesan cheese**

½ **of a 10-ounce package frozen chopped spinach, thawed and drained well**

8 **ounces sliced mozzarella cheese**

1 Remove casings from sausage, if present. For meat sauce, in a medium saucepan cook sausage and onion over medium heat until meat is brown and onion is tender; drain. Stir in drained tomatoes, tomato sauce, and Italian seasoning. Bring to boiling; reduce heat. Simmer, uncovered, for 15 to 20 minutes or until desired consistency.

2 Meanwhile, cook lasagna noodles according to package directions until tender but still firm; drain. Rinse with cold water; drain well. For filling, in a medium bowl combine egg, ricotta cheese, and ¼ cup of the Parmesan cheese. Fold in spinach.

3 Place 3 noodles in bottom of an ungreased 2-quart rectangular baking dish. Spread half of the filling over noodles. Top with half of the meat sauce and half of the mozzarella cheese. Repeat layers. Sprinkle with remaining Parmesan cheese. Cover with plastic wrap and chill for up to 24 hours.

4 To serve, preheat oven to 375°F. Remove and discard plastic wrap. Cover baking dish with foil. Bake for 40 minutes. Uncover and bake about 20 minutes more or until heated through.

Makes 8 servings

Nutrition Facts per serving: 343 cal., 19 g total fat (9 g sat. fat), 87 mg chol., 796 mg sodium, 19 g carbo., 2 g fiber, 24 g pro.

TO SERVE RIGHT AWAY: Preheat oven to 375°F. Bake, uncovered, about 30 minutes or until heated through. Let stand for 10 minutes before serving.

VEGETABLE SHEPHERD'S PIE

A golden mashed-potato crust gives way to a creamy vegetable-filled center in this savory pie. If you're short on prep time, for the potato topper, just stir the thyme, milk, and cheese into refrigerated mashed potatoes (omit the butter and salt).

Prep: 25 minutes   Bake: 1 hour   Cook: 30 minutes   Chill: up to 24 hours   Oven: 350°F

1	**14-ounce can vegetable broth or chicken broth**
¾	**cup water**
1	**cup dry lentils, rinsed and drained**
1½	**teaspoons bottled minced garlic (3 cloves)**
1½	**pounds parsnips or carrots, peeled and cut into ½-inch slices (about 3½ cups)**
6	**purple boiling onions (8 ounces), quartered, or 1 medium red onion, cut into wedges**
1	**14.5-ounce can diced tomatoes with Italian herbs, undrained**
2	**tablespoons tomato paste**
4	**medium potatoes, peeled and cut up**
3	**tablespoons butter**
1	**tablespoon snipped fresh thyme or ½ teaspoon dried thyme, crushed**
½	**teaspoon salt**
¼	**to ⅓ cup milk**
1½	**cups shredded Colby and Monterey Jack or cheddar cheese (6 ounces)**

1 In a large saucepan stir together broth, water, lentils, and garlic. Bring to boiling; reduce heat. Cover and simmer for 20 minutes. Add parsnips and onions. Return to boiling; reduce heat. Cover and simmer for 10 to 15 minutes more or just until vegetables and lentils are tender. Remove from heat. Stir in undrained tomatoes and tomato paste.

2 Meanwhile, in a 2-quart saucepan cook potatoes in lightly salted boiling water for 20 to 25 minutes or until tender; drain. Mash with a potato masher or beat with an electric mixer on low speed. Add butter, thyme, and salt. Gradually beat in enough milk to make light and fluffy. Stir in 1 cup of the cheese until melted.

3 Spread lentil mixture in a 2- to 2½-quart au gratin dish. Spoon potato mixture over lentil mixture. Cover dish with plastic wrap; chill in refrigerator for up to 24 hours.

4 To serve, preheat oven to 350°F. Remove plastic wrap; cover dish with foil. Bake for 50 minutes. Uncover and bake for 10 to 15 minutes more or until heated through. Sprinkle with remaining ½ cup cheese.

Makes 6 servings

Nutrition Facts per serving: 449 cal., 16 g total fat (10 g sat. fat), 42 mg chol., 1,122 mg sodium, 58 g carbo., 17 g fiber, 20 g pro.

TO SERVE RIGHT AWAY: Preheat oven to 350°F. Bake for 30 to 35 minutes or until heated through. Sprinkle with the remaining ½ cup cheese.

BAKED PENNE with MEAT SAUCE

Quick-to-grab ingredients make this hearty pasta dish super easy to put together. Pictured on page 266.

Prep: 30 minutes   Bake: 75 minutes or 50 minutes   Freeze: up to 1 month   Oven: 350°F

8   ounces dried penne

1   14.5-ounce can diced
     tomatoes, undrained

½   of a 6-ounce can (⅓ cup)
     Italian-style tomato paste

⅓   cup dry red wine
     or tomato juice

⅓   cup water

½   teaspoon sugar

½   teaspoon dried oregano,
     crushed, or 2 teaspoons
     snipped fresh oregano

¼   teaspoon salt

¼   teaspoon ground black
     pepper

1   pound lean ground beef

1   medium onion, chopped
     (½ cup)

¼   cup sliced pitted ripe olives

1   cup shredded reduced-fat
     mozzarella cheese
     (4 ounces)

1 Cook pasta according to package directions; drain well.

2 Meanwhile, in a medium bowl stir together undrained tomatoes, tomato paste, wine, water, sugar, dried oregano (if using), salt, and pepper. Set aside.

3 In a large skillet cook ground beef and onion over medium heat until meat is brown. Drain off fat. Stir in tomato mixture. Bring to boiling; reduce heat. Cover and simmer for 10 minutes. Stir in pasta, fresh oregano (if using), and olives.

4 Divide the pasta mixture among six 10- to 12-ounce individual casseroles (or one 3-quart rectangular baking dish*). Cover with freezer wrap, label, and freeze for up to 1 month.

5 To serve, preheat oven to 350°F. Remove freezer wrap; cover each casserole with foil. Bake about 70 minutes or until heated through. Sprinkle with mozzarella cheese. Bake, uncovered, about 5 minutes more or until cheese melts. (Or, thaw casseroles overnight in the refrigerator. Remove freezer wrap; cover each casserole with foil. Bake in a preheated 350°F oven about 45 minutes or until heated through. Sprinkle with cheese and bake about 5 minutes more or until cheese melts.)

Makes 6 servings

Nutrition Facts per serving: 342 cal., 10 g total fat (4 g sat. fat), 51 mg chol., 465 mg sodium, 37 g carbo., 2 g fiber, 22 g pro.

*TO SERVE IN A 3-QUART BAKING DISH: Cover dish with foil. Bake in the 350°F oven about 1½ hours or until heated through, stirring carefully once. Sprinkle with mozzarella cheese. Bake, uncovered, about 5 minutes more or until cheese melts. (Or, thaw baking dish overnight in the refrigerator. Remove freezer wrap; cover baking dish with foil. Bake in a 350°F oven about 55 minutes or until heated through, stirring carefully once. Sprinkle with cheese and bake about 5 minutes more or until cheese melts.)

SHORTCUT LASAGNA

No-boil lasagna noodles simplify the assembly of this family favorite.
Replacing half the ground beef with Italian sausage boosts the flavor.
Choose either sweet or hot sausage. Pictured on page 267.

Prep: 30 minutes   Bake: 40 minutes   Stand: 5 minutes   Freeze: up to 1 month   Oven: 350°F

8   **ounces lean ground beef**

8   **ounces bulk Italian sausage**

1   **26-ounce jar tomato-basil pasta sauce**

1   **egg, lightly beaten**

1   **15-ounce carton low-fat ricotta cheese or cream-style cottage cheese**

1   **2.25-ounce can sliced pitted ripe olives**

9   **no-boil lasagna noodles**

1   **8-ounce package sliced mozzarella cheese**

¼   **cup grated Parmesan cheese**

Snipped fresh basil (optional)

1 In a large saucepan cook ground beef and sausage over medium heat until brown. Drain off fat. Stir pasta sauce into meat in saucepan; bring to boiling. Remove from heat.

2 Meanwhile, in a medium bowl stir together egg, ricotta cheese, and olives.

3 To assemble lasagna, spread about 1 cup of the hot meat mixture in the bottom of two 9×5-inch loaf pans* or dishes. Cover with three of the lasagna noodles, breaking noodles as necessary to fit and making sure that noodles do not touch the edge of the pan or dish. Cover with one-third of the ricotta mixture, one-third of the remaining meat mixture, and one-third of the mozzarella cheese. Repeat with two more layers of noodles, meat mixture, ricotta cheese mixture, and mozzarella. (Make sure that noodles are covered with sauce.) Sprinkle with Parmesan cheese.

4 Cool lasagna slightly. Chill lasagna in pans or dishes for at least 1 hour. Using two spatulas, carefully remove lasagna from pans or dishes. Transfer each to a large resealable plastic bag. Seal and freeze for up to 1 month.

5 To serve, thaw lasagna in the refrigerator for 1 to 2 days. Preheat oven to 350°F. Carefully place the lasagna back in the 9-inch loaf pans or dishes. Bake for 40 to 45 minutes or until heated through. Let stand for 5 minutes before serving. If desired, garnish with basil.

Makes 8 servings

Nutrition Facts per serving: 492 cal., 26 g total fat (12 g sat. fat), 109 mg chol., 987 mg sodium, 34 g carbo., 2 g fiber, 31 g pro.

TO SERVE RIGHT AWAY: Preheat oven to 350°F. Cover pans with foil. Bake for 30 minutes. Uncover and bake for 10 to 15 minutes more or until cheese is golden and noodles are tender. Let stand for 5 minutes before serving. If desired, garnish with fresh basil.

***NOTE:** Lasagna also can also be made in a 3-quart rectangular baking dish.

TACO SPAGHETTI

Some kids could eat tacos and spaghetti night after night. Why fight it? Here, these two kid-pleasing favorites get rolled into one great casserole. And with the bonus batch, you can have a repeat performance on demand.

Prep: 40 minutes   Bake: 1 hour   Freeze: up to 1 month   Oven: 375°F

10   ounces dried spaghetti, linguine, or fettuccine, broken

2   pounds lean ground beef or ground uncooked turkey

2   large onions, chopped (2 cups)

1½   cups water

1   1.25-ounce envelope (2 tablespoons) taco seasoning mix

2   11-ounce cans whole kernel corn with sweet peppers, drained

1   cup sliced, pitted ripe olives

3   cups shredded Colby and Monterey Jack or cheddar cheese (12 ounces)

1   cup bottled salsa

2   4-ounce cans diced green chile peppers, drained

Shredded lettuce

Chopped fresh tomato

Broken tortilla chips (optional)

Dairy sour cream (optional)

1 Cook pasta according to package directions; drain.

2 In a 4-quart Dutch oven cook ground meat and onions over medium heat until meat is brown. Drain off fat. Stir in water and taco seasoning; bring to boiling. Reduce heat; simmer, uncovered, for 2 minutes, stirring occasionally. Stir in cooked pasta, drained corn, olives, 1 cup of the cheese, the salsa, and chile peppers.

3 Divide mixture evenly among 2 lightly greased 2-quart casseroles. Wrap, label, and freeze the casseroles for up to 1 month.

4 To serve, thaw frozen casseroles in refrigerator overnight. Preheat oven to 375°F. Bake, covered, about 1 hour or until heated through, stirring once about halfway through baking time. Sprinkle each casserole with 1 cup shredded cheese. Serve with lettuce, chopped tomato, and, if desired, tortilla chips and sour cream.

Makes 2 (6-serving) portions

Nutrition Facts per serving: 352 cal., 17 g total fat (7 g sat. fat), 66 mg chol., 772 mg sodium, 30 g carbo., 3 g fiber, 24 g pro.

TO SERVE RIGHT AWAY: Preheat oven to 350°F. Cover and bake casserole(s) for 20 to 25 minutes or until heated through. Sprinkle with remaining cheese.

LAMB AND POLENTA BAKE

Lots of good-old American Mom-style casseroles started with ground beef, onions, and celery. For a tasty update, this one starts with ground lamb and fennel. It's decidedly different, but equally easy and comforting.

Prep: 40 minutes   Bake: 35 minutes (for serving immediately)   Freeze: up to 1 month   Oven: 375°F

1½   **pounds ground lamb**

1   **large onion, chopped (1 cup)**

2   **small fennel bulbs, chopped (about 1½ cups)**

1   **tablespoon bottled minced garlic (6 cloves)**

2   **tablespoons snipped fresh oregano or 2 teaspoons dried oregano, crushed**

½   **teaspoon coarsely ground black pepper**

2   **14.5-ounce cans whole Italian-style tomatoes, undrained and cut up**

   Nonstick cooking spray

2   **16-ounce tubes refrigerated cooked polenta**

¾   **cup crumbled feta or garlic-and-herb feta cheese (3 ounces)**

1   **15-ounce can Italian-style tomato sauce**

   For make ahead:

¼   **cup crumbled feta or garlic-and-herb feta cheese (1 ounce)**

1 In a 12-inch skillet cook lamb, onion, fennel, garlic, oregano, and pepper until lamb is brown and onion is tender. Drain off fat. Add undrained tomatoes. Bring to boiling; reduce heat. Simmer, uncovered, for 10 to 15 minutes or until most of the liquid is evaporated, stirring occasionally.

2 Meanwhile, line four 10- to 12-ounce casseroles with large pieces of plastic wrap, allowing excess to extend over edges. Coat the plastic wrap lightly with nonstick cooking spray; set individual casseroles aside. Lightly coat a 1½-quart casserole with cooking spray (but don't line with plastic wrap); set aside.

3 Slice each polenta tube in half lengthwise. Slice each half into ¼-inch slices. Using one-fourth of the slices, press into the bottoms of the prepared individual casseroles. Press another fourth of the slices into the bottom of the prepared 1½-quart casserole, overlapping slices as necessary.

4 Preheat oven to 375°F. Divide half of the lamb mixture among the individual casseroles, spooning over polenta. Spoon remaining half of the lamb mixture over polenta in the 1½-quart casserole. Sprinkle ¼ cup of the cheese over the lamb mixture in the individual casseroles. Sprinkle another ¼ cup cheese over lamb mixture in 1½-quart casserole. Wrap and chill the remaining ¼ cup cheese. Divide half of the remaining polenta slices among the individual casseroles; pressing down firmly. Arrange remaining polenta slice over the 1½-quart casserole, overlapping as necessary.

5 Bring the plastic wrap together over the mixture in the individual casseroles. Seal. Place casseroles in freezer for a few hours or just until firm. Remove from the individual casserole dishes. Overwrap each with foil, or place in an airtight freezer container. Label and freeze the individual casseroles up to 1 month. Pour half of the remaining tomato sauce into an airtight freezer container; seal, label, and freeze.

6 Cover and bake the 1½-quart casserole for 35 to 40 minutes or until heated through, uncovering the last 10 minutes. Sprinkle the reserved cheese on top. Let stand for 10 minutes. Meanwhile, in a small saucepan heat the remaining tomato sauce just to boiling. To serve, spoon heated tomato sauce over casserole.

Makes 2 (4-serving) portions

Nutrition Facts per serving: 405 cal., 20 g total fat (10 g sat. fat), 75 mg chol., 1165 mg sodium, 34 g carbo., 10 g fiber, 21 g pro.

TO REHEAT FROZEN PORTIONS: Remove individual frozen casseroles from overwrap, if using, or from freezer containers. Remove plastic wrap. Return to the same 4 greased 10- to 12-ounce casseroles. Cover and let frozen casseroles and tomato sauce thaw overnight in refrigerator. To serve, preheat oven to 350°F. Bake casseroles, covered with foil, for 45 to 55 minutes or until heated through, uncovering the last 10 minutes of baking. Sprinkle ¼ cup feta cheese over casseroles. Let stand for 10 minutes. Heat tomato sauce in a small saucepan just to boiling. Spoon heated tomato sauce over casseroles.

MAKE-AHEAD PIZZA

Your own frozen pizza beats purchased frozen pizza any day. Mix and match toppings as you like. Pictured on page 138.

Prep: 30 minutes   Bake: 25 minutes   Freeze: up to 1 month   Oven: 375°F

1 **15-ounce can pizza sauce**

2 **12-inch (10-ounces each) thin Italian bread shells* (Boboli) or purchased baked pizza crust**

1 **pound bulk Italian sausage, ground beef, or ground pork, cooked and drained; or 1½ cups diced cooked ham or Canadian-style bacon (6 ounces)**

1 **cup green sweet pepper strips and/or sliced mushrooms**

4 **green onions, sliced (½ cup), or ½ cup sliced, pitted ripe olives**

3 **cups shredded mozzarella cheese (12 ounces)**

1 Spread pizza sauce evenly on crusts. Top pizzas with meat, vegetables, and cheese.

2 Cover pizzas with plastic wrap and freeze until firm. Wrap frozen pizzas in moisture- and vaporproof wrap. Wrap in heavy foil or place in a large resealable freezer bag; seal. Label and freeze for up to 1 month.

3 To serve, preheat oven to 375°F. Unwrap a frozen pizza and place on baking sheet. Bake about 25 minutes or until cheese is bubbly.

Makes 3 to 4 servings per pizza

Nutrition Facts per serving: 685 cal., 37 g total fat (14 g sat. fat), 100 mg chol., 1586 mg sodium, 18 g carbo., 2 g fiber, 36 g pro.

FOR CRISPER CRUST: Bake pizza directly on center oven rack.

***NOTE:** If you prefer to use a thick pizza crust, increase baking time to about 35 minutes.

CHICKEN AND BEAN BURRITOS

Burritos are Mexican or Tex-Mex sandwiches that originally were filled with refried beans. Today's variation are now large flour tortillas wrapped around a variety of fillings, such as tomato, avocado, and cheese.

Prep: 25 minutes   Bake: 40 minutes   Freeze: up to 3 months   Oven: 350°F

Nonstick cooking spray

1 **medium red sweet pepper, cut into thin strips**

1 **medium onion, chopped (½ cup)**

1 **teaspoon bottled minced garlic (2 cloves)**

1 **16-ounce can fat-free refried beans**

2 **skinless, boneless chicken breast halves, cooked and shredded (about 1½ cups)**

8 **8-inch flour tortillas**

1 **cup shredded Monterey Jack cheese or cheddar cheese (4 ounces)**

Avocado slices, chopped tomato, and/or salsa (optional)

1 Preheat oven to 350°F. Coat a large, heavy skillet with cooking spray. Cook sweet pepper, onion, and garlic until tender. Remove from heat. Stir in refried beans and chicken.

2 Meanwhile, wrap tortillas tightly in foil. Heat in preheated oven about 10 minutes or until heated through.

3 To assemble each burrito, spoon about ⅓ cup of the filling onto each tortilla just below center. Top with cheese. Fold edge nearest filling up and over just until filling is covered. Fold in 2 adjacent sides just until they meet; roll up.

4 Wrap each burrito in foil and place in a freezer container. Freeze for up to 3 months.

5 To reheat, preheat oven to 350°F. Place frozen burritos, loosely wrapped in foil, on a baking sheet. Heat in oven about 30 minutes. Open foil and bake for 10 to 15 minutes more or until heated through. (To reheat in microwave oven, remove foil and place 1 or 2 burritos on a microwave-safe plate. Cover loosely with waxed paper. Microwave on 50 percent power {medium} for 5 to 6 minutes for 1 burrito or 6 to 8 minutes for 2, or until heated through.) If desired, serve burritos with avocado, tomato, and/or salsa.

Makes 8 burritos

Nutrition Facts per serving: 242 cal., 8 g total fat (3 g sat. fat), 35 mg chol., 482 mg sodium, 25 g carbo., 4 g fiber, 17 g pro.

TO SERVE RIGHT AWAY: Preheat oven to 350°F. Arrange burritos, seam side down, on a baking sheet. Bake, covered, for 10 minutes. Uncover and bake for 5 minutes more. If desired, serve burritos with avocado, tomato, and/or salsa.

ROASTED TURKEY CALZONES

Keep a batch of these foldover pizzas on hand in the freezer. They'll make a soothing, satisfying supper for those days when overwhelmed is an understatement. Pictured on page 267.

Prep: 30 minutes   Bake: 12 minutes   Freeze: up to 1 month   Oven: 350°F

3   **cups chopped cooked turkey breast, chopped (about 1 pound)**

2½ **cups chopped fresh spinach**

1½ **cups shredded 4-cheese pizza cheese (6 ounces)**

1   **14- or 15-ounce jar pizza sauce**

2   **13.8-ounce packages refrigerated pizza dough**

    Milk

    Grated Parmesan or Romano cheese (optional)

1 In a large bowl combine turkey, spinach, pizza cheese, and ½ cup of the pizza sauce. On a lightly floured surface, roll one package of pizza dough out to a 12×12-inch square. Cut into four 6×6-inch squares.

2 Place about ⅔ cup of the turkey mixture onto half of each square to within about ½ inch of edge. Moisten edges of dough with water and fold over, forming a triangle or rectangle. Pinch or press with a fork to seal edges. Prick tops of calzones with a fork; brush with milk and place on an ungreased baking sheet. Repeat with remaining dough and turkey mixture.

3 Freeze until firm. Transfer to a resealable freezer bag or an airtight freezer container. Seal, label, and freeze up to 1 month. Transfer the remaining pizza sauce to an airtight freezer container. Seal, label, and freeze.

4 To serve frozen calzones, thaw frozen calzones and frozen pizza sauce in the refrigerator overnight. Preheat oven to 350°F. Unwrap calzones and place on a lightly greased baking sheet. If desired, sprinkle with Parmesan cheese. Bake calzones, uncovered, for 12 to 15 minutes or until heated through. Heat pizza sauce in a small saucepan. Serve with calzones.

Makes 2 (4-serving) portions (8 calzones)

Nutrition Facts per serving: 295 cal., 9 g total fat (3 g sat. fat), 35 mg chol., 1221 mg sodium, 31 g carbo., 1 g fiber, 22 g pro.

TO SERVE RIGHT AWAY: Preheat oven to 375°F. If desired, sprinkle the tops of calzones with Parmesan cheese. Bake calzones about 18 minutes or until golden brown. Heat remaining pizza sauce and serve with calzones.

PICADILLO CHICKEN LOAVES

The Latin American dish, picadillo, varies from country to country but always features a pleasing mix of sweet and spicy. These two great tastes come together again in this chicken loaf.

Prep: 15 minutes   Bake: 38 minutes   Freeze: up to 3 months   Oven: 350°F

- 2   eggs, lightly beaten
- ½   cup fine dry bread crumbs
- ½   cup raisins
- ¼   cup thinly sliced pimiento-stuffed olives
- ¼   cup apple juice or milk
- 1   teaspoon onion salt
- 1   teaspoon ground cinnamon
- 1   teaspoon ground cumin
- 2   pounds ground uncooked chicken or turkey
- ½   cup chopped almonds or pecans, toasted
- ¼   cup shredded cheddar or Monterey Jack cheese

1 In a large bowl stir together eggs, bread crumbs, raisins, olives, apple juice, onion salt, cinnamon, and cumin. Add the ground chicken and nuts; mix well.

2 Shape the chicken mixture into eight 4×2½ × 1-inch loaves. Place loaves in a shallow baking pan. Freeze until firm. Place in an airtight freezer container or in resealable freezer bags. Seal, label, and freeze for up to 3 months.

3 To serve, preheat oven to 350°F. Bake frozen loaves, uncovered, for 35 to 40 minutes or until done (165°F). Sprinkle each loaf with 1 tablespoon cheese. Bake about 3 minutes more or until cheese melts.

Makes 8 chicken loaves

Nutrition Facts per chicken loaf: 289 cal., 16 g total fat (1 g sat. fat), 53 mg chol., 508 mg sodium, 14 g carbo., 2 g fiber, 24 g pro.

TO SERVE RIGHT AWAY: Preheat oven to 350°F. Bake loaves, uncovered, about 25 minutes or until done (165°F). Sprinkle each loaf with 1 tablespoon shredded cheese. Bake about 3 minutes more or until the cheese melts.

PARMESAN CHICKEN AND BROCCOLI

With just a few flavorful touches, including rich Parmesan cheese, and a little ham, a quick chicken-and-rice casserole becomes a dinnertime event worth savoring.

Prep: 30 minutes   Bake: 40 minutes   Freeze: up to 3 months   Oven: 350°F

1	cup converted rice
2	green onions, sliced (¼ cup)
1	tablespoon cooking oil
12	ounces skinless, boneless chicken breast halves, cut into bite-size strips
¾	teaspoon dried Italian seasoning, crushed
½	teaspoon bottled minced garlic (1 clove)
1	16-ounce jar reduced-fat Alfredo pasta sauce
3	cups frozen cut broccoli
⅓	cup grated Parmesan cheese
¼	cup diced cooked ham
1	2-ounce jar diced pimiento, drained
	Ground black pepper

1 Cook rice according to package directions; remove from heat and stir in green onions. Divide the rice mixture among four 12- to 16-ounce individual au gratin dishes or casseroles; set aside.

2 In a large skillet heat oil over medium heat. Add chicken strips, Italian seasoning, and garlic; cook and stir for 4 to 6 minutes or until chicken is no longer pink. Remove from heat. Stir in Alfredo sauce, broccoli, Parmesan cheese, ham, and pimiento. Season to taste with pepper.

3 Spoon chicken mixture over rice in dishes. Cover with freezer wrap, label, and freeze for up to 3 months.

4 To serve, thaw frozen dishes overnight in the refrigerator (they may still be icy). Preheat oven to 350°F. Remove freezer wrap; cover each dish with foil. Bake for 20 minutes. Uncover and bake about 20 minutes more or until heated through.

Makes 4 servings

Nutrition Facts per serving: 660 cal., 25 g total fat (12 g sat. fat), 109 mg chol., 1277 mg sodium, 71 g carbo., 5 g fiber, 39 g pro.

TO SERVE RIGHT AWAY: Preheat oven to 350°F. Bake for 15 minutes. Uncover and bake about 15 minutes more or until heated through.

MINESTRONE

Here's a fix-and-freeze favorite that empowers you to bring a satisfying soup supper to the table in minutes. You also can freeze it in individual portions for take-along meals or the family that eats in shifts.

Prep: 50 minutes   Cook: 25 to 30 minutes   Freeze: up to 1 month

6   **cups water**

1   **28-ounce can tomatoes, cut up**

1   **8-ounce can tomato sauce**

1   **large onion, chopped (1 cup)**

1   **cup chopped cabbage**

1   **medium carrot, chopped (½ cup)**

1   **stalk celery, chopped (½ cup)**

1   **tablespoon instant beef bouillon granules**

1   **tablespoon dried Italian seasoning, crushed**

1   **teaspoon salt**

1   **teaspoon bottled minced garlic (2 cloves)**

¼   **teaspoon ground black pepper**

1   **15-ounce can cannellini (white kidney), undrained**

1   **10-ounce package frozen lima beans**

4   **ounces dried linguini or spaghetti, broken**

1   **small zucchini, halved lengthwise and sliced**

2   **to 3 tablespoons purchased pesto (optional)**

Grated Parmesan cheese

1 In a 5- to 6-quart Dutch oven combine water, undrained tomatoes, tomato sauce, onion, cabbage, carrot, celery, bouillon granules, Italian seasoning, salt, garlic, and pepper. Bring to boiling; reduce heat.

2 Cover and simmer for 10 minutes. Stir in undrained cannellini beans, lima beans, linguini, and zucchini. Return to boiling; reduce heat. Simmer, uncovered, for 15 minutes. Remove from heat. Cool.

3 Divide the soup between two 2-quart freezer containers. Seal, wrap, label, and freeze for up to 1 month.

4 To serve, thaw soup overnight in the refrigerator. Transfer frozen soup to a large saucepan. Cover and cook over low heat until heated through, stirring occasionally to break up mixture. Ladle into soup bowls. If desired, top each serving with 1 teaspoon pesto. Sprinkle individual servings with Parmesan cheese.

Makes 2 (4-serving) portions

Nutrition Facts per serving: 177 cal., 3 g total fat (1 g sat. fat), 5 mg chol., 992 mg sodium, 32 g carbo., 5 g fiber, 10 g pro.

TO SERVE RIGHT AWAY: Do not cool soup. Serve as directed.

WORKDAY DINNERS

Both working and stay-at-home moms value quick-to-the-table meals and with this chapter, they've hit the mother lode. These 30-minute, 10-ingredients-or-less recipes take advantage of shortcut cooking techniques and various convenience products. Packed with plenty of family-pleasing appeal, these main dishes are sure to please the cook as well as the hungry family.

PEPPERY STEAK WITH BORDELAISE SAUCE

Bordelaise means "from Bordeaux," and generally signifies that a dish will be served with a brown sauce flavored with the region's famous red wine. The wine-laced sauce here gets a head start with brown gravy mix.

Start to Finish: 25 minutes

1¼   **cups water**

1   **cup packaged sliced fresh mushrooms**

1   **medium onion, finely chopped (½ cup)**

1   **0.87- to 1.2-ounce package brown gravy mix**

¼   **cup dry red wine**

2   **teaspoons garlic-pepper seasoning**

4   **beef ribeye, top sirloin, or tenderloin steaks, cut ¾ inch thick (about 1½ pounds)**

2   **tablespoons olive oil**

1 For sauce, in a medium saucepan bring the water to boiling. Add mushrooms and onion. Reduce heat. Cover and cook for 3 minutes. Stir in dry gravy mix; stir in red wine. Cook about 3 minutes or until thickened, stirring occasionally. Cover; keep warm.

2 Sprinkle garlic-pepper seasoning evenly over steaks; rub in with your fingers. In a large heavy skillet heat oil over medium-high heat. Add steaks. Reduce heat to medium; cook until desired doneness, turning once. Allow 7 to 12 minutes for medium-rare (145°F) to medium doneness (160°F).

3 Serve steaks with the sauce on warmed plates.

Makes 4 servings

Nutrition Facts per serving: 366 cal., 18 g total fat (5 g sat. fat), 81 mg chol., 954 mg sodium, 7 g carbo., 1 g fiber, 39 g pro.

BEEF KABOBS WITH BLUE CHEESE DIPPING SAUCE

Take kabobs to a new level of sophistication by serving them with blue cheese salad dressing.

Prep: 20 minutes   **Grill:** 8 minutes

1   **pound boneless beef sirloin steak, cut 1 inch thick**

2   **teaspoons steak seasoning**

12 **fresh cremini or white mushrooms, halved**

6   **green onions, cut into 2-inch pieces**

1   **cup bottled blue cheese salad dressing**

1 Trim fat from steak. Cut steak into 1-inch cubes. In a medium bowl combine steak cubes and steak seasoning; toss to coat. On eight 8-inch metal skewers, alternately thread steak cubes, mushrooms, and green onions, leaving a ¼-inch space between pieces.

2 For a charcoal grill, grill kabobs on the rack of an uncovered grill directly over medium coals until meat reaches desired doneness, turning once. Allow 8 to 12 minutes for medium (160°F). (For a gas grill, preheat grill. Reduce heat to medium. Place kabobs on grill rack over heat. Cover and grill as above.)

3 Serve kabobs with salad dressing.

Makes 4 servings

Nutrition Facts per serving: 475 cal., 38 g total fat (8 g sat. fat), 79 mg chol., 1071 mg sodium, 8 g carbo., 1 g fiber, 29 g pro.

GRILLED STEAK, MANGO, AND PEAR SALAD

Look for jars of sliced mango in the produce section of your supermarket. They're always perfectly ripe, already peeled and sliced, and make a sweet addition to this steak salad.

Prep: 15 minutes   Grill: 14 minutes

12	ounces boneless beef top loin steak, cut 1 inch thick
½	teaspoon salt
¼	teaspoon ground black pepper
1	10-ounce package torn mixed salad greens (about 8 cups)
1	24-ounce jar refrigerated sliced mango, drained
1	medium pear, peeled, cored, and chopped
¾	cup refrigerated fat-free blue cheese salad dressing
	Cracked black pepper

1 Sprinkle both sides of steak with salt and the ¼ teaspoon pepper.

2 For a charcoal grill, place steak on the rack of an uncovered grill directly over medium coals. Grill until desired doneness, turning once. Allow 14 to 18 minutes for medium-rare (145°F) or 18 to 22 minutes for medium (160°F). (For a gas grill, preheat grill. Reduce heat to medium. Place meat on grill rack over heat. Cover and grill as above.)

3 To serve, thinly slice steak across the grain. Arrange greens on a serving platter; top with meat, mango, and pear. Drizzle with salad dressing. Sprinkle with cracked black pepper.

Makes 4 servings

Nutrition Facts per serving: 307 cal., 5 g total fat (2 g sat. fat), 50 mg chol., 900 mg sodium, 49 g carbo., 4 g fiber, 19 g pro.

ITALIAN BEEF SOUP

Keep canned broth and a package of frozen pasta and vegetables on hand
for this easy meal and you'll always be prepared to stir up a hearty supper.

Start to Finish: 25 minutes

1	**pound lean ground beef**
2	**14-ounce cans beef broth**
1	**16-ounce package frozen pasta with broccoli, corn, and carrots in garlic-seasoned sauce**
1	**14.5-ounce can diced tomatoes, undrained**
1½	**cups no-salt-added tomato juice**
2	**teaspoons dried Italian seasoning, crushed**
¼	**cup grated Parmesan cheese**

1 In a 4-quart Dutch oven cook ground beef until brown. Drain off fat. Add beef broth, pasta with mixed vegetables, undrained tomatoes, tomato juice, and Italian seasoning.

2 Bring to boiling; reduce heat. Simmer, uncovered, about 10 minutes or until pasta and vegetables are tender. Sprinkle individual servings with Parmesan cheese.

Makes 6 to 8 servings

Nutrition Facts per : 279 cal., 13 g total fat (6 g sat. fat), 56 mg chol., 827 mg sodium, 21 g carbo., 3 g fiber, 20 g pro.

SKILLET TOSTADAS

Because this recipe uses nacho cheese soup, bottled salsa, and preshredded taco cheese, you'll be saying olé to these tostadas in no time at all.

Start to Finish: 25 minutes

- 8 **ounces lean ground beef**
- I **medium onion, chopped (½ cup)**
- I **15-ounce can red kidney beans, rinsed and drained**
- I **II-ounce can condensed nacho cheese soup**
- ⅓ **cup bottled salsa**
- 8 **tostada shells**
- I **cup shredded taco cheese (4 ounces)**

  Shredded lettuce

  Chopped tomato

  Dairy sour cream or guacamole (optional)

1 In a large skillet cook ground beef and onion until meat is brown and onion is tender. Drain off fat. Stir in kidney beans, soup, and salsa. Heat through.

2 Divide beef mixture among tostada shells. Top with cheese, lettuce, and tomato. If desired, serve with sour cream.

Makes 4 servings

Nutrition Facts per serving: 576 cal., 33 g total fat (15 g sat. fat), 81 mg chol., 1277 mg sodium, 42 g carbo., 11 g fiber, 26 g pro.

ITALIAN STEAK AND CHEESE SANDWICH

Use leftover or deli roast beef for this flavor-packed sandwich. If you like, serve it with your favorite soup.

Start to Finish: 25 minutes

10 tablespoons bottled zesty-style clear Italian salad dressing

2 medium green sweet peppers, cut into thin strips

1 medium onion, sliced

12 ounces thinly sliced deli roast beef

6 French-style rolls, split and toasted

½ cup shredded mozzarella cheese (2 ounces)

1 In a large skillet heat 2 tablespoons of the salad dressing over medium heat. Add sweet peppers and onion; cook and stir about 5 minutes or until vegetables are tender. Remove vegetable mixture from skillet; keep warm.

2 Add another 2 tablespoons salad dressing to the same skillet. Add beef; cook over medium heat for 2 to 3 minutes or until heated through. Fill rolls with meat and vegetable mixture. Drizzle meat and vegetables in each sandwich with 1 tablespoon salad dressing. Top with cheese.

Makes 6 sandwiches

Nutrition Facts per sandwich: 311 cal., 13 g total fat (3 g sat. fat), 45 mg chol., 732 mg sodium, 26 g carbo., 2 g fiber, 23 g pro.

FRENCH ONION AND BEEF SOUP

The addition of beef transforms a traditional French onion soup into a satisfying main dish. Take your pick—use leftover roast beef or buy some from the deli.

Start to Finish: 25 minutes

3	**tablespoons butter**
1	**medium onion, thinly sliced and separated into rings**
2	**10.5-ounce cans condensed French onion soup**
2½	**cups water**
1½	**cups cubed cooked beef (8 ounces)**
4	**1-inch slices French bread**
½	**cup shredded Gruyère or Swiss cheese (2 ounces)**

1 In a large skillet melt butter over medium heat. Add onion; cook about 5 minutes or until very tender, stirring occasionally. Stir in onion soup, water, and cooked beef. Bring to boiling, stirring occasionally.

2 Meanwhile, preheat broiler. Place the bread slices on a baking sheet. Broil 4 inches from the heat about 1 minute or until toasted on one side. Top the toasted sides with cheese; broil about 1 minute more or until cheese is melted.

3 To serve, ladle soup into soup bowls. Top with bread, cheese sides up.

Makes 4 servings

Nutrition Facts per serving: 465 cal., 21 g total fat (10 g sat. fat), 82 mg chol., 1701 mg sodium, 40 g carbo., 3 g fiber, 28 g pro.

HURRY-UP BEEF AND VEGETABLE STEW

Step aside, sandwiches—here's a tastier way to use leftover roast beef.

Start to Finish: 20 minutes

- **2 cups water**
- **1 10.75-ounce can condensed golden mushroom soup**
- **1 10.75-ounce can condensed tomato soup**
- **½ cup dry red wine or beef broth**
- **2 cups chopped cooked beef (10 ounces)**
- **1 16-ounce package frozen sugar snap stir-fry vegetables or one 16-ounce package frozen cut broccoli**
- **½ teaspoon dried thyme, crushed**

In a 4-quart Dutch oven combine water, mushroom soup, tomato soup, and wine. Stir in beef, frozen vegetables, and thyme. Cook over medium heat until bubbly, stirring frequently. Continue cooking, uncovered, for 4 to 5 minutes more or until vegetables are crisp-tender, stirring occasionally.

Makes 5 servings

Nutrition Facts per serving: 231 cal., 4 g total fat (1 g sat. fat), 42 mg chol., 906 mg sodium, 21 g carbo., 4 g fiber, 20 g pro.

CHIPOTLE BRISKET SANDWICHES

Cooked and sliced beef brisket is the ultimate in convenience and makes a meaty filling for these hefty sandwiches. Chipotle peppers give a mouthwatering smokiness.

Start to Finish: 15 minutes

1   **17-ounce package refrigerated cooked, seasoned, and sliced beef brisket with barbecue sauce**

1   **to 2 canned chipotle peppers in adobo sauce, chopped**

½   **of a 16-ounce package shredded cabbage with carrot (coleslaw mix) (about 4 cups)**

⅓   **cup bottled coleslaw dressing**

6   **kaiser rolls, split and toasted**

1 In a large saucepan combine the beef brisket with barbecue sauce and chipotle peppers. Cook and stir about 5 minutes or until heated through.

2 Meanwhile, in a large bowl combine shredded cabbage mixture and coleslaw dressing.

3 To serve, spoon beef mixture onto roll bottoms. Top with coleslaw mixture. Top with roll tops.

Makes 6 sandwiches

Nutrition Facts per sandwich: 414 cal., 18 g total fat (5 g sat. fat), 39 mg chol., 1085 mg sodium, 47 g carbo., 2 g fiber, 16 g pro.

SPEEDY SWEDISH MEATBALLS

For a healthful twist, serve these saucy meatballs with whole green beans or spaghetti squash instead of the traditional noodles.

Start to Finish: 10 minutes

- 1 **cup water**
- 1 **1.1-ounce envelope mushroom gravy mix**
- ¼ **teaspoon ground black pepper**
- 1 **8-ounce carton dairy sour cream**
- ¼ **teaspoon ground allspice**
- 1 **16-ounce package frozen cooked meatballs, thawed**
- 1 **4.5-ounce can sliced mushrooms, drained**

1 In a large skillet combine water, gravy mix, and pepper. Cook and stir over medium-high heat for 3 to 5 minutes or until thickened and bubbly.

2 Remove skillet from heat; stir in sour cream and allspice. Stir in meatballs and mushrooms. Return skillet to heat; heat through.

Makes 4 servings

Nutrition Facts per serving: 509 cal., 42 g total fat (19 g sat. fat), 65 mg chol., 1407 mg sodium, 17 g carbo., 3 g fiber, 17 g pro.

PORK SLICES WITH APPLES

Pork and apples are a classic combination—and for good reason! They taste great together. What's more, in just 25 minutes you can have this dinner on the table thanks to a can of sliced apples.

Start to Finish: 25 minutes

- 1 **1-pound pork tenderloin**
- 2 **tablespoons olive oil or butter**
- 1 **teaspoon bottled minced garlic (2 cloves)**
- 1 **20-ounce can sliced apples, drained**
- 2 **teaspoons snipped fresh thyme or ½ teaspoon dried thyme, crushed**

1 Trim fat from pork. Cut pork crosswise into ½-inch slices. Set pork aside.

2 In a 12-inch skillet heat oil over medium-high heat. Add garlic; cook for 15 seconds. Carefully add pork slices to skillet; reduce heat to medium. Cook about 4 minutes or until brown and juices run clear, turning once. Add drained apples and thyme. Cover and cook about 1 minute or until apples are heated through.

Makes 4 servings

Nutrition Facts per serving: 292 cal., 11 g total fat (2 g sat. fat), 73 mg chol., 61 mg sodium, 24 g carbo., 2 g fiber, 24 g pro.

BALSAMIC AND GARLIC PORK

Pork loin chops sizzle in a skillet, then get sauced with drippings cooked with balsamic dressing, roasted garlic, honey mustard, and woodsy rosemary. Serve them with mashed potatoes and another favorite vegetable.

Start to Finish: 15 minutes

- **4 boneless pork loin chops, cut ¾ inch thick (about 1 pound)**
- **½ teaspoon dried rosemary, crushed**
- **¼ teaspoon salt**
- **1 tablespoon olive oil**
- **2 teaspoons bottled minced roasted garlic**
- **½ cup bottled balsamic salad dressing**
- **1 tablespoon honey mustard**

1 Trim fat from chops. Sprinkle chops with rosemary and salt, pressing into surface of meat.

2 In a large nonstick skillet heat oil over medium heat. Add chops; cook for 8 to 12 minutes or until slightly pink in center and juices run clear (160°F), turning once halfway through cooking time. Remove chops, reserving drippings in skillet; keep chops warm while preparing sauce.

3 For sauce, in same skillet cook garlic in hot drippings for 30 seconds. Stir in salad dressing and honey mustard. Bring to boiling. To serve, spoon sauce over chops.

Makes 4 servings

Nutrition Facts per serving: 276 cal., 18 g total fat (4 g sat. fat), 54 mg chol., 562 mg sodium, 5 g carbo., 0 g fiber, 22 g pro.

ASIAN APRICOT-GLAZED CHOPS

Treat the very spicy Oriental chili-garlic sauce the same way you would hot pepper sauce: A little goes a long way.

Prep: 15 minutes   Grill: 7 minutes

⅓   **cup apricot preserves**

1   **tablespoon Oriental chili-garlic sauce**

2   **teaspoons soy sauce**

¼   **teaspoon ground ginger**

4   **boneless pork sirloin chops, cut ¾ inch thick (about 1 pound)**

Salt and ground black pepper

1 For glaze, place apricot preserves in a small bowl; snip any large pieces of fruit. Stir in chili-garlic sauce, soy sauce, and ginger. Set glaze aside. Sprinkle both sides of chops with salt and pepper.

2 For a charcoal grill, grill chops on the rack of an uncovered grill directly over medium coals for 7 to 9 minutes or until chops are slightly pink in the center and juices run clear (160°F), turning once halfway through grilling and brushing with glaze during the last 2 to 3 minutes of grilling. (For a gas grill, preheat grill. Reduce heat to medium. Place chops on grill rack over heat. Cover and grill as above.)

Makes 4 servings

Nutrition Facts per serving: 317 cal., 9 g total fat (3 g sat. fat), 106 mg chol., 515 mg sodium, 20 g carbo., 0 g fiber, 36 g pro.

MAPLE-PECAN GLAZED PORK CHOPS

Think pecan-roll topping melting over a succulent chop. Sweet and savory make a sensational combination.

Start to Finish: 15 minutes

4   **boneless pork loin chops, cut about ¾ inch thick (about 1 pound)**

   Salt and ground black pepper

4   **tablespoons butter, softened**

2   **tablespoons pure maple syrup or maple-flavored syrup**

⅓   **cup chopped pecans, toasted**

1 Trim fat from chops. Sprinkle chops with salt and pepper. In a very large skillet melt 1 tablespoon of the butter over medium-high heat. Add chops; cook for 8 to 12 minutes or until chops are slightly pink in the center and juices run clear (160°F), turning once halfway through cooking. Transfer chops to a serving platter.

2 Meanwhile, in a small bowl combine the remaining 3 tablespoons butter and the maple syrup. Spread butter mixture evenly over cooked chops. Let stand about 1 minute or until melted. Sprinkle with pecans.

Makes 4 servings

Nutrition Facts per serving: 333 cal., 23 g total fat (10 g sat. fat), 98 mg chol., 310 mg sodium, 8 g carbo., 1 g fiber, 23 g pro.

SMOKED PORK CHOP SKILLET

The skillet is one of the most versatile pans in your kitchen—and this recipe makes good use of it. Not only are you cooking meat to perfection, you're preparing the veggies at the same time.

Start to Finish: 25 minutes

- **2 tablespoons olive oil**
- **4 cooked smoked pork chops, cut ¾ inch thick (about 1¾ pound)**
- **1 16-ounce package frozen French-style green beans or mixed vegetables**
- **⅓ cup bottled roasted red sweet pepper, cut into strips**
- **¼ cup water**
- **1½ teaspoons snipped fresh sage or ½ teaspoon dried sage leaves, crushed**
- **½ cup balsamic vinegar**

1 In a 12-inch skillet heat oil over medium heat. Add chops and cook for 3 to 5 minutes on each side or until light brown. Remove chops from skillet; set aside. Add green beans, roasted pepper strips, water, and sage to skillet; place chops on top. Cover and cook for 5 minutes.

2 Meanwhile, in a small saucepan gently boil balsamic vinegar about 5 minutes or until reduced to ¼ cup. Brush chops with reduced vinegar; drizzle remaining vinegar over the bean mixture.

Makes 4 servings

Nutrition Facts per serving: 309 cal., 14 g total fat (3 g sat. fat), 75 mg chol., 1627 mg sodium, 18 g carbo., 3 g fiber, 27 g pro.

CRANBERRY-SAUCED PORK AND SWEET POTATOES

Just five ingredients make more than a main dish; this is an entire meal packed with flavor and family appeal.

Start to Finish: 20 minutes

4 **boneless pork loin chops, cut ¾ inch thick (about 1 pound)**

   Salt and ground black pepper

   Nonstick cooking spray

1 **17-ounce can vacuum-pack sweet potatoes**

1 **tablespoon butter**

1 **cup orange juice**

¼ **cup dried cranberries**

1 Trim fat from chops. Sprinkle chops lightly with salt and pepper. Coat an unheated large skillet with cooking spray. Preheat skillet over medium-high heat. Add chops; cook for 8 to 12 minutes or until chops are slightly pink in the center and juices run clear (160°F), turning once.

2 Meanwhile, place sweet potatoes in a medium saucepan. Mash with a potato masher. Stir in butter. Cook and stir over medium heat until potatoes are heated through. If desired, season with additional salt and pepper.

3 Transfer pork to a serving platter; cover to keep warm. Add orange juice and cranberries to skillet. Bring to boiling; reduce heat. Simmer, uncovered, about 7 minutes or until liquid is reduced by half. Spoon sauce over pork. Serve with mashed sweet potatoes.

Makes 4 servings

Nutrition Facts per serving: 312 cal., 8 g total fat (4 g sat. fat), 54 mg chol., 267 mg sodium, 38 g carbo., 3 g fiber, 22 g pro.

BLACK BEAN SOUP WITH SALSA VERDE

Cumin is the star spice in this soup. Its smoky flavor adds richness and depth.

Start to Finish: 15 minutes

1	**16-ounce jar mild or medium thick and chunky salsa**
2	**14-ounce cans reduced-sodium chicken broth**
1	**15- to 16-ounce can black beans, rinsed and drained**
8	**ounces reduced-sodium cooked ham, cubed (1½ cups)**
1	**teaspoon ground cumin**
½	**cup bottled salsa verde**

1 In a large saucepan combine salsa, chicken broth, beans, ham, and cumin. Bring to boiling; reduce heat. Cover and simmer for 5 minutes.

2 Ladle soup into bowls. Top individual servings with salsa verde.

Makes 4 servings

Nutrition Facts per serving: 197 cal., 4 g total fat (1 g sat. fat), 27 mg chol., 1603 mg sodium, 26 g carbo., 6 g fiber, 18 g pro.

MEATY ORZO GOULASH

Smoked paprika gives a more pungent hit than the familiar mild paprika.
It's becoming easier to find but if your supermarket doesn't have it, check
out a gourmet shop.

Start to Finish: 20 minutes

3   slices bacon

I   pound bulk sweet Italian
    sausage or uncooked
    chorizo sausage, casings
    removed

I   sweet red pepper, finely
    chopped (I cup)

I   small onion, cut in thin
    wedges

I   tablespoon smoked paprika

I½ 14.5-ounce cans stewed
    tomatoes, undrained (about
    22 ounces)

I   cup frozen whole kernel
    corn, thawed (optional)

2   cups hot cooked orzo, rice,
    noodles, or polenta slices

1 In a large skillet cook bacon until crisp; drain on paper towels.
When cool, coarsely crumble bacon; set aside. Discard bacon
drippings.

2 In the same skillet cook sausage, sweet pepper, and onion about
8 minutes or until sausage is brown and pepper is tender. Drain
off fat. Blot sausage dry with paper towels, if necessary.

3 Stir in smoked paprika; cook and stir for 1 minute. Add undrained
tomatoes, reserved bacon, and, if desired, corn. Cook and stir
until heated through. Serve over hot cooked orzo.

Makes 4 servings

Nutrition Facts per serving: 600 cal., 37 g total fat (I2 g sat. fat), 82 mg chol., II89 mg sodium, 37 g carbo.,
6 g fiber, 25 g pro.

CHICKEN WITH SALSA

Give chicken plenty of Tex-Mex kick with just five ingredients and less than 25 minutes. For a less fiery version, use medium or mild salsa.

Prep: 10 minutes   Grill: 12 minutes

1 tablespoon cooking oil

1 teaspoon chili powder

¾ teaspoon salt

4 skinless, boneless chicken breast halves

½ cup hot-style thick and chunky salsa

1 tablespoon tomato paste

1 In a small bowl stir together oil, chili powder, and salt; brush onto chicken breast halves.

2 In a blender or food processor combine salsa and tomato paste. Cover and blend until nearly smooth.

3 For a charcoal grill, grill chicken on the rack of an uncovered grill directly over medium coals for 12 to 15 minutes or until chicken is no longer pink (170°F), turning once halfway through grilling and brushing often with salsa mixture during the last 2 minutes of grilling. (For a gas grill, preheat grill. Reduce heat to medium. Place chicken on grill rack over heat. Cover and grill as above.)

Makes 4 servings

Nutrition Facts per serving: 207 cal., 6 g total fat (1 g sat. fat), 82 mg chol., 752 mg sodium, 3 g carbo., 0 g fiber, 33 g pro.

MAPLE CHICKEN FETTUCCINE

This special-day dish features oodles of noodles, tender chicken breast halves, and a medley of peppers, ingredients which are sure to please everyone around the table. Pictured on page 268.

Start to Finish: 30 minutes

10   ounces dried fettuccine

5   skinless, boneless chicken
      breast halves (about
      1½ pounds total)

      Salt and ground black
      pepper

1   tablespoon olive oil

1   16-ounce package frozen
      pepper stir-fry vegetables
      (yellow, green, and red
      sweet peppers and onion)

¾   cup chicken broth

1   tablespoon cornstarch

1   teaspoon snipped fresh
      rosemary

⅛   teaspoon ground black
      pepper

¼   cup maple syrup

1 Cook pasta according to package directions; drain. Set aside and keep warm.

2 Meanwhile, season chicken with salt and black pepper. In a 12-inch skillet heat oil over medium heat. Add chicken; cook for 10 to 12 minutes or until chicken is no longer pink (170°F), turning to brown evenly. Remove chicken from skillet; keep warm.

3 Increase heat to medium-high. Add frozen vegetables to skillet; cook and stir for 6 to 8 minutes or until vegetables are crisp-tender.

4 In a small bowl stir together chicken broth, cornstarch, rosemary, and the ⅛ teaspoon black pepper. Add to skillet. Cook and stir until thickened and bubbly. Cook and stir for 1 minute more. Stir in maple syrup.

5 To serve, arrange hot pasta on dinner plates or in shallow bowls. Top with chicken. Spoon vegetable mixture over chicken and pasta.

Makes 5 servings

Nutrition Facts per serving: 466 cal., 6 g total fat (1 g sat. fat), 79 mg chol., 285 mg sodium, 60 g carbo., 2 g fiber, 40 g pro.

WARM CHICKEN SPINACH SALAD

Toasted walnuts add a rich favor and pleasant crunch to this
wilted spinach salad.

Start to Finish: 20 minutes

4	**skinless, boneless chicken breast halves**
	Salt and ground black pepper
2	**tablespoons cooking oil**
1½	**cups packaged sliced fresh mushrooms**
1	**10-ounce package prewashed fresh spinach**
½	**cup chopped walnuts, toasted**
2	**tablespoons finely shredded Parmesan cheese**

1 Season chicken with salt and pepper. In a 12-inch skillet heat oil over medium heat. Add chicken; cook for 8 to 12 minutes or until chicken is no longer pink (170°F), turning to brown evenly. Remove chicken from skillet; keep warm.

2 Add mushrooms to skillet. Cook and stir for 2 minutes. Add spinach to mushrooms in skillet. Cover and cook for 1 to 2 minutes or just until spinach is wilted, gently stirring once. Stir in walnuts. Season to taste with additional salt and pepper. Transfer spinach mixture to a serving bowl; sprinkle with Parmesan cheese. Serve chicken with spinach.

Makes 4 servings

Nutrition Facts per serving: 347 cal., 19 g total fat (2 g sat. fat), 84 mg chol., 192 mg sodium, 6 g carbo., 3 g fiber, 39 g pro.

ITALIAN CHICKEN SKILLET

This Italian-inspired chicken skillet is a winner at any dinner table. Make sure you use fresh basil for rich flavor.

Start to Finish: 25 minutes

2	tablespoons olive oil
1½	pounds skinless, boneless chicken breast halves, cut into thin bite-size strips*
¼	teaspoon salt
⅛	teaspoon ground black pepper
1	14.5-ounce can diced tomatoes with basil, garlic, and oregano, drained
2	tablespoons snipped fresh basil
1	10-ounce package prewashed fresh spinach
1	cup shredded mozzarella cheese (4 ounces)

1 In a 12-inch skillet heat oil over medium-high heat. Cook chicken, half at a time, in hot oil until no longer pink (170°F). Drain off fat. Return all of the chicken to the skillet. Sprinkle chicken with salt and pepper.

2 Add drained tomatoes and basil to skillet. Bring to boiling. Add spinach to skillet, half at a time, tossing with tongs just until wilted. Remove from heat. Sprinkle with cheese. Let stand for 3 to 5 minutes or until cheese melts.

Makes 4 servings

Nutrition Facts per serving: 380 cal., 14 g total fat (4 g sat. fat), 116 mg chol., 998 mg sodium, 12 g carbo., 2 g fiber, 50 g pro.

*NOTE: To save time, look for packaged chicken breast strips for stir-frying in the meat section of your supermarket.

TWO-STEP CRUNCHY CHICKEN STRIPS

Starting with uncooked chicken breast tenderloins, this recipe produces plump, crunchy chicken strips in 20 minutes. Pictured on page 269.

Prep: 10 minutes   Bake: 10 minutes   Oven: 425°F

Nonstick cooking spray

2½ cups crushed bite-size cheddar fish-shape crackers or pretzels

⅔ cup bottled buttermilk ranch salad dressing or honey Dijon mustard

1 pound chicken breast tenderloins

Bottled buttermilk ranch salad dressing or honey Dijon mustard (optional)

1 Preheat oven to 425°F. Line a 15×10×1-inch baking pan with foil; lightly coat foil with cooking spray. Set aside.

2 In a shallow dish place the crushed crackers. In another shallow dish place the salad dressing. Dip chicken tenderloins into the dressing, allowing excess dressing to drip off; dip chicken into cracker crumbs to coat. Arrange chicken in prepared pan.

3 Bake for 10 to 15 minutes or until chicken is no longer pink (170°F). If desired, serve with additional ranch dressing or mustard for dipping.

Makes 4 to 6 servings

Nutrition Facts per serving: 517 cal., 21 g total fat (2 g sat. fat), 66 mg chol., 1060 mg sodium, 51 g carbo., 2 g fiber, 33 g pro.

QUICKER VERSION: Use a 10-ounce package refrigerated cooked chicken breast strips instead of the chicken breast tenderloins. Prepare as above except bake for 5 to 8 minutes or until heated through.

CHICKEN IN PHYLLO NESTS

The phyllo nests are surprisingly easy to make. Simply bake strips of phyllo dough and then use them to line the serving bowls. Nestle the chicken mixture in the nests, add a drizzle of balsamic vinaigrette, and serve!

Start to Finish: 30 minutes   Oven: 425°F

Nonstick cooking spray

10   sheets frozen phyllo dough
       (14×9-inch rectangles),
       thawed

2   tablespoons olive oil

1   bunch green onions, cut
       into 2-inch pieces (1 cup)

12   ounces refrigerated
       grilled chicken breast
       strips (3 cups)

1   6-ounce package
       prewashed fresh baby
       spinach

¾   cup cherry tomatoes,
       halved or quartered

1   tablespoon snipped fresh
       tarragon

¼   teaspoon black pepper

¼   cup bottled balsamic
       vinaigrette

1 Preheat oven to 425°F. Lightly coat a 15×10×1-inch baking pan with cooking spray; set aside. Roll up the stack of phyllo sheets into a cylinder. With a sharp knife cut phyllo roll crosswise into ¼- to ½-inch slices. Place slices in the prepared baking pan. Gently separate into strips and spread into an even layer. Coat phyllo generously with additional nonstick cooking spray. Bake, uncovered, for 8 to 10 minutes or until phyllo is golden brown.

2 Meanwhile, in a 12-inch skillet heat oil over medium-high heat. Add green onion; cook for 1 minute or just until tender. Add chicken; cook and stir until heated through. Remove skillet from heat. Add spinach, cherry tomatoes, tarragon, and pepper. Toss to combine.

3 Divide phyllo among 6 serving bowls. Spoon chicken mixture over phyllo. Drizzle with balsamic vinaigrette. Serve immediately.

Makes 6 servings

Nutrition Facts per serving: 197 cal., 10 g total fat (2 g sat. fat), 40 mg chol., 760 mg sodium, 14 g carbo., 1 g dietary fiber, 14 g protein.

CHICKEN WITH CREAMY MUSHROOMS

Sliced mushrooms sizzled in butter add a woodsy accent to the marinated chicken. If you prefer, substitute plain chicken breast halves for the marinated ones.

Start to Finish: 30 minutes

3 tablespoons butter

1 pound packaged sliced fresh mushrooms

6 purchased Italian-marinated skinless, boneless chicken breast halves

3 tablespoons rice vinegar or white wine vinegar

1½ cups whipping cream

3 tablespoons capers, rinsed and drained

¼ teaspoon ground black pepper

Steamed fresh vegetables (optional)

1 In a 12-inch skillet melt 1 tablespoon of the butter over medium-high heat. Add mushrooms; cook about 5 minutes or until tender. Remove mushrooms from skillet.

2 Reduce heat to medium. Add the remaining 2 tablespoons butter and the chicken breast halves to skillet. Cook for 8 to 12 minutes or until no longer pink (170°F), turning once to brown evenly. Remove chicken from skillet; keep warm.

3 For mushroom sauce, remove skillet from heat; add vinegar, stirring to loosen brown bits in bottom of skillet. Return skillet to heat. Stir in whipping cream, capers, and pepper. Bring to boiling; boil gently, uncovered, for 2 to 3 minutes or until sauce is slightly thickened. Stir mushrooms into cream mixture in skillet; heat through.

4 To serve, spoon mushroom sauce over chicken. If desired, serve with steamed vegetables.

Makes 6 servings

Nutrition Facts per serving: 456 cal., 34 g total fat (19 g sat. fat), 183 mg chol., 967 mg sodium, 7 g carbo., 1 g fiber, 33 g pro.

CHICKEN FOCACCIA SANDWICHES

Here's a simple solution for days you're extra rushed. These sandwiches are a fast meal in a package that every member of the family will like.

Start to Finish: 15 minutes

1   8- to 10-inch tomato or onion Italian flatbread (focaccia) or 1 loaf sourdough bread

⅓   cup mayonnaise dressing or salad dressing

1   cup lightly packed fresh basil

8   ounces sliced or shredded cooked chicken

½   cup bottled roasted red sweet peppers, drained and cut into strips

1 Using a long serrated knife, cut bread in half horizontally. Spread cut sides of bread halves with mayonnaise.

2 Layer basil leaves, chicken, and roasted peppers on bottom half of bread. Replace top half of bread. Cut into quarters; serve immediately.

Makes 4 sandwiches

Nutrition Facts per sandwich: 435 cal., 22 g total fat (3 g sat. fat), 65 mg chol., 486 mg sodium, 38 g carbo., 1 g fiber, 24 g pro.

SAVORY CHICKEN SALAD

Get a head start on the salad preparations by purchasing a roasted chicken from the supermarket. Buy the mushrooms already sliced and you'll save additional preparation time.

Start to Finish: 30 minutes

- 1 **2- to 2¼-pound purchased deli-roasted chicken**
- 2 **tablespoons olive oil**
- 1 **pound packaged sliced fresh mushrooms**
- ½ **cup bottled dried tomato pesto**
- 3 **tablespoons balsamic vinegar**
- ½ **cup cherry tomatoes, halved**
- 1 **5-ounce package mixed salad greens (about 8 cups)**

1 Remove and chop enough meat from the chicken to make 2 cups. Save any remaining chicken for another use.

2 In a large skillet heat oil over medium heat. Add mushrooms; cook about 10 minutes or until tender, stirring occasionally. Stir in pesto and balsamic vinegar. Bring to boiling; stir in chopped chicken. Heat through. Gently stir in tomatoes.

3 To serve, line a platter with salad greens and top with the chicken mixture. Serve warm.

Makes 4 servings

Nutrition Facts per serving: 419 cal., 24 g total fat (6 g sat. fat), 96 mg chol., 330 mg sodium, 14 g carbo., 3 g fiber, 38 g pro.

TOWERING TOSTADAS

Here's a chance to pile on extra veggies if you think your kids won't notice.
For an extra taste of Mexican-style creamy flavor, top each tostada with a
dollop of light dairy sour cream.

Start to Finish: 15 minutes

1	18-ounce tub taco sauce with shredded chicken*
8	to 12 6-inch tostada shells
¾	cup packaged shredded broccoli (broccoli slaw mix)
¾	cup canned black beans, rinsed and drained
⅔	cup shredded Colby and Monterey Jack cheese

In a medium saucepan cook taco sauce with chicken until heated through. Spoon chicken mixture onto tostada shells. Top with broccoli, beans, and cheese.

Makes 4 to 6 servings

Nutrition Facts per serving: 336 cal., 15 g total fat (6 g sat. fat), 74 mg chol., 1197 mg sodium, 29 g carbo., 3 g fiber, 17 g pro.

*TEST KITCHEN TIP: If you can't find tubs of taco sauce with shredded chicken, combine bottled taco sauce and shredded cooked chicken; heat through as directed.

BARBECUE CHICKEN QUESADILLAS

Dip the quesadilla wedges into salsa and green onion–topped sour cream. Or spoon the salsa and sour cream on top of the quesadillas and eat them with a knife and fork.

Prep: 20 minutes   **Cook:** 4 minutes per batch   **Oven:** 300°F

- 4   **7- or 8-inch flour tortillas**
      Nonstick cooking spray
- 1   **cup shredded extra-sharp cheddar cheese or finely shredded Mexican cheese blend (4 ounces)**
- 1   **4-ounce can diced green chile peppers, drained**
- 1   **18-ounce tub refrigerated shredded chicken with barbecue sauce (2 cups)**
- 1   **cup bottled salsa**
- ¼   **cup dairy sour cream**
- 2   **green onions, sliced (¼ cup)**

1 Coat one side of each tortilla with cooking spray. Place tortillas sprayed sides down on a cutting board or waxed paper. Sprinkle ¼ cup of the cheese over half of each tortilla. Top with chile peppers and barbecued chicken. Fold tortillas in half, pressing gently.

2 Heat a large nonstick skillet over medium heat. Cook quesadillas, 2 at a time, in hot skillet for 4 to 6 minutes or until light brown, turning once. Remove quesadillas from skillet; place on a baking sheet. Keep warm in a 300°F oven. Repeat with remaining quesadillas. To serve, cut each quesadilla into 3 wedges. Serve with salsa, sour cream, and green onions.

Makes 4 servings

Nutrition Facts per serving: 469 cal., 21 g total fat (10 g sat. fat), 86 mg chol., 1629 mg sodium, 46 g carbo., 1 g fiber, 25 g pro.

HONEYED CRANBERRY TURKEY

If you like, substitute 4 skinless, boneless chicken breast halves for the halved turkey breast tenderloins.

Start to Finish: 20 minutes

2 **turkey breast tenderloins (about 1¼ pounds)**

   Salt and ground black pepper

1 **tablespoon butter**

½ **cup whole cranberry sauce**

1 **tablespoon honey**

½ **teaspoon finely shredded lemon peel**

1 **tablespoon lemon juice**

1 Split each turkey breast tenderloin in half horizontally to make a total of 4 pieces. Sprinkle turkey with salt and pepper. In a 12-inch skillet melt butter over medium-high heat. Add turkey; cook for 12 to 15 minutes or until no longer pink (170°F), turning once to brown evenly. Transfer turkey to a serving platter; reserve drippings in skillet. Cover turkey to keep warm.

2 For sauce, stir cranberry sauce, honey, lemon peel, and lemon juice into the reserved drippings in skillet. Cook and stir until heated through. Spoon sauce over turkey.

Makes 4 servings

Nutrition Facts per serving: 252 cal., 4 g total fat (2 g sat. fat), 96 mg chol., 246 mg sodium, 18 g carbo., 0 g fiber, 35 g pro.

APPLE-GLAZED TURKEY

The lively tastes of garlic, sage, and apple jelly come together in an impressive brush-on glaze.

Prep: 10 minutes   **Broil:** 9 minutes

2   **turkey breast tenderloins (about 1¼ pounds)**

1   **tablespoon lemon juice**

1   **tablespoon olive oil**

½   **teaspoon seasoned salt**

½   **teaspoon dried sage leaves, crushed**

2   **teaspoons bottled minced garlic (4 cloves)**

2   **tablespoons apple jelly, melted**

1 Preheat broiler. Split each turkey breast tenderloin in half horizontally to make a total of 4 pieces. Place turkey on the unheated rack of a broiler pan. In a small bowl combine lemon juice, oil, seasoned salt, sage, and garlic. Brush mixture on both sides of each turkey portion.

2 Broil turkey 4 to 5 inches from the heat for 5 minutes. Turn turkey; broil for 2 minutes more. Using a clean brush, brush with apple jelly. Broil for 2 to 3 minutes more or until no longer pink (170°F).

Makes 4 servings

Nutrition Facts per serving: 192 cal., 5 g total fat (1 g sat. fat), 68 mg chol., 247 mg sodium, 8 g carbo., 0 g fiber, 27 g pro.

TURKEY DINNER BURGERS

A peppery sweet glaze tops the burgers. For a colorful accompaniment, try a medley of vegetables cooked in the microwave oven and tossed with your favorite salad dressing.

Prep: 15 minutes   Grill: 7 minutes

- 1   **egg, lightly beaten**
- ½   **teaspoon salt**
- ¼   **teaspoon ground black pepper**
- 1   **pound uncooked ground turkey or ground chicken**
- ¼   **cup fine dry bread crumbs**
- 1   **tablespoon olive oil**
- ¼   **cup jalapeño pepper jelly, melted, or barbecue sauce**
- **Prepackaged shredded red cabbage, thinly sliced red onion, and/or your favorite toppings**
- 4   **potato rolls, kaiser rolls, or hamburger buns, split and toasted**

1 In a medium bowl combine egg, salt, and black pepper. Add turkey and bread crumbs; mix well. Shape mixture into four ¾-inch-thick patties.

2 Lightly grease the rack of an indoor electric grill. Preheat grill. Place patties on the grill rack. If using a covered grill, close lid. Grill patties until done (165°F). For a covered grill, allow 5 to 7 minutes. For an uncovered grill, allow 14 to 18 minutes, turning once halfway through grilling. Brush patties with pepper jelly and cook for 1 minute more on each side.

3 To serve burgers, place cabbage, red onion, or other toppings on bottom halves of rolls. Add burgers and roll tops.

Makes 4 burgers

Nutrition Facts per burger: 504 cal., 20 g total fat (2 g sat. fat), 55 mg chol., 900 mg sodium, 52 g carbo., 2 g fiber, 28 g pro.

Broiler Method: Place patties on the unheated rack of a broiler pan. Broil 4 to 5 inches from the heat about 10 minutes or until turkey is no longer pink (165°F). Brush patties on each side with jalapeño jelly or barbecue sauce. Cook 1 minute more on each side.

Skillet Method: Cook patties over medium heat in hot oil in a large nonstick skillet about 10 minutes or until turkey is no longer pink (165°F). Brush each side of patties with jalapeño jelly or barbecue sauce. Cook 1 minute more on each side.

THAI TURKEY BURGERS

It's easy to give your burgers an Asian flair. Simply add Thai seasoning and top with peanut sauce.

Prep: 15 minutes   Broil: 14 minutes

- 1   egg, lightly beaten
- 1   teaspoon Thai seasoning
- 1   pound uncooked ground turkey or ground chicken
- ¼   cup fine dry bread crumbs
- 4   kaiser rolls or hamburger buns, split and toasted
- ¾   cup fresh basil leaves
- 2   tablespoons purchased peanut dipping sauce

    Green onions, bias-sliced (optional)

1 Preheat broiler. In a medium bowl combine egg and Thai seasoning. Add turkey and bread crumbs; mix well. Shape mixture into four ¾-inch-thick patties.

2 Place patties on the unheated rack of a broiler pan. Broil 3 to 4 inches from the heat for 14 to 18 minutes or until done (165°F),* turning once halfway through broiling.

3 To serve burgers, top bottom halves of buns with basil. Add patties. Spoon peanut dipping sauce over patties. If desired, garnish with green onions. Add bun tops.

Makes 4 burgers

Nutrition Facts per burger: 389 cal., 13 g total fat (3 g sat. fat), 123 mg chol., 739 mg sodium, 36 g carbo., 2 g fiber, 31 g pro.

*****TEST KITCHEN TIP:** The internal color of a burger is not a reliable doneness indicator. A turkey or chicken patty cooked to 165°F is safe, regardless or color. To measure the doneness of a patty, insert an instant-read thermometer through the side of the patty to a depth of 2 to 3 inches.

LEMONY COD WITH ASPARAGUS

Cod is a mild-flavored lean, white fish. It is incredibly versatile in cooking and can be found in most supermarkets either fresh or frozen.

Prep: 10 minutes   Broil: 5 minutes

- **4   purchased soft breadsticks**
- **2   tablespoons butter, melted**
- **¼   teaspoon garlic salt**
- **1   pound fresh or frozen cod fillets, ½ inch thick**
- **12 ounces fresh asparagus spears, trimmed**
- **1   tablespoon lemon juice**
- **½   teaspoon dried thyme, crushed**
- **⅛   teaspoon ground black pepper**
- **Lemon wedges (optional)**

1 Preheat broiler. Place breadsticks on the unheated rack of a broiler pan. Brush with 1 tablespoon of the melted butter and sprinkle with garlic salt. Broil 4 inches from heat for 1 to 2 minutes or until golden, turning breadsticks once. Remove breadsticks from pan and keep warm.

2 Arrange fish and asparagus in a single layer on the broiler pan rack. In a small bowl stir together the remaining 1 tablespoon melted butter and lemon juice. Drizzle butter mixture over fish and brush over asparagus. Sprinkle fish and asparagus with thyme and pepper.

3 Broil 4 inches from heat for 4 to 6 minutes or until fish begins to flake when tested with a fork and asparagus is crisp-tender, turning asparagus once. Serve fish and asparagus with breadsticks and, if desired, lemon wedges.

Makes 4 servings

Nutrition Facts per serving: 293 cal., 8 g total fat (4 g sat. fat), 64 mg chol., 454 mg sodium, 29 g carbo., 3 g fiber, 27 g pro.

HALIBUT WITH TOMATOES AND OLIVES

Fished from cold northern waters, halibut is white and firm with a mild flavor. Steaks are more commonly available than fillets. Pictured on page 270

Prep: 15 minutes   Broil: 8 minutes

4   **5- to 6-ounce fresh or frozen halibut steaks, cut 1 inch thick**

2   **tablespoons olive oil**

    Salt and ground black pepper

1   **small tomato, chopped (⅓ cup)**

⅓   **cup Greek black olives, pitted and chopped**

2   **tablespoons snipped fresh flat-leaf parsley or 1 tablespoon snipped fresh oregano or thyme**

1 Thaw fish, if frozen. Rinse fish; pat dry with paper towels. Brush fish with 1 tablespoon of the oil; sprinkle with salt and black pepper.

2 Preheat broiler. Place fish on the greased unheated rack of a broiler pan. Broil fish 4 inches from heat for 8 to 12 minutes or until fish begins to flake when tested with a fork, turning once halfway through cooking.

3 Meanwhile, in a small bowl stir together the remaining 1 tablespoon oil, tomato, olives, and parsley. To serve, spoon tomato mixture over fish.

Makes 4 servings

Nutrition Facts per serving: 262 cal., 12 g total fat (2 g sat. fat), 54 mg chol., 264 mg sodium, 2 g carbo., 1 g fiber, 36 g pro.

FISH FILLETS WITH SALSA VERDE

Snipped cilantro freshens the taste of bottled green salsa.

Prep: 10 minutes   **Broil: 4 to 6 minutes per ½-inch thickness**

1 **pound fresh or frozen cod or orange roughy fillets**
1 **tablespoon lime juice**
1 **tablespoon olive oil**
⅛ **teaspoon salt**
⅛ **teaspoon ground black pepper**
½ **cup bottled green salsa**
3 **tablespoons snipped fresh cilantro**
Lime wedges (optional)

1 Thaw fish, if frozen. Rinse fish; pat dry with paper towels. Preheat broiler. In a small bowl combine lime juice, oil, salt, and pepper. Brush both sides of fish with lime juice mixture.

2 Measure thickness of fish. Place fish on the greased unheated rack of a broiler pan, tucking under any thin edges to make fish of uniform thickness. Broil 4 inches from heat until fish begins to flake when tested with a fork. (Allow 4 to 6 minutes per ½-inch thickness of fish. If fish is 1 inch or more thick, turn once halfway through cooking.)

3 Meanwhile, stir together salsa and 2 tablespoons of the cilantro. To serve, top fish with salsa mixture; sprinkle with the remaining 1 tablespoon cilantro. If desired, garnish with lime wedges.

Makes 4 servings

Nutrition Facts per serving: 125 cal., 4 g total fat (1 g sat. fat), 42 mg chol., 157 mg sodium, 1 g carbo., 0 g fiber, 20 g pro.

ITALIAN-STYLE FISH

You're just 20 minutes to dinner with this recipe! Simply drape a quick, mushroom-studded tomato sauce over broiled fish fillets and top with a little Parmesan. Serve with couscous and your favorite frozen vegetable.

Start to Finish: 20 minutes

1½ **pounds fresh or frozen fish fillets, ½ to 1 inch thick**

¼ **teaspoon salt**

¼ **teaspoon ground black pepper**

1 **tablespoon cooking oil**

2 **cups packaged sliced fresh mushrooms**

1 **14.5-ounce can Italian-style stewed tomatoes, undrained**

1 **10.75-ounce can condensed tomato bisque soup**

⅓ **cup finely shredded Parmesan cheese**

3 **cups hot cooked pasta**

1 Thaw fish, if frozen. Rinse fish; pat dry with paper towels. Cut fish into 6 serving-size pieces, if necessary. Measure thickness of fish. Place fish on the greased unheated rack of a broiler pan, tucking under any thin edges to make fish of uniform thickness. Sprinkle with salt and ⅛ teaspoon of the pepper.

2 Preheat broiler. Broil 4 inches from the heat for 4 to 6 minutes per ½-inch thickness or until fish begins to flake when tested with a fork. (If fillets are 1 inch thick, carefully turn once halfway through broiling.)

3 Meanwhile, for sauce, in a medium saucepan heat oil over medium-high heat. Add mushrooms; cook until tender, stirring occasionally. Stir in undrained tomatoes, soup, and the remaining ⅛ teaspoon pepper. Cook and stir over medium heat until heated through.

4 Spoon the sauce over fish fillets. Sprinkle with Parmesan cheese. Serve with hot cooked pasta.

Makes 6 servings

Nutrition Facts per serving: 415 cal., 14 g total fat (6 g sat. fat), 71 mg chol., 1218 mg sodium, 35 g carbo., 2 g fiber, 37 g pro.

CAJUN CATFISH WITH COLESLAW

Salt-free Cajun seasoning has a zippier flavor and richer color than regular Cajun seasonings, most of which contain salt. If you use regular Cajun seasoning, omit the salt.

Prep: 10 minutes   Bake: 15 minutes   Oven: 350°F

1   **pound fresh or frozen skinless catfish fillets, ½ inch thick**

2½   **teaspoons salt-free Cajun seasoning**

¼   **teaspoon salt**

2   **cups shredded cabbage with carrot (coleslaw mix)**

3   **tablespoons mayonnaise or salad dressing**

     Salt and ground black pepper

     Bottled hot pepper sauce (optional)

1 Thaw fish, if frozen. Preheat oven to 350°F. Rinse fish; pat dry with paper towels. Cut fish into 4 serving-size pieces, if necessary. Combine 2 teaspoons of the Cajun seasoning and the ¼ teaspoon salt; sprinkle both sides of fish with seasoning mixture. Arrange fish in a greased 3-quart rectangular baking dish, tucking under any thin edges to make fish of uniform thickness.

2 Bake, uncovered, for 15 to 20 minutes or until fish begins to flake when tested with a fork.

3 Meanwhile, in a medium bowl stir together cabbage, mayonnaise, and the remaining ½ teaspoon Cajun seasoning. If desired, season to taste with salt and black pepper. Cover and chill until serving time. Serve catfish with coleslaw and, if desired, hot pepper sauce.

Makes 4 servings

Nutrition Facts per serving: 241 cal., 17 g total fat (3 g sat. fat), 57 mg chol., 127 mg sodium, 3 g carbo., 1 g fiber, 18 g pro.

PARMESAN BAKED FISH

A simple sauce of mayonnaise, chives, Worcestershire, and Parmesan makes a tangy crisp crust for this quick-baking meal.

Prep: 10 minutes   Bake: 12 minutes   Oven: 450°F

4   **4- to 5-ounce fresh or frozen skinless salmon or other firm fish fillets, ¾ to 1 inch thick**

¼   **cup mayonnaise or salad dressing**

2   **tablespoons grated Parmesan cheese**

1   **tablespoon snipped fresh chives or sliced green onion**

1   **teaspoon Worcestershire sauce for chicken**

1 Thaw fish, if frozen. Preheat oven to 450°F. Rinse fish; pat dry with paper towels. Place fish in a greased 2-quart square or rectangular baking dish, tucking under any thin edges to make fish of uniform thickness. Set aside.

2 In a small bowl stir together mayonnaise, Parmesan cheese, chives, and Worcestershire sauce. Spread mayonnaise mixture evenly over fish.

3 Bake, uncovered, for 12 to 15 minutes or until fish begins to flake when tested with a fork.

Makes 4 servings

Nutrition Facts per serving: 302 cal., 22 g total fat (4 g sat. fat), 77 mg chol., 185 mg sodium, 0 g carbo., 0 g fiber, 25 g pro.

SESAME-COATED TILAPIA WITH SPINACH

Fish in a salad? Why not! Coating the tilapia with sesame seeds before cooking makes it look attractive and gives it an agreeable crunch.

Start to Finish: 20 minutes

1   **pound fresh or frozen tilapia fillets**

¼   **cup all-purpose flour**

¼   **cup sesame seeds**

½   **teaspoon ground black pepper**

⅔   **cup bottled honey-Dijon salad dressing**

2   **tablespoons cooking oil**

1   **5-ounce package baby spinach and red leaf lettuce or baby spinach with radicchio**

1 Thaw fish, if frozen. Rinse fish; pat dry with paper towels. Cut fish into 4 serving-size pieces, if necessary.

2 In a shallow bowl combine flour, sesame seeds, and pepper. Place 2 tablespoons of the salad dressing in a small bowl. Brush all sides of the fish pieces with the 2 tablespoons salad dressing. Firmly press both sides of each fish piece into sesame mixture.

3 In a 12-inch skillet heat oil over medium heat. Cook fish in hot oil about 6 minutes or until fish begins to flake when tested with a fork, turning once halfway through cooking.

4 Divide spinach among 4 dinner plates; top each with a fish piece. Drizzle with the remaining salad dressing.

Makes 4 servings

Nutrition Facts per serving: 418 cal., 30 g total fat (3 g sat. fat), 0 mg chol., 247 mg sodium, 16 g carbo., 4 g fiber, 22 g pro.

CAJUN FISH SOUP

Jazz up the mild fish in this soup with peppery Cajun seasoning.

Start to Finish: 20 minutes

12   **ounces fresh or frozen sea bass, cod, or orange roughy fillets**

4   **cups assorted stir-fry vegetables from salad bar or produce department, or one 16-ounce package frozen stir-fry vegetables (any combination)**

4   **cups reduced-sodium chicken broth**

2   **teaspoons Cajun seasoning**

1   **14.5-ounce can diced tomatoes, undrained**

1 Thaw fish, if frozen. Rinse fish; pat dry with paper towels. Cut fish into 1-inch pieces; set fish aside.

2 In a large saucepan combine vegetables, chicken broth, and Cajun seasoning. Bring to boiling; reduce heat. Cover and simmer for 3 to 5 minutes or until vegetables are crisp-tender. Stir in fish and undrained tomatoes. Return to boiling; reduce heat. Simmer, covered, for 2 to 3 minutes or until fish begins to flake when tested with a fork.

Makes 4 servings

Nutrition Facts per serving: 157 cal., 2 g total fat (0 g sat. fat), 35 mg chol., 968 mg sodium, 12 g carbo., 3 g fiber, 21 g pro.

SKILLET TUNA AND BISCUITS

Easy to prepare and enjoy, this saucy biscuit-topped skillet dinner will be a dish your family will ask for often.

Prep: 15 minutes   Bake: 12 minutes   Oven: 400°F

- 1   **10-ounce container Alfredo pasta sauce**
- 1   **10-ounce package frozen peas and carrots**
- 1   **4-ounce can (drained weight) sliced mushrooms, drained**
- ¼   **teaspoon dried dill**
- 1   **12-ounce can tuna, drained and flaked**
- 1   **cup packaged biscuit mix**
- ⅓   **cup milk**
- ¼   **cup shredded cheddar cheese (1 ounce)**

1 Preheat oven to 400°F. In a large oven-going skillet combine Alfredo sauce, peas and carrots, mushrooms, and dill. Cook and stir over medium heat until bubbly and heated through. Stir in tuna. Cover to keep warm.

2 In a medium bowl stir together biscuit mix, milk, and half of the cheese. Drop mixture into 4 mounds on top of tuna mixture in skillet. Sprinkle with the remaining cheese.

3 Bake for 12 to 15 minutes or until biscuits are golden.

Makes 4 servings

Nutrition Facts per serving: 481 cal., 24 g total fat (12 g sat. fat), 86 mg chol., 1431 mg sodium, 35 g carbo., 3 g fiber, 31 g pro.

MEDITERRANEAN SHRIMP AND COUSCOUS

A packaged couscous mix and canned seasoned tomatoes make this shrimp dish as easy as it is delicious.

Start to Finish: 15 minutes

12 **ounces fresh or frozen peeled and deveined medium shrimp***

1 **14.5-ounce can diced tomatoes with garlic and onion, undrained**

¾ **cup water**

1 **5.6-ounce package toasted pine nut couscous mix**

½ **cup golden raisins**

¾ **cup crumbled feta cheese**

1 **cup arugula leaves**

1 Thaw shrimp, if frozen.

2 In a large skillet combine undrained tomatoes, water, and seasoning packet from the couscous mix to boiling. Bring to boiling. Stir in shrimp; cook over high heat for 2 to 3 minutes or until shrimp turn opaque. Stir in couscous and raisins. Remove from heat. Cover and let stand about 5 minutes or until liquid is absorbed.

3 Once the couscous has absorbed all the water, fluff with a fork. Add feta cheese and arugula; toss to mix.

Makes 4 servings

Nutrition Facts per serving: 405 cal., 10 g total fat (5 g sat. fat), 154 mg chol., 187 mg sodium, 52 g carbo., 5 g fiber, 28 g pro.

*NOTE: If peeled shrimp are unavailable, purchase 1 pound fresh shrimp in shells. Peel and devein shrimp. Rinse shrimp; pat dry with paper towels.

RAVIOLI WITH RED CLAM SAUCE

Refrigerated ravioli and canned clams make this a great off-the-shelf dinner with restaurant style.

Start to Finish: 20 minutes

- 1 **9-ounce package refrigerated cheese-filled ravioli or tortellini**
- 1 **6.5-ounce can minced clams**
- 1 **14.5-ounce can stewed tomatoes, undrained**
- 1 **medium zucchini, halved lengthwise and thinly sliced (about 1½ cups)**
- 2 **teaspoons dried Italian seasoning, crushed**
- 1 **8-ounce can tomato sauce**
- 1 **tablespoon cornstarch**
   Grated Parmesan cheese (optional)

1 Cook ravioli according to package directions. Drain; keep warm.

2 Meanwhile, drain clams, reserving liquid; set clams aside. In a large saucepan combine the clam liquid, the undrained stewed tomatoes, zucchini, and Italian seasoning. Bring to boiling; reduce heat. Simmer, uncovered, for 2 minutes.

3 In a small bowl stir together the tomato sauce and cornstarch until smooth. Stir cornstarch mixture into hot mixture in saucepan. Cook and stir over medium heat until thickened and bubbly. Cook and stir for 2 minutes more. Stir in clams and ravioli. Heat through. If desired, sprinkle individual servings with Parmesan cheese.

Makes 4 servings

Nutrition Facts per serving: 271 cal., 4 g total fat (2 g sat. fat), 46 mg chol., 960 mg sodium, 42 g carbo., 4 g fiber, 18 g pro.

SAUCY PIZZA SKILLET DINNER

Lasagna dinner mix is the base for this skillet dish that's studded with olives and mushrooms and full of flavor.

Start to Finish: 30 minutes

- 1   **6.4-ounce package lasagna dinner mix**
- 3   **cups water**
- 1   **4-ounce can (drained weight) mushroom stems and pieces**
- ½   **cup chopped green sweet pepper**
- ½   **cup sliced, pitted ripe olives (optional)**
- ½   **cup shredded mozzarella cheese (2 ounces)**

1 If the noodles in the dinner mix are large, break them into bite-size pieces. In a large skillet combine noodles and seasoning from dinner mix, water, undrained mushrooms, and sweet pepper.

2 Bring to boiling, stirring occasionally; reduce heat. Cover and simmer about 13 minutes or until pasta is tender. Uncover and cook for 2 to 3 minutes more or until sauce is of desired consistency.

3 If desired, sprinkle with olives. Top with cheese. Remove from heat; let stand for 1 to 2 minutes or until cheese melts.

Makes 4 servings

Nutrition Facts per serving: 318 cal., 14 g total fat (5 g sat. fat), 28 mg chol., 1774 mg sodium, 37 g carbo., 3 g fiber, 14 g pro.

TUSCAN RAVIOLI STEW

Broccoli rabe, a leafy green with stalks and broccoli-like buds that is popular in Italian cuisine, has a pungent, somewhat bitter flavor. If it is not available, substitute broccoli florets. Pictured on page 271.

Start to Finish: 20 minutes

- 1 tablespoon olive oil
- ⅓ cup sliced leek
- 1½ teaspoons bottled minced garlic (3 cloves)
- 1 14-ounce can vegetable or beef broth
- ¾ cup water
- ¼ teaspoon crushed red pepper (optional)
- 5 cups coarsely chopped broccoli rabe or broccoli florets
- 1 14.5-ounce can no-salt-added stewed tomatoes, undrained
- 1 9-ounce package refrigerated cheese-filled ravioli
- 1 tablespoon snipped fresh rosemary or 1 teaspoon dried rosemary, crushed
- ¼ cup grated Asiago or Parmesan cheese (optional)

1 In a large saucepan heat oil. Add leek and garlic; cook and stir over medium heat for 5 minutes. Add broth, water, and, if desired, crushed red pepper. Bring to boiling.

2 Add broccoli rabe, undrained tomatoes, ravioli, and rosemary. Return to boiling; reduce heat. Cover and simmer for 7 to 8 minutes or until broccoli rabe and ravioli are tender. If desired, sprinkle individual servings with cheese.

Makes 4 servings

Nutrition Facts per serving: 363 cal., 16 g total fat (9 g sat. fat), 55 mg chol., 995 mg sodium, 41 g carbo., 5 g fiber, 13 g pro.

LEMONY ALFREDO-STYLE FETTUCCINE

Cream cheese and evaporated milk pair up to make this easy Alfredo-like sauce. Lemon peel keeps the flavor fresh.

Start to Finish: 20 minutes

8 **ounces dried spinach fettuccine or plain fettuccine**

2 **cups frozen California blend, Oriental blend, or Italian blend mixed vegetables**

1 **5-ounce can evaporated milk**

2 **ounces cream cheese, cut up**

¼ **cup grated Parmesan cheese**

½ **teaspoon finely shredded lemon peel**

¼ **teaspoon ground black pepper**

Dash ground nutmeg

1 In a Dutch oven cook pasta according to package directions, adding frozen vegetables for the last 6 minutes of cooking. When the pasta is nearly done, carefully remove ¼ cup of the cooking water with a ladle. Set aside. Drain pasta and vegetables; return to pan.

2 Add evaporated milk, cream cheese, Parmesan cheese, lemon peel, pepper, and nutmeg to pasta mixture. Cook, tossing constantly, over low heat until cheese is melted. If necessary, stir in some of the reserved pasta liquid to make desired consistency. Serve immediately.

Makes 4 servings

Nutrition Facts per serving: 349 cal., 10 g total fat (6 g sat. fat), 30 mg chol., 189 mg sodium, 50 g carbo., 8 g fiber, 14 g pro.

CAJUN BEANS ON CORN BREAD

Beans and tomatoes cook with onion and hot pepper sauce to meld the flavors. Mound the beans on top of corn bread and add a sprinkle of cheese. Pictured on page 272.

Start to Finish: 30 minutes

| 8.5-ounce package corn muffin mix

| tablespoon cooking oil

| medium green sweet pepper, chopped (¾ cup)

| 15- to 16-ounce can Great Northern beans, rinsed and drained

| 14.5-ounce can diced tomatoes with garlic and onion, undrained

| teaspoon instant chicken bouillon granules

¼ teaspoon ground black pepper

¼ to ½ teaspoon bottled hot pepper sauce

½ cup shredded cheddar cheese (2 ounces)

1 Prepare corn muffin mix according to package directions for corn bread. Cool slightly.

2 Meanwhile, in a medium saucepan heat oil over medium heat. Add sweet pepper; cook and stir just until tender. Add beans, undrained tomatoes, bouillon granules, black pepper, and hot pepper sauce. Bring to boiling; reduce heat. Cover and simmer for 10 minutes.

3 Cut corn bread into 4 portions and place on dinner plates or in shallow bowls. Spoon bean mixture over corn bread. Sprinkle with cheese.

Makes 4 servings

Nutrition Facts per serving: 485 cal., 17 g total fat (4 g sat. fat), 70 mg chol., 1563 mg sodium, 68 g carbo., 6 g fiber, 17 g pro.

ITALIAN VEGGIE BURGERS

Start with frozen veggie burgers and and choose either the basic recipe or one of the tasty variations.

Start to Finish: 15 minutes

4	**refrigerated or frozen meatless burger patties**
¼	**cup tomato paste**
4	**to 5 tablespoons water**
2	**teaspoons snipped fresh basil**
8	**slices firm-textured whole wheat or oatmeal bread, toasted if desired**
4	**slices mozzarella cheese (1 ounce)**
16	**small fresh basil leaves**

1 Cook burger patties according to package directions. Meanwhile, for sauce, in a small bowl combine tomato paste, water, and snipped basil.

2 To serve, place each burger patty on 1 slice of bread. Top with sauce, cheese, and basil leaves. Top with another slice of bread. If desired, cut each sandwich into quarters.

Makes 4 burgers

Nutrition Facts per burger: 332 cal., 12 g total fat (2 g sat. fat), 25 mg chol., 819 mg sodium, 33 g carbo., 8 g fiber, 26 g pro.

Tomato-Mayo Veggie Burgers: Prepare as above except omit tomato paste, water, basil, and cheese. In a small bowl combine ¼ cup mayonnaise or salad dressing, 3 tablespoons ketchup, and dash garlic powder. Top each burger with some of the mayonnaise mixture and a lettuce leaf. Serve as above.

Barbecue Veggie Burgers: Prepare as above except omit tomato paste, water, basil, and cheese. Top each burger with 1 rounded tablespoon bottled barbeque sauce and a lettuce leaf. Serve as above.

CHEESE-and-VEGETABLE-FILLED FOCACCIA

Brimming with zesty pickled vegetables and herbed cheese, this stuffed focaccia makes an instant meal. Save time by buying prewashed spinach from the produce department and getting the cheese at the deli counter so you can have it very thinly sliced or shaved.

Start to Finish: 20 minutes

⅓ **cup mayonnaise or salad dressing**

2 **tablespoons honey mustard**

1 **8- to 10-inch tomato or onion focaccia bread, halved horizontally**

1 **cup lightly packed fresh spinach**

6 **ounces dilled Havarti cheese, very thinly sliced**

1 **16-ounce jar pickled mixed vegetables, drained and chopped**

In a small bowl stir together mayonnaise and honey mustard. Spread mayonnaise mixture over bottom half of focaccia. Top with spinach and half of the cheese. Spoon vegetables over; top with remaining cheese. Replace bread top. Cut into quarters.

Makes 4 sandwiches

Nutrition Facts per sandwich: 364 cal., 32 g total fat (2 g sat. fat), 67 mg chol., 1251 mg sodium, 10 g carbo., 0 g fiber, 10 g pro.

INDEX

Note: Page references in **bold** refer to photographs.

METRIC INFORMATION

The charts on this page provide a guide for converting measurements from the U.S. customary system, which is used throughout this book, to the metric system.

PRODUCT DIFFERENCES

Most of the ingredients called for in the recipes in this book are available in most countries. However, some are known by different names. Here are some common American ingredients and their possible counterparts:
- Sugar (white) is granulated, fine granulated, or castor sugar.
- Powdered sugar is icing sugar.
- All-purpose flour is enriched, bleached, or unbleached white household flour. When self-rising flour is used in place of all-purpose flour in a recipe that calls for leavening, omit the leavening agent (baking soda or baking powder) and salt.
- Light-colored corn syrup is golden syrup.
- Cornstarch is cornflour.
- Baking soda is bicarbonate of soda.
- Vanilla or vanilla extract is vanilla essence.
- Green, red, or yellow sweet peppers are capsicums or bell peppers.
- Golden raisins are sultanas.

VOLUME AND WEIGHT

The United States traditionally uses cup measures for liquid and solid ingredients. The chart, top right, shows the approximate imperial and metric equivalents. If you are accustomed to weighing solid ingredients, the following approximate equivalents will be helpful.
- 1 cup butter, castor sugar, or rice = 8 ounces = ½ pound = 250 grams
- 1 cup flour = 4 ounces = ¼ pound = 125 grams
- 1 cup icing sugar = 5 ounces = 150 grams

Canadian and U.S. volume for a cup measure is 8 fluid ounces (237 ml), but the standard metric equivalent is 250 ml.

1 British imperial cup is 10 fluid ounces.

In Australia, 1 tablespoon equals 20 ml, and there are 4 teaspoons in the Australian tablespoon.

Spoon measures are used for smaller amounts of ingredients. Although the size of the tablespoon varies slightly in different countries, for practical purposes and for recipes in this book, a straight substitution is all that's necessary. Measurements made using cups or spoons always should be level unless stated otherwise.

COMMON WEIGHT RANGE REPLACEMENTS

Imperial / U.S.	Metric
½ ounce	15 g
1 ounce	25 g or 30 g
4 ounces (¼ pound)	115 g or 125 g
8 ounces (½ pound)	225 g or 250 g
16 ounces (1 pound)	450 g or 500 g
1¼ pounds	625 g
1½ pounds	750 g
2 pounds or 2¼ pounds	1,000 g or 1 Kg

OVEN TEMPERATURE EQUIVALENTS

Fahrenheit Setting	Celsius Setting*	Gas Setting
300°F	150°C	Gas Mark 2 (very low)
325°F	160°C	Gas Mark 3 (low)
350°F	180°C	Gas Mark 4 (moderate)
375°F	190°C	Gas Mark 5 (moderate)
400°F	200°C	Gas Mark 6 (hot)
425°F	220°C	Gas Mark 7 (hot)
450°F	230°C	Gas Mark 8 (very hot)
475°F	240°C	Gas Mark 9 (very hot)
500°F	260°C	Gas Mark 10 (extremely hot)
Broil	Broil	Grill

*Electric and gas ovens may be calibrated using celsius. However, for an electric oven, increase celsius setting 10 to 20 degrees when cooking above 160°C. For convection or forced air ovens (gas or electric) lower the temperature setting 25°F/10°C when cooking at all heat levels.

BAKING PAN SIZES

Imperial / U.S.	Metric
9×1½-inch round cake pan	22- or 23×4-cm (1.5 L)
9×1½-inch pie plate	22- or 23×4-cm (1 L)
8×8×2-inch square cake pan	20×5-cm (2 L)
9×9×2-inch square cake pan	22- or 23×4.5-cm (2.5 L)
11×7×1½-inch baking pan	28×17×4-cm (2 L)
2-quart rectangular baking pan	30×19×4.5-cm (3 L)
13×9×2-inch baking pan	34×22×4.5-cm (3.5 L)
15×10×1-inch jelly roll pan	40×25×2-cm
9×5×3-inch loaf pan	23×13×8-cm (2 L)
2-quart casserole	2 L

U.S. / STANDARD METRIC EQUIVALENTS

⅛ teaspoon = 0.5 ml	⅓ cup = 3 fluid ounces = 75 ml
¼ teaspoon = 1 ml	½ cup = 4 fluid ounces = 125 ml
½ teaspoon = 2 ml	⅔ cup = 5 fluid ounces = 150 ml
1 teaspoon = 5 ml	¾ cup = 6 fluid ounces = 175 ml
1 tablespoon = 15 ml	1 cup = 8 fluid ounces = 250 ml
2 tablespoons = 25 ml	2 cups = 1 pint = 500 ml
¼ cup = 2 fluid ounces = 50 ml	1 quart = 1 litre

Dinnertime just got easier,
thanks to hundreds of quick and easy mealtime solutions

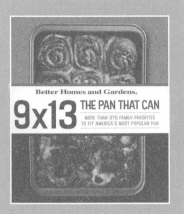

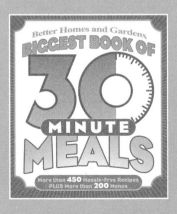